Heritage, Place and Community

HERITAGE, PLACE
AND COMMUNITY

BELLA DICKS

*Published on behalf of the Board of Celtic Studies
of the University of Wales*

UNIVERSITY OF WALES PRESS
CARDIFF
2000

British Library Cataloguing-in-Publication Data.
A catalogue record for this book is available from the British Library.

ISBN 0–7083–1668–9

Typeset by Aarontype Limited, Easton, Bristol
Printed in Great Britain by Dinefwr Press, Llandybïe

This book is dedicated to Kevin and Louis

Contents

List of Illustrations, Figures and Tables

Illustrations

Figures

Tables

Acknowledgements

Parts of chapter 5 have appeared as B. Dicks, 'The view of our town from the hill: communities on display as local heritage', *International Journal of Cultural Studies*, 2(3) (1999), 349–68, and in B. Dicks and J. Van Loon, 'Territoriality and heritage in south Wales: space, time and imagined communities', in R. Fevre and A. Thompson (eds.), *Nation, Identity and Social Theory*, Cardiff, University of Wales Press, 1999. Parts of the Introduction and chapter 6 have appeared as B. Dicks, 'Regeneration versus representation in the Rhondda: the story of the Rhondda Heritage Park', *Contemporary Wales*, 9 (1996), 56–73. Parts of chapter 10 have appeared as B. Dicks, 'Encoding and decoding the people: circuits of communication at a local heritage museum', *European Journal of Communication*, 15(1) (2000), 61–78. All of these have been substantially reworked for inclusion in the present volume.

A view of the Rhondda Heritage Park in the 1990s. Reproduced by permission of Rhondda Heritage Park.

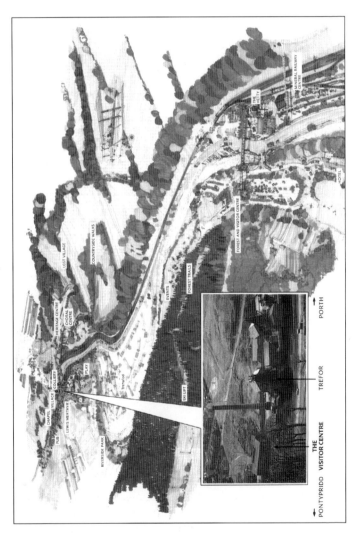

A plan of the Rhondda Heritage Park with proposed associated developments, as envisaged in the early 1990s. Reproduced by permission of Rhondda Heritage Park.

Introduction

On the A4058 from Pontypridd to Porth, in Mid Glamorgan, is a sign announcing the Rhondda Valleys. Just beyond the sign, the mainly green and wooded landscape is suddenly interrupted by an image from the past: to the right is an old pit winding house, with the year 1875 inscribed on its stone wall, and a few minutes later there emerges on the left an entire colliery in surprisingly fine condition, complete with winding wheels silhouetted before rows of steeply terraced housing. The first is the Hetty winding house, now a listed building and part of the old Tŷ Mawr colliery which closed in 1983. The second is the Rhondda Heritage Park. This is the former Lewis Merthyr colliery, which was connected to the Tŷ Mawr underground, and which also closed in 1983. Tŷ Mawr was razed to the ground when it ceased production, but the Lewis Merthyr met a different fate, setting out on a new life as a heritage attraction. This book tells its biography.

New grass is now growing on the steep, regraded Llwyncelyn waste tip on the other side of the bypass from the Heritage Park. A large area of derelict land at its feet is where the old pithead baths used to be. Miners would park their cars here, change into their work clothes, and then cross a long, covered footbridge, over the road, the River Rhondda and the railway, to the colliery. Now a heritage museum, it is the only colliery building left in a valley which at one time supported sixty-six deep mines. No smoke emerges from the towering brick-built chimney that guards the two winding wheels. The air is clean and still and no noise issues from behind walls which are made of stone rather than the traditional concrete. The visitor's attention is suddenly caught by an incongruous glint of colour. Looking up, a huge yellow sun-face appears, mounted on a vast children's slide and smiling over the top of the wall.

A little further on is a turning into a car park. On a summer Saturday there are groups of visitors and families making their way from their cars to a modern-looking reception building. This used to be the old colliery stores. Inside is a gift shop where visitors queue to buy entrance tickets. Nearby is a row of old Rhondda shop fronts: a hardware shop and a butcher's. While waiting to join the next guided tour, visitors can wander through these old shops to further displays behind: a collection of cobbler's equipment, for example, and a draper's. There is a miner's cottage, on the left, consisting of a series of interconnecting rooms furnished with genuine old domestic artefacts and furniture from the local area. In the parlour is an old pianola, a hearth and a dresser; in the kitchen visitors witness different time periods, seeing the appliances updated as they move from one end of the kitchen to the other. On the walls are fragments of texts seemingly torn from the writings of Rhondda poets and novelists, as well as photographic displays explaining local social conditions before and after the First World War: 'We came back to a land fit for heroes: aye, you had to be a bloody hero to live here.'

Every half an hour, the visitors are mustered by a guide, himself an ex-miner, who is dressed in the garb of a 1950s collier, with lamp, helmet, battery case, work clothes and blackened face. He takes his assembled group outside into the colliery yard and explains the functions of the buildings, chimney, two winding houses (named after the colliery owner's two sons, Bertie and Trefor), and various mining artefacts and machinery dotted around the yard. Then he leads them inside the Bertie winding house engine room, where they sit down. The lights go off. Suddenly, a tableau is illuminated in front, composed of life-sized figures. It is a mid-nineteenth-century family, speaking in Welsh, just at the start of the Rhondda's rapid industrial expansion as a world-class producer of coal. A disembodied voice booms out of the darkness. It belongs to Bryn Rees, a Lewis Merthyr miner, who is the cipher for the story that is about to unfold. As he speaks, a series of slides begins to flash across a suspended screen high up in the roof space, showing scenes from the Rhondda and describing the contours of this 'unique' place. Bryn introduces his grandfather and father too, who, together with voices projected from life-size historical figures illuminated in *tableaux vivants* in different areas of the building, tell the history of the origins and development of the *Black Gold* community.

At the end of the show, the guide returns to pick up his group, and escorts them out of the back of the Bertie winding house, into the cage at the top of the shaft, to make the descent down into the underground experience: *A Shift in Time*. With their helmets on, visitors follow the guide along underground roadways, as he explains the various techniques of shot-firing, pit-propping, coal-cutting, ventilation and so forth which made up the working day of different classes of miner. At the end of their tour underground, visitors are led into an awaiting carriage, resembling the 'drams' in which coal was piled to carry to the surface. The lights go out, an underground roadway suddenly stretches out on a screen in front, and the dram 'sets off' on a jerky and disorientating thrill ride back to the 'surface'.

When visitors emerge back into the daylight, their guide is ready to escort them to the fan-house, where a second audio-visual show begins. Narrated by Neil Kinnock, it tells the social and cultural history of the *Black Gold* community. Here, there is a particular emphasis on the role that women played in the life of the coalfield, detailing the arduous nature of their daily lives as wives, daughters and mothers of miners. All kinds of Rhondda social and cultural traditions are described and illustrated by means of a slide show projected onto the screen. Visitors then have the option of watching the third and final audio-visual show, which takes place in the Trefor winding house. This houses the colliery's original steam winding engine, restored to working order. Bryn Rees reappears and, with the aid of life-size figures, projected images and sound effects, he tells of his working life as a miner at the Lewis Merthyr colliery. Visitors hear about the changes in working conditions and organization of the colliery since his grandfather's day, and they also hear about the hustle and bustle of life in the colliery and its community:

Collieries are peculiar animals. I've 'eard some men talk about pits they've worked in as if they were alive. It's difficult to explain but, see, in the Rhondda the pits just dominated our lives. You take it now, just before the First World War, when I was born – we 'ad almost 60 collieries at work in these two valleys. And that's well over 40,000 men working the coal. In Lewis Merthyr, here, we 'ad five shafts at one time and if we're talking about the whole of south Wales, there was a quarter of a million coalminers with trains rattling day and night down those valleys to the docks, at Cardiff and Barry and all over the world ...

Rhondda was world famous, mun. And a magnet for people. By the early 1920s we 'ad almost 168,000 people living, crammed tight, in these two valleys. And just 70 years before that, when my grandfather was born, in the 1850s – there was scarcely a thousand here ...

I suppose, through it all, we survived because, in a way, the getting of coal had made us a community. We've 'ad our famous sons and daughters, like everyone else, but it's the ordinary people who really gave salt to our lives. Ordinary? They were bloody extra-ordinary.

When the narrative reaches the 1950s, the lights come back on and visitors have come to the end of their encounter with the *Black Gold* community. If they want, they can now visit the Energy Zone outside, where children climb onto the sun-face slide and play at loading coal in a pretend colliery. Otherwise, they can go to the café back in the reception building or visit the gift shop before taking their leave.

When visitors leave the car park, most drive straight off back on to the A4058. However, if they turn left into Trehafod, the village in which the heritage museum stands, they encounter a stillness and calmness that is palpable. It is hard to square the images and stories told inside the museum, of vast crowds and bustling human activity, of huge numbers of coal mines all busily bellowing smoke and filled with the noise of clanking machinery, with the quiet, orderly and tidy streets of the village as it is now. There are a few shops, a couple of pubs, and rows of neat terraces steeply rising up the valley sides. An impressive looking though disused miners' institute and a chapel testify to the past life of the mining community, but, apart from a sign for a coal-carving workshop, there is little indication that the village has much to do with its former industrial life or, indeed, its current heritage one. Instead, it seems strangely detached from the silent colliery in its midst.

How did such a transformation happen? How and when did the colliery take on its new life? Why did the other Rhondda collieries disappear, leaving only this one standing? How can we connect today's Rhondda – with its forested valley sides and regraded waste tips, new roundabouts and bypasses, factory units and super-stores – with the Rhondda of yesterday that the heritage museum describes? There are still ribbons and ribbons of terraces snaking on up the valley and several small, still lively high streets stretching through Pontypridd, then Porth and up through Treorchy and Treherbert or Tylorstown, Ferndale and Maerdy. But there are also abundant signs of decay and dilapidation, albeit held at bay by the evidence of environmental improvement grants, bringing new infra-structure and plenty of green all around. Looking at the rather bleak environment of today and contrasting it with the warm evocation of community presented inside the preserved colliery, it is hard not to feel a sense of loss and nostalgia.

If the heritage museum exudes this sense of sadness, one also wonders, with Umberto Eco, whether these are crocodile tears. How did the mining industry become the raw material for a heritage museum? The Rhondda Heritage Park betrays a certain determined amnesia in 'forgetting' that it was the embrace of leisure and tourism in the 1980s that helped consign the mining industry to the history books. Perhaps it is the 'entrepreneurial colonisation by the New World that makes the Old World's condition critical' with heritage crying the tears of 'the Roman patrician who reproduced the grandeurs of the very Greece that his country had humiliated and reduced to a colony' (Eco, 1986: 39). Is heritage not the 'bad conscience' of economic restructuring, in that it takes the fact of a people's decline as its necessary building blocks, whilst at the same time celebrating and displaying that same people's heroic traditions (and charging an entrance fee to see them)?

Another way of thinking about this, however, is that the Heritage Park provides the only significant public memorial the Rhondda has to its mining industry. The well-preserved buildings themselves offer up an account of colliery life that can be read, or at least imagined, from the machinery, pityard, chimney and winding wheels of its material presence. If these were cleared away, as so many other Rhondda collieries have been, there would be no material sign left of its once-dominant industrial identity. The guides tell the story of the mine and its community, day in and day out, for visitors to hear. In this sense, the heritage museum is a space in which encounters with the past and with different ways of life are on offer as a public resource – albeit a commercial one.

Of course, such stories, and undoubtedly more detailed, varied and harsher versions of them, are also told by grandparents within ex-mining family homes, and in the local pubs and working men's clubs that ex-miners still frequent. But these are private conversa-tions, dying away as the years pass and mining recedes into distant family memory. The Heritage Park offers an ongoing, public and institutionalized forum for the display and reconstruction of those stories, which is qualitatively different from the private ebbs and flows of local oral culture. It provides them with a backdrop of three-dimensional spectacle, a dedicated service personnel and a technology, which grant them an authority and a stature that does more than simply provide a space for the recording of history.

For children, it perhaps offers more than history books alone. As Ivor – one of the original instigators behind preserving the Lewis Merthyr colliery and now a guide at the Rhondda Heritage Park – explains:

> Books are not enough. I've always had a love of books and read books all my life, and I certainly hope that the school curriculum includes the local history. I don't know if these people that make the decisions say that coal mining and the history of these valleys and the history of your grandparents, your great-grandparents and the people who came to these valleys to work in the pits, has to be told. There are kids here – like the kids that came in only last week with their boards and said 'we are going to be asking questions because we're doing something on coal'. We're doing something on coal. But I say to the teacher, but not only *coal* – are you doing something on the mining *community*? You can tell people that coal is a certain number of million years old and that it came here as a result of primeval forests and what have you, but it's the mining *community* [that's important].
>
> (Personal interview with Ivor England; emphasis in original interview)

In Ivor's view, the Rhondda Heritage Park succeeds in communicating local social, as opposed to merely technical, knowledge that would not be otherwise accessible. It provides this knowledge in the form of a visitable attraction, a day out and a leisure destination. But it does so not only for the tourist from afar, but also for the next generation of local residents, in whose lives and homes the stories of miners would not otherwise enter.

Such issues go right to the heart of the heritage problematic. The potential of heritage to offer a representation of local life which is thought-provoking, accessible and which provides an ongoing public forum for the expression of local identities, constitutes one side of what has become known as the 'heritage debate' (see Lumley, 1994). On the other side are lined up the heritage critics, pointing to heritage's pretensions, banalities and failures and to its tainted, entrepreneurial character. Outside of this entrenched ideological warfare are, in addition, more ambivalently located questions concerning the role of heritage in the formation and negotiation of social identity. What do visitors actually take away with them when they step out from the heritage museum into the glare of the present? How does the local history they have seen assume a form and a narrative in their minds, and how do these images fit into their wider, political consciousness, personal reminiscences or collective identifications, if at all? In what ways are national and proto-national identifications, like Welshness, articulated to the heritage on display – identifications which are often either flagged or ignored at heritage museums dealing with more local identities. Indeed, how does 'Wales – the Nation' fit into the Rhondda Heritage Park, and how does the museum itself register such wider tensions over the imagining of community, collectivity and nation?

This book does not pretend to provide comprehensive answers to such questions. However, in exploring them, I hope to offer the reader an insight into the complexity of the heritage phenomenon. I also hope to contribute to an understanding of the Rhondda and the Valleys as social spaces within the wider regional culture of south Wales. In this sense, the book aspires to do more than provide a record of the Rhondda Heritage Park's development. It seeks to trace some of the ways in which the study of heritage opens up wider questions of representation and politics. These include the questions of how culture is intertwined with the economy, how the local is implicated in wider spatial and social formations, how the past is produced as a set of stories told in the present, and how 'community' is appropriated in the business of representing both the past, the present and the future. In contrast to approaches which disaggregate heritage into separate areas of enquiry, this book provides an analysis which brings together the economic, cultural, social and political dimensions of heritage production and consumption.

Part I situates heritage within its social contexts, by examining its position in both the local social space of south Wales (chapter 1) and the UK (chapter 2) and within the academic debates that have characterized its reception in recent years (chapter 3). Part II turns to a consideration of heritage as a form of historical, place-based representation. It addresses the construction of 'imagined communities' both in Wales (chapter 4) and specifically in the Rhondda (chapter 5). In Part III, I address the cultural and social production of heritage through examining the political governance of the Rhondda project in the 1980s and 1990s (chapter 6), its relationship with local people (chapter 7) and the professional interpretative practices that structured its development (chapter 8). The final two chapters, in Part IV, discuss the question of visiting heritage museums, and provide an overview of the kinds of interaction that heritage offers (chapter 9), as well as a case-study drawn from the Rhondda Heritage Park of how particular groups of visitors interpreted the history on display (chapter 10). The intention throughout is to provide a linked analysis which examines heritage as political, social and economic resource (production), as cultural representation (text) and as a framework for people's historical understanding (consumption).

I. CONTEXTS OF HERITAGE

1

Tourism and heritage in the Valleys: the local context

Heritage museums, as many critics point out, have been mushroom-ing in the UK for several decades. But they do not simply spring from the ground as the metaphor suggests. Rather, they take shape within the context of specific social, cultural and economic relations – contexts which, especially during the 1980s, shifted in response to political developments at the UK government level. Local authorities were being urged to invest in their areas' cultural 'assets' in order to encourage the leisure-led regeneration of failing industrial economies. Leisure and tourism were to take over where manufacturing had receded, and this was to be achieved by assembling a new alliance between a backward-looking heritage and a forward-looking 'enterprise' (Corner and Harvey, 1991). Enterprise tied the provision of public funds for urban regeneration projects (such as the Urban Development and Urban Regeneration Grants of the 1980s) to success in the market-place. Marketing strategies aimed at replacing public subsidy with private investment and sponsorship became key aspects of both new heritage ventures and the reimaging of older museums. In many ways, then, heritage is a quintessential product of enterprise culture in Britain in the 1980s and 1990s.

However, although many critics of heritage have seen this entre-preneurial ideal as its defining characteristic, heritage projects rarely embody a 'pure' principle of free enterprise. Most arise from quite particular local contexts in which a variety of agencies, parties, motivations and processes are involved. Very often, local councils are centrally involved in their promotion, funding and management, and the public grants system is fundamental to their development. Urban development grants have to be applied for, secured, match-funded and deployed – a process which is fraught with all kinds of complex inter-relations and cultural dissonances at the local level. Glib central government rhetoric about free enterprise does not overwrite established local patterns, but rather interlocks, in unpredictable ways, with the sedimented historical relations, allegiances, interests and cultural discourses of the local political sphere. These variables mean that it is impossible to subsume all projects under the same banner. Instead, we need to consider how local, regional and national alliances evolve along certain policy trajectories rather than others, and how these in turn shape the development of heritage projects.

The present chapter maps the particular relations through which heritage enterprise began to emerge at a local policy level in the south Wales Valleys. Local social relations, however, are always embedded in wider, regional contexts, and it makes little sense to isolate the economic context of the Valleys from the fortunes of the south Wales industrial region as a whole. It is that wider regional economic context, both now and in the heyday of heritage enterprise, which exposes the particular faultlines running through the uneven social space of industrial south Wales, and which formed the backdrop to the adoption of heritage solutions in the Rhondda in the 1980s. In what follows, I shall begin with the present-day situation in the region, and work back to the origins of the Rhondda heritage project.

1. Economic decline in the south Wales Valleys

The 1990s saw the culmination of decades of unrelenting de-industrialization in south Wales, centred on the virtual disappearance of deep coalmining and the steep decline of steel-making and related manufacturing industries. Some 90,000 jobs were lost in the region between 1978 and 1987, of which nearly 70,000 were manufacturing jobs. In Llanwern and Port Talbot, the south Wales steelworks lost 61 per cent of their jobs, and in the Valleys the collieries shed 70 per cent in the decade up to 1988. A total of 18,000 coalmining jobs were lost between 1980 and 1988 as twenty-three collieries in the region closed down (Fretter, 1993). The 1980s and 1990s were also decades in which governmental economic policy became directed towards private-sector, market-orientated strategies for urban regeneration (Prentice, 1993). During the 1980s, various public funding packages were made available: for example, the Welsh Office's 1988 Programme for the Valleys and the European Commission's granting of Objective 2 funding status to the coalfield area. These packages were designed to foster an 'entrepreneurial' approach to economic development on the part of local agencies of governance (Harvey, 1989b), in which promoting the area's cultural assets and heritage became a central element.

The ongoing problem of economic regeneration in the Valleys

Before turning the clock back to the 1980s when the Rhondda Heritage Park was founded, it is worth reflecting on the situation that the south Wales Valleys currently face, two decades after the Conservative Party came to power in London in 1979 and just a year after the election of Wales's first National Assembly in Cardiff – under the political control of Labour. In some respects, the Welsh economy as a whole looks brighter at the beginning of the twenty-first century than it did at the close of the 1970s. Some commentators, indeed, came to see the 1990s as the decade of Wales's long-awaited 'economic miracle', impelled by the modernization of the region's industrial structure and its supposed revealing of a regional innovation 'renaissance' (Rees and Morgan, 1991; Price et al., 1994). However, such a conclusion has also been roundly contested, with studies pointing to the entrenched spatial unevenness of economic growth. Lovering (1998), for example, argues that the recent gains in manufacturing have done little to compensate for the massive job losses resultant from the earlier closure of the coalmining industry.

Wales in 2000 has left its twentieth-century industrial identity behind and become, like England, a service economy. However, although the service sector, as in England, was trumpeted throughout the 1980s as the prime means of achieving economic renewal, the restructuring of employment around service industries was not as marked in Wales as in England (Prentice, 1993). A countervalent trend has been the growth of consumer goods manufacturing along the Wales end of the M4 corridor, which has pulled the economy ever further eastwards, giving the impression of economic buoyancy and even prosperity in south Wales, and helping the region to avoid the worst effects of the UK service-led recession of the early 1990s. The electronics industry has been hailed as Wales's new 'sunrise' industry, held up as evidence that Wales is succeeding in attracting high levels of large-scale inward foreign investment. The Welsh Development Agency was particularly active in the 1990s in encouraging these foreign-owned companies to come to Wales, organizing vast public grants and providing infrastructure in the form of road-building, training and recruitment services (B. Morgan, 1997).

The electronics sector, however, is largely composed of assembly functions relying on cheap labour, rather than research and development, and remains a branch plant operation with investment and managerial decisions made outside Wales. This is the same problem that English-owned plants brought to Welsh manufacturing in the 1970s. Lovering (1998) points out that, notwithstanding the optimism that greeted these arrivals, the electronics sector actually expanded much less rapidly in the 1980s and the 1990s than it did in the 1970s, as is also true of the automotive sector. Wages, too, have remained lower than in other parts of the UK, and the vulnerability of jobs in the large branch assembly plants to global restructuring is painfully evident – as the recent downsizing of the vast LG electronics development at Newport has indicated.

More importantly for the present arguments, there has been little evidence that those economic gains brought by manufacturing growth are drifting up towards the Valleys (Adamson, 1999). New growth sectors, such as the 'producer' service industries, have been almost exclusively located in Cardiff, whilst economic depression continues unchecked in the Valleys (European Commission, 1994–6). As Prentice (1993) concludes, geographical location remains the prime determinant of whether an individual in south Wales is likely to become unemployed. A recent UK-wide study which set out to measure the extent of 'real unemployment' (as opposed to the official claimant count) identified Merthyr Tydfil as having the highest unemployment rate, at 33.4 per cent, in the whole of the UK (Beatty et al., 1997). Parts of the Valleys are now home to socially excluded communities whose members have little opportunity to access jobs, services and adequate housing. Out-migration continues to take people away from the Valleys towards

Cardiff: the boroughs of Merthyr Tydfil, Caerphilly, Blaenau Gwent and Torfaen lost 10,000 residents among them between 1991 and 1996, whilst Cardiff alone gained 8,800 (Dunkerley, 1999).

The 'problem of the Valleys' was thus still exercising the minds of economic planners throughout the 1990s, just as it had in the 1970s. This is in spite of a second five-year renewal period granted to the Programme for the Valleys. The Programme was designed to encourage new industrial investment through combining the Regional Development and Regional Selective Assistance grants with private-sector funding. Much of the criticism it has attracted has stemmed from its apparent reliance on administering existing, rather than new, funds – such as the European Regional Development Fund. In 1988, the Welsh Office promised 25,000–30,000 new jobs; however, by 1992 manufacturing employment had actually fallen faster in the Valleys than the average fall for Wales as a whole, and male unemployment had actually increased (Rees, 1997). In addition, total regional aid to the programme area was substantially reduced during the first three years of the programme, in line with wider central government insistence on cutting expenditure on regional assistance. The second phase of the programme, announced in 1993, sought to distance central government even further from direct control over the Valleys' economic future, by placing appeals to local community solutions at the heart of its rhetoric. This rehashes a familiar refrain in Valleys initiatives, and one which has not – so far – managed to bridge the economic divide between the Valleys and the coastal belt (Rees, 1997).

A recent Wales-wide survey (Morris and Wilkinson, 1993, 1995) used a variety of prosperity indicators (social class, qualifications, unemployment rate, permanent sickness, etc.) to make a comparison between the socio-economic well-being of each of the thirty-seven local authority districts (LADs) of Wales, before local government reorganization in 1997. Pointing to the substantial uneven development within Wales as a whole, the amalgamated statistics produced by this study show that the four northern valley LADs – Rhondda, Merthyr Tydfil, Blaenau Gwent and the Cynon Valley – performed worst on all indicators both in 1981 and 1991. The Vale of Glamorgan and Monmouth, on the other hand, both consistently come within the top 25 per cent of LADs in Wales as a whole, demonstrating the considerable discrepancies between districts *within* south Wales. In both the 1971–81 and 1981–91

census periods, the Rhondda was consistently at the bottom of the
league, with a significant gap between it and the next 'worst' LADs,
Blaenau Gwent and the Cynon Valley. Morris and Wilkinson
conclude that 'the benefits of economic developments enjoyed
in South Wales over the last ten years or so have been limited to certain segments of the population' (1993: 53). They go on to observe
that the Programme for the Valleys 'has either largely failed the
core valley problem areas, or has an immense amount of work
remaining, depending on one's level of cynicism' (1993: 66).

Dunkerley (1999), similarly, reports research employing a variety
of economic and social indicators to measure material and social
deprivation in Wales, which shows that Mid Glamorgan in 1991
had by far the highest level of deprivation – almost twice as high as
the next county ranked (West Glamorgan). Of course, there is also
considerable variation within counties and districts too: Cardiff
had both Wales's lowest deprivation ward (Rhiwbina) and three of
the highest four (Ely, Adamsdown and Butetown). Nevertheless, it
is clear that some of the Valleys areas (notably Rhondda, Cynon
Valley, Merthyr Tydfil, Rhymney, Blaenau Gwent and Torfaen)
have a high concentration of deprived wards without the balance
provided by prosperous wards nearby. Studies such as these indicate that the socio-economic situation of the Valleys in the 1990s
is still in a chronic state of decline. Objective 1 status has recently
been granted by the European Commission to the coalfield area,
showing the ongoing nature of the Valleys' economic and social
problems.

Meanwhile, at Cardiff Bay, the massive redevelopment of the
docklands (under the control of the Cardiff Bay Development
Corporation) contrasts painfully with the situation in the Valleys, a
disparity which has been described as 'the great cultural divide'
between 'deprived Welsh valley communities' and 'the brave new
world of Cardiff Bay' (*Western Mail*, 17 March 1995). Also located
in the Bay is the National Assembly for Wales. It has not yet been in
session for a year at the time of writing, and it is too early to judge
what kind of effect, if any, it is going to have on the socio-spatial
inequalities outlined above. The Assembly's powers are limited, in
that it cannot raise taxation or pass primary legislation, and will
therefore remain tethered to the economic and political framework
of Westminster and Whitchall in ways that Scotland will not. This

suggests that its capacity to institute a radically different philosophy of economic development will be similarly constrained.

The Programme for the Valleys has now come to an end. Yet hopes continue to be placed in accepted entrepreneurial approaches, such as renewed efforts to 'rebrand' the Valleys to attract new businesses (see the recent Welsh Office brochure *The Valleys: New Opportunities, New Future*, launched by Peter Hain, MP, in March 1999). A Valleys Forum, composed of the new unitary local authorities, along with the Welsh Development Agency, the TECs, and other agencies, is supporting the creation of industrial villages, small and medium business enterprises and a new marketing campaign for the Valleys; in other words, a continuation of the same entrepreneurial public–private policy approach that has so far failed to bring noticeable economic regeneration to the area. At the time of writing, the Forum has only met once, in August 1998, and awaits new initiatives and guidance from the Assembly.

The National Assembly debated a Plaid Cymru motion on the 'Revitalization of the Valleys' on 23 November 1999, which made repeated calls for an 'integrated', 'co-ordinated' and 'comprehensive' strategy of regeneration for the Valleys, targeting education and training, health inequalities, job creation, environmental improvement, transport infrastructure and community development. A few months after this debate, at the time of writing, the First Secretary, Alun Michael, had resigned before a potentially humiliating vote of 'no confidence' by the opposition Assembly parties. This was due, in no small measure, to the Assembly Labour Government's failure publicly to commit funds to match European Objective 1 allocations, betraying its continued dependence on budgetary decisions and schedules decided at Westminster. Such developments further postpone optimism in a new era for the Valleys under devolution.

Nevertheless, the Assembly does have under its control a budget of billions of pounds, which is no longer directly administered by London. There is some hope to be invested in the expectation that a Wales-wide representative body, accountable directly to the people of Wales, will have to make progress on redistributing the benefits of economic regeneration more evenly, not least because the ex-coalmining areas contain some of the most populous constituencies in Wales. The task of drawing up a distinctive urban policy which will redress the blatant imbalances within Wales will surely be a major area of activity and argument in the first decade of the twenty-first century.

Valleys tourism and heritage in 2000

As we shall see below, in the 1980s tourism and leisure were considered the big new ideas for the Valleys, charged with the task of turning their industrial heritage and their re-greened landscapes to economic advantage and replacing some of the jobs lost through deindustrialization. Tourism was one of the prime fronts which the Programme for the Valleys singled out for attention, through encouraging local borough and county councils to play a more proactive role in developing the infrastructure and image necessary to attract tourism development from the private sector. This optimism started to wane in the early 1990s, however, as the UK-wide recession in the tourist trade depressed visitor numbers and curtailed large-scale developments in the leisure industry as a whole.

Tourism in industrial south Wales remains largely undeveloped in 2000, and in parts of the Valleys there has been no tradition of tourism whatsoever (European Commission, 1994–6). Again, the familiar, uneven pattern emerges of growth along the M4 corridor, with major leisure and tourism investment at Cardiff Bay and Swansea, and under-development in the Valleys. The existent new heritage attractions in the Valleys – such as the Rhondda Heritage Park, Llancaiach Fawr and Big Pit – are limited to the day-visitor market. Whilst hope continues to be invested in tourism for the Valleys, with the Wales Tourist Board's *Tourism 2000* report delineating the area as a 'Special Action Programme', the challenges remain considerable. A recent report for the European Commission (Ecotec Research and Consulting Ltd., 1993) recognizes that tourism cannot hope to solve the current economic problems of the Valleys, which need to be tackled instead by attracting new industry and encouraging existing firms to expand and reinvest.

A further problem stems from local government reorganization. As Prentice (1993) points out, it brings the danger that, with the county-wide level of tourism planning and concomitant funding levels abolished, Valleys local authorities will now simply compete with each other on much-reduced budgets, and any overall region-wide tourism policy will be difficult to pursue. Current financial deficits in Rhondda Cynon Taff certainly suggest that these fears are well-founded. This is indicative of a more generalized trend in urban redevelopment since the 1980s, which has produced an increasingly fragmented, competitive and specialized urban environ-ment in which different zones develop according to the logic of disaggregated 'islands of regeneration' and 'flagship' redevelopment areas (Bianchini and Schwengel, 1991; Harvey, 1989b). The tour-ism, leisure and retail projects at Cardiff Bay, for instance, have developed within the ambit of the self-contained and inward-looking gaze of the Cardiff Bay Development Corporation, rather than as part of a strategic or redistributive development plan for the whole of Glamorgan or industrial south Wales.

The south Wales Valleys currently have half a dozen heritage sites dedicated to the coalmining industry. Of these, only two – Big Pit mining museum and the Rhondda Heritage Park (RHP) – represent sizeable visitor attractions with clear economic development func-tions. However, Big Pit stands way ahead of the RHP in terms of the numbers of visitors and the levels of funding that it attracts. Indeed, the future of Big Pit now looks rather rosy, in that it sits in the middle of a landscape, surrounding the small town of Blaenavon, which is currently being considered for inclusion in the list of World Heritage Sites compiled by UNESCO. The Rhondda Heritage Park, on the other hand, continues to operate at a deficit and to under-perform in terms of visitor numbers. The Rhondda is still urged to capitalize on its heritage for tourism purposes, but the economic returns of such a strategy are difficult to see so far. In addition, the use of the past for the purposes of entrepreneurial and tourist-orientated place promotion involves hitching together two iden-tities – a past and a future one – that pull in opposite directions. A tourism consultant's report in the 1990s warned:

> Rhondda, like other Valleys, has to take tourism advantage of its heritage yet prevent that image from endangering today's economic development prospects. The Borough Council is at pains to stress that it is not living in or on the past by adopting the slogan 'A living tribute to the past and a strong commitment to the future.'
>
> (Cole, 1995: 2)

Some of the further problems involved in turning the Rhondda's past into a heritage asset will begin to become clear both below and in successive chapters.

2. *The Valleys in the 1970s and 1980s*

Tracing the story of the Valleys' fortunes back in time from the year 2000, one is unavoidably faced with the bleak and dulling realization that little has been achieved in the sphere of economic regeneration since the 1970s and 1960s. The entrenched social and economic inequality that divides the coastal areas of south Wales from the Valleys is merely the unchanging inheritance of decades of uneven development. The Valleys emerge as an area of seemingly intractable decline, and it is this fact – unaltered by the development of heritage projects, the building of new factory units or the clearing of ex-industrial land along the way – which forms the real context for the discussion of heritage presented in this book. In spite of its promises, there is no doubt that heritage and the other entrepreneurial initiatives adopted in the Valleys during the last decades of the twentieth century have singularly failed to turn around their economic fortunes. No doubt the planners and sponsors of the Rhondda Heritage Park would retort that, had its initial grand scale been fully realized, this picture could have been different. Chapter 6 will examine this question through tracing the development of the Heritage Park in detail. In the mean time, let us turn the clock back to the immediate historical context of the 'turn to heritage' in the 1970s.

At the end of the 1970s, significant swathes of south Wales's traditional heavy industry were still intact: thirty-six collieries remained open, employing 27,000 people, and the steel plants of Port Talbot and Llanwern still employed over 20,000 (European Commission, 1994–6). However, it was already clear that both coal and steel had an uncertain future. By the beginning of the 1980s, a major restructuring of employment had already occurred, from the extractive and heavy manufacturing industries to the service sector and light manufacturing. Even by 1981, six out of ten employees were working in service industries (Prentice, 1993). In spite of this economic diversification, however, the Valleys entered the 1980s with considerable problems of high unemployment, out-migration and a growing economically inactive section of the population (Rees and Rees, 1980).

What was to be done with the Valleys?

The increasing sense of crisis at the end of the 1970s was represented in a widespread perception that 'something had to be done' in the Valleys. However, a question remained over what route the Valleys should take: a renewed effort to reindustrialize through manufacturing and to retain existing industry wherever possible, or an alternative, service-sector-orientated solution which would accept the relocation of manufacturing along the M4 corridor and develop a more leisure-orientated economic base for the ex-mining valleys. This dilemma was intensely sensitive and highly politicized in the local arena. Both district and county councils were publicly committed to resisting vigorously any suggestion that the closure of the coalmining industry was an inevitability. To some extent, this political atmosphere resulted in a reluctance to embrace new solutions, especially those associated with replacement policies for coal, steel and manufacturing. The suggestion that the pursuit of 'proper jobs' in the Valleys (that is, those in the traditional industries) might be replaced by service-industry solutions was still a controversial and contested idea. However, the question remained of what kind of alternative employment was to be generated and how.

An indication of the immediate historical context of this dilemma is to be found in the 1970s' community initiatives in the south Wales Valleys. In the early 1970s, fears of the further entrenchment of the northern Valleys' economic marginalization had suddenly increased when the Welsh Office announced plans to designate Llantrisant, at the mouth of the Ely valley, a New Town (cf. Clavel, 1983). This would have been a further coastal 'pull' factor, disadvantaging the northern Valleys, and was stridently resisted by local Valleys councils.[1] In the light of these concerns, a coalition of local councils and voluntary organizations designated 1974 the 'Year of the Valleys'. This initiative, which grew out of a sense that little had been achieved to aid the valley communities since the Aberfan disaster of 1966, resulted in a series of inter-disciplinary conferences and meetings amongst academics, churches, planners, local spokespeople, residents and others throughout the year (and which continued, more spasmodically, for a decade). The Year resulted in the publication of a series of papers, entitled *The Valleys Call* (Ballard and Jones, 1975).

This book, reflecting as it does the views of a range of local academics and community leaders who were concerned to try and halt the economic decline of the Valleys, expresses one dimension of the 'structure of feeling' – to use Raymond Williams's phrase – in the Valleys at the time. Above all, it reflects a common theme: that the Valleys were in a state of crisis and that *something had to be done*:

> Unless something is done, the Valleys will die ... the present time is one of crisis for the valleys, due to economic rundown, and it is urgent that the communities should come together and pledge themselves firmly to change it.
> (Report of general discussion at the 'Call to the Valleys' conference in March 1973 – Ballard and Jones, 1975: 39–40)

This sense of crisis was based on a fear that the Valleys communities were on the brink of disintegration, and that their whole identity was threatened with extinction. This threat was understood, in particular, to come from the 'long-standing debate over the relative needs of the valley communities and the coastal belt' (1975: 279), reflecting fears of the industrial peripheralization of the Valleys.

It is worth quoting at length the contribution of Harold Carter, then Professor of Human Geography at Aberystwyth. He singles out one scenario proposed for the Valleys' future:

> There is a widely held view, often expressed in private but rarely propounded in public, that the Valleys constitute a dying area, indeed one of the classic areas in decline within the E.E.C., where an old resource-based heavy industry is retracting in favour of new industrial areas based on accessibility and the ease of assembly of diverse materials. The economic disadvantages of the Valleys are, therefore, so great that the only sensible policy is to give way to what is inevitable, and salvage what is possible, by encouraging development at the valley mouths and along the line of the M4 ... It might be proper to speculate that no strategy exists for South Wales because in the end there is no conviction that a real future exists for the Valleys; the myth has become a conviction.
> (Ballard and Jones, 1975: 372)

The papers gathered together in the volume, specifically directed at countering this conviction, insisted that the future of the Valleys lay in industrial redevelopment and regeneration as economic areas in their own right, and not as commuter-belt zones for the coastal plain. An underlying fear was that the Valleys were going to be turned away from production to become leisure spaces for 're-greening'. Many contributors took as their starting-point the Welsh Office declaration in the White Paper of 1967 that 'for both economic and social reasons the Government rejects any policy which would assume disintegration of the substantial valley communities' (Welsh Office, 1967: 337, quoted in Ballard and Jones, 1975: 279; see also K. O. Morgan, 1995). This commitment from central government, however, was seen as inadequate, as it was not backed up by a coherent regional policy for the Valleys as an economic area in their own right.

The rhetoric of impending disintegration is bound up with the feeling of a loss of a *way of life*. This, I want to argue, is based upon an appeal to the distinctive cultural identity of the Valleys, imagined in terms of strong images of community, solidarity and mutual aid. Carter elaborates again:

> The Year of the Valleys has ... sought through every possible means to contribute towards the reinvigoration of the life and character of the Valleys, an area where a fatalistic acceptance of future decline has been clearly evident. That *way of life* and *distinctive character* are impossible to specify briefly, if at all, in words ... But they are made up of an extremely complex and interlocking array of *customs and traditions*, *patterns of behavior*, out of which some tangible manifestations emerge ... The Year of the Valleys has tried to give expression to very many aspects of that *culture* or *way of life* but in the end, underpinning everything, is one foundation – and that is economic prosperity, or at least economic *viability*. Without such a foundation, and the population it supports, there can only be gradual decay and ultimate dissolution, and a rich contributor to the *national character of Wales* will become attenuated and the *whole life of the nation* impoverished. This conference, therefore, deals with a crucial issue as everything else derives from it.
>
> (1975: 368–9; my italics)

Here, the only proper objectives of regeneration are held to be those which will sustain the 'economic viability' of the Valleys – not as an end in itself, but as the very means through which they are to survive as places with 'a way of life and a distinctive character'. In other words, the sense of crisis that underpins this volume articulates a much deeper concern centred on the survival of place identity, understood as the need to maintain the *cultural distinctiveness* of the Valleys. We can see the influence here of well-rehearsed narratives that picture the Valleys as a community, a term that has been absolutely central to repeated efforts – both at a grass-roots and a bureaucratic level – to mobilize resources for the Valleys and to resist pit closures (Rees, 1997). Indeed, the slogan 'Cau Pwll, Lladd Cymuned' (Close a Pit, Kill a Community) was a key rallying cry in the Valleys during the year-long miners' strike (Francis, 1990: 112). We shall see, in later chapters, how the ideal of the distinctive Valleys community became a central organizing plat-form, too, in the development of heritage in the Rhondda.

This image of community is constructed around the values of self-reliance, solidarity and social cohesion which coalmining is held to encapsulate (Dicks, 1997a). In the 1970s, the conviction still held that the survival of these values depended upon the recovery of productive economic capacity. The ability of the Valleys to provide employment for their own indigenous workforce was seen as the central foundation of their distinctive identity. As Rees notes, the economic regeneration of the area has continued to be couched in such terms throughout the succeeding decades:

> Central government policies ... for regional economic development in South Wales have universally been couched in terms which take as *axiomatic* the need to regenerate the economy of the Valleys, despite the collapse and, by the 1980s, the virtual disappearance of the region's initial economic raison d'être ... It is the special vibrancy and popular currency of the social imagery of the Valleys which, in no small part, accounts for the effectiveness of this presentation.
>
> (1997: 100; italics in original)

Thus, in the 1970s, hopes continued to rest on the regeneration of the Valleys around traditional industrial production, in terms of the generation of wealth from extraction and manufacture.

Re-greening my valley?

Yet by the 1980s there were signs of an increasing willingness to envisage the Valleys as spaces of consumption, rather than centres of production. The dam which had tried to shore up the old identity had, it seems, begun to give way. In the process, the fear of losing Valleys identity to the 're-greening' option continued to haunt local political sensibilities, and this – in no small measure I would argue – helps to account for the controversy that the Rhondda Heritage Park attracted at its inception. This fear was intensified in the 1980s, when the Rhondda Heritage Park was already a proposal under investigation by the Welsh Development Agency, and had already been floated in the local newspapers. In 1985, just after the end of the year-long national miners' strike aimed at preventing pit closures, the Commons Select Committee on Welsh Affairs was receiving submissions concerning the potential for tourism in the ex-coalmining Valleys. John Brown, a tourism and heritage consultant from England (who was also a key consultant for the Rhondda Heritage Park), presented evidence built on the re-greening option:

> Today, it may be kindest and wisest to let the population of valleys like the Rhondda and the Rhymney drift gently down to much, much lower levels, to enable, in 20 or 50 years, smaller towns and villages to offer a higher quality of life and environment. It seems perverse to build another generation of factories, with no innate raison d'être, on small difficult sites in inaccessible valleys, rather than where they are more likely to succeed, on the coastal plain and in the M4 corridor, within the same travel to work area.
>
> (Committee on Welsh Affairs, 1986–7: 130)

Such a statement reflects a view that the withdrawal of industry should bring a 'rational' realignment of the social and economic identity of the area, so that tourism can 'naturally' take over. What tourists do not, apparently, want to see are endless ribbons of dilapidated housing: as John Brown puts it, 'the built environment would often be delightful if there were not so much of it' (p. 129).

Such a vision belongs to a 1980s political discourse that has been described by Humphreys (1995) as the 'new new Wales'. It is a reincarnation of the images of a 'new Wales's prevalent in the 1950s, during the period of economic growth and diversification which saw the rapid development of new plants and factories along the coastal belt. Based on a right-wing call for the re-greening of the Valleys and the celebration of the decline of the coal industry as heralding a new psychological perspective, it sees Wales's future as lying in 'new' and 'modern' forms of employment, in small and medium business enterprises organized around leisure and consumption (Humphreys, 1995: 140). Hywel Francis (1990) sees the 1980s as a period in which an ideological shift was engineered in the Valleys, away from the proletarian values of *Cwmardy* (the title of the book by Rhondda's famous socialist novelist Lewis Jones) towards the entrepreneurial new world of 'Greater Cardiff', in which the Valleys' identity was to be subsumed into that of the metropolis (1990: 111).

The re-greening scenario was hotly contested, however, and John Brown's report was met, on the whole, with considerable local hostility. The Wales Tourist Board, which had not been consulted on its drafting, was highly embarrassed. Its chairman, Prys Edwards, interviewed in *Planet* magazine at the time, made strenuous efforts to distance the Board from the report. On John Brown's suggestions to re-green the Valleys for leisure consumption, he says:

> No – we are working hard to make sure that there is employment in the Valleys, so we are doing the opposite of what he says ... to undertake any development in Wales which is alien to its character is not the way we are looking at things ... My own feeling was that after twelve months of trying to present tourism in a constructive way that was commensurate with the character of the country, this report set me back many many months in my public relations exercise, and I was not happy about it, I must say.
>
> (Barnie, 1985: 9–10)

This defensiveness on behalf of the Wales Tourist Board indicates the political sensitivity of the 'character' of the Valleys – their cultural and economic identity – and the role of tourism within it. The Rhondda Heritage Park, seeming to stand for the replacement of 'proper' jobs with menial and casual ones and of a productive colliery with a theme park, managed to encapsulate all these fears of deindustrialization, peripheralization and depopulation. In many ways, this fear lay at the root of the troubled relationship between the park and local people, a matter which will be further explored in chapter 7.

Labourism, local government and community in the Rhondda

The determination to buttress what was seen as the crumbling edifice of community in the Valleys was not merely an abstract ideal. It needs to be understood in the light of enduring social and political relations in the Valleys, and particularly in the Rhondda, which are encapsulated in the idea of 'labourism'. The Valleys were (until local government reorganization in March 1996) divided up into administrative boroughs. Of these, the coalmining boroughs have, since 1922 and the collapse of the Liberal vote, consistently returned huge Labour majorities in both local and national elections. Whilst other political traditions, such as the Communist Party's strength in 1930s Rhondda, should not be ignored, most analyses of the post-war period acknowledge the undisputed primacy of the Labour Party (Francis and Smith, 1980; C. Williams, 1996). In the first National Assembly elections of May 1999, Plaid Cymru's ground-breaking victory in the Rhondda finally seems to have broken the long-standing local hegemony of the Labour Party. In the 1970s and 1980s, though, it had seemed unassailable.[2]

The industrial, working-class, anglophone areas of Wales, where the Labour Party's dominance was most firmly rooted, have been described as 'Welsh Wales's as opposed to 'British Wales's or 'Y Fro Gymraeg' (Balsom, 1985), reflecting the distinctive, 'anglicized Welsh' political identity of the area. Labourism had been forged on the social and cultural fit between the coalfields and the Party, and had historically defined itself as the modern, forward-looking alternative to the Welsh-speaking, rural traditions (Thomas, 1999). Ensuring the survival of the traditional community identity of the Valleys was its central mission. It represented a political culture that still, in the 1970s, defined the 'true' identity of the Valleys in terms of industrial production, skilled manual work, the family wage and a strong community spirit. It held on to policy approaches dominant during the immediate post-war period, which demanded state intervention to resolve local social and economic problems (Rees, 1985). Chris Williams traces the genesis of these values to the Labour Party's gradual consolidation of local politics in the inter-war and post-war period, resulting in a broad consensus over policies such as full employment, comprehensive education and the provision of leisure time and amenities for workers (1996: 211).

An interview extract from one of the councillors involved in the Rhondda Heritage Park from its inception gives an insight into this labourist identity. This councillor is from neighbouring Taff Ely, lying to the south of the Rhondda, yet identifies his interests very much with Rhondda coalmining traditions: he had spent forty-five

years working in the pits. He makes it clear that he sees his political
position as automatic, secure and enduring:

> We've got a lot in common with the Rhondda people. It's a mining
> community, we're a mining community. We're not separated ... I've
> been here thirty years. Nobody asked me to be a councillor. I put my
> name up, and that was it. I top the poll every year at elections, and that's
> it. I'm not worried.
>
> (Personal interview with Taff Ely borough councillor)

This account shows the clear alignment of a 'we' identity between
the speaker and the mining community. This particular councillor
had also been a magistrate for thirty-eight years, as well as serving
on various charitable committees and societies, and was fully
committed to the traditional public-service model that, according
to Williams, was a trademark of the typical Rhondda Labour
councillor (C. Williams, 1996).

Increasingly, however, in the 1970s and 1980s, Valleys labourism
had become associated with anachronism, traditionalism, parochialism and complacency. As Boyne et al. (1991) point out, 'Safe
Labour wards provide councillors with the prospect of unchal-
lenged occupancy of their position ... A traditional and still largely
working-class Labour establishment dominates local government in
urban Wales' (1991: 6). Within its virtual monopoly of the political
scene, the Labour Group on most councils was characterized by
consensus and stability, an absence of factionalism and a rather
ageing council membership. Griffiths (1987) observes:

> The relationships between the [Mid Glamorgan] council leadership,
> other councillors and Labour Party members are ones of deference and
> patronage. With no acceptable means of challenge and succession, the
> leadership is elderly ... Intra-party disputes in so far as they do emerge
> are based in the main on geographical, ward-based interests and
> committee loyalties.
>
> (Griffiths, 1987: 216)

The typical Valleys councillor – up until the electoral shake-up of
1999 – was usually male, over sixty years old and from a manual
working-class background. Quite a number of Valleys councillors
were still from mining backgrounds even in the 1990s. These
councillors retained strong contacts with local constituents from

similar circles, who shared similar backgrounds and life-experiences. Such a culture, as many critics have pointed out, tended in places to generate a self-serving parochialism manifested in the 'who you know' syndrome (Rees, 1997; Boyne et al., 1991; Betts, 1993).

This rooted and traditionalist labourism has dominated local policy responses to deindustrialization in the Valleys.[3] It pictures its responsibilities towards its constituents largely in terms of the provision of opportunities for productive labour, organized around two appeals: skilled manual *work* in the form of a 'labour aristocracy', and *community* in the form of localist power-bases. The focus on (waged, productive) work betrays a further, masculinist strand, predicated on a traditional gender division of labour. Ideals of hard manual work, 'decent' living, a strict demarcation between work and leisure, the male family wage, community spirit, are all central aspects of what we could term the 'imaginary' of labourism – that is, its characteristic images, symbols and narratives. The values of individual enterprise, consumerism, leisure and marketization – with which the arrival of heritage came to be associated in the 1980s – are not part of the picture.

What happened to labourist political culture during the 1970s and early 1980s, when, as the above discussion has shown, attempts to replace an occupational identity based on coalmining with other manufacturing initiatives were finally seen to be exhausted? Did labourism collapse along with the eclipse of the 'old working class' (Adamson, 1991; W. Thompson, 1993)? The Rhondda Heritage Park, it could be argued, emerged as a timely container for this labourist imaginary: a repository for the traditions of the past, and yet also an irreproachable economic 'solution' (in the best entrepreneurial spirit) to the area's future regeneration. This apparently paradoxical synergy between heritage's cultural functions (of representing the old identity) and economic functions (of replacing that identity with a new economic base) has certain hyper-real qualities. It suggests that heritage tries to effect a magical solution to a problem that is, in fact, intractable: the problem of both regenerating *and* also culturally relocating Britain's ex-industrial periphery.

The insistence on the Rhondda's productive viability and distinctive character is a central element of the identity crisis of deindustrialization. It is an appeal that can only be made through mythologizing an attached way of life, through the labourist ideals of work and community discussed above. This type of discourse leads to calls for reindustrialization around manufacturing and 'proper jobs', but it is not difficult to see how it also helps prepare the ground for a heritage initiative – both in economic and cultural terms. Economically, the call for community survival is increasingly made in the context of the turn to service-sector solutions, so that reindustrialization is gradually accepted as embracing service industries, too. Culturally, it canonizes a particular imaginary for the Rhondda, in that it publicly insists on the *distinctiveness* of the local way of life. The ground is thus prepared for the magical solution of heritage enterprise – celebrating traditional cultural identity at the same time as embracing a forward-looking economic identity based on the obliteration of the old. Pragmatically, heritage could thus allow labourist political culture publicly to display its own historical credentials, yet also enable the local area to grasp its fair share of new development grants for leisure and tourism in the 1980s.

The turn to heritage in the Rhondda

By the early 1980s, government agencies in Wales, notably the Welsh Development Agency and the Wales Tourist Board, were convinced that what the Rhondda needed was a grand 'flagship' leisure and tourism project to herald a new identity for the Valleys, and lead them away from the traditional reliance on heavy industry. In 1983, the year when Lewis Merthyr closed, the Wales Tourist Board commissioned a substantial report, entitled *Realising the Tourism Potential of the South Wales Valleys*. It concluded that 'the Valleys have considerable potential for growth in a different and largely new field of economic activity – tourism'.[4] The report lists various resources that the Valleys can market to the outsider: built resources (including industrial archaeology and heritage, architecture and leisure amenities), cultural resources (covering 'famous sons and daughters', literature, art, sports, music, crafts, famous events, etc.) and natural resources (forest trails, conservation, parks and gardens, outdoor pursuits, etc.). In this way, by compiling a compendium of indigenous characteristics that can be marketed as tourist attractions, the report seeks to promote the Valleys as 'a region which must emphasise its own special, unique blend of characteristics ... [and] express [its] own identity and images – clearly, strongly and proudly' (Leisure and Tourism Unit: 1983: 9).

The report is resolutely uncommitted, however, as to exactly what the 'unique' identity consists of, reducing it to a general list of attributes, or what could aptly be termed an 'inventory of traditions'. These cover just about every general resource the average tourist could reasonably hope to find. It is noticeable that, instead of specifying the exact nature of local attractions, the report spends considerable time addressing itself to the 'residents of the Valleys' – whose psychological characteristics are held to be in need of some improvement:

Industrial South Wales for long has been seen wrongly as a joke-location – based on 'How Green Was My Valley', where all are coal miners, singing their way to the chapel, or playing rugby, or steaming in pithead baths. There is a great and wide array of realisable resources which are far wider than the unreal images of the Valleys. Changed attitudes to conserving the resources of South Wales have come almost too late. The region has been busy destroying its past, before realising that these resources are among its greatest potential assets [...] Past suffering has led to problems of self-image, of lack of pride, and even lack of respect for people in the Valleys ... There seems to be a lack of pride and belief in a great past, and in great achievements. Tourism, conservation and interpretation are not only matters of telling the story of your culture to others, but also of transmitting it to your *own* children and grandchildren in the Valleys.

However modest were the housing conditions, or the financial circumstances of families in the Valleys, the great tradition of warm and generous hospitality offered to visiting family and friends, was maintained. Dealing with the stranger is not such a strong local tradition. [...] An even bigger psychological challenge is to get the residents of the Valleys to think of their area as a real and desirable tourism-destination area ... there is need for attitudinal change on the part of local people as hosts. [...]

Last, but not least, in the area of Values and the approach to tourism, is the need to deal with residual feelings found in chapel-going Wales, and elsewhere, that holidays, play, leisure and free time relaxation are shameful, sinful and indulgent. The Protestant Work Ethic itself diminishes as a declining percentage of our population finds their economic support via permanent full-time jobs ... The case for leisure as a desirable thing in its own right is the first step. The second step is to see that holiday tourism can give those leisure experiences which may be the pinnacle of our year, whereby we are restored, stimulated, renewed and refuelled for the future.

(Leisure and Tourism Unit, 1983: 9–10)

This extract is worth quoting at length, for it provides a particularly clear example of the visionary 'brave new world of leisure' rhetoric which was beginning to be aired in central government pronouncements and from New Right think-tanks and newspapers in the early 1980s.

Beginning with a ritual disavowal of the 'joke-location', disassociating the report from the standard-bearer of Valleys stereotypes, *How Green was My Valley*,[5] the extract is clear about what is *not* the true Valleys identity, but rather reticent about specifying what *is*. The 'story', 'great achievements' and 'potential assets' are left disingenuously vague. Instead, considerable space is devoted to specifying the *current characteristics* of the 'residents of the Rhondda'. These are framed by an image of community which is in many ways opposed to the image of the heroic, labourist community of collective action and hard work. These images belong rather to a discourse that represents working-class communities as deprived, backward and recalcitrant. Images of working-class communities as downtrodden, isolated and underclass have, in fact, often been mobilized in both right-wing free-market rhetoric and in welfarist, 'social exploration' studies documenting the ills of the working class (Dicks, 1999).

The report describes Valleys people as lacking in self-confidence, pride and awareness of history (depriving their grandchildren of an appreciation of past greatness), inward-looking (generous to friends but not to strangers), obstinately clinging to old ways of thinking (the 'challenge' is to 'get' them to change), anachronistically puritanical (having 'residual feelings' about shame and sin), and, above all, in need of enlightenment through a two-step Gestalt philosophy proposing a magically 'restored and stimulated' new 'we'. This imaginary produces a clear 'then versus now' discourse, in which the Valleys play the role of the reluctant participant – ushered along by the Wales Tourist Board – in new realities, which involve the decline of 'full-time permanent jobs'. In contrast to the determined resistance put up in the labourist call for reindustrialization, here the future is embraced as a brave new world far removed from labourist coalmining inheritance (cf. Humphreys, 1995). Thus, the tourism-heritage option requires local residents to 'pull their socks up', and seeks to enlist them as proactive heritage entrepreneurs.

Some of the complexity involved in this representational strategy can be grasped by noting how determinedly the above report recommends the transformation of the *ways of thinking* of residents of the Rhondda. It is clear, indeed, that if the Rhondda's heritage is to be tapped for tourism, some aspects of that heritage – such as its labourist inheritance and 'habitual attitudes' – might appear a burden (see also Robins, 1991, on the North-East's ambivalence regarding its cultural icon, Andy Capp, during Newcastle's attempts to harness heritage for economic regeneration). If the Wales Tourist Board was to be successful in capitalizing on the Valleys' past, it had to approach the area as a flexible hybrid, capable of generating images of both post-industrial renewal and the traditional industrial heritage. In a sense, it involved proclaiming 'How Green was My Valley is dead – long live How Green was My Valley'.

Whilst the proletarian identity of the Rhondda might be a burden to enterprise culture, the presentation of the Rhondda people as an *underclass* neatly provides a reason for the Wales Tourist Board to intervene in the area and change this image. Thus, the call for tourism – though affirming the need for Rhondda people to change – also depends upon *advertising* their neediness so as to shore up funding claims. Images of the self-sufficient, labourist community are unhelpful in this respect, but images of a deprived and under-confident community are just what is required. Thus, heritage as economic regeneration depends upon the simultaneous proclamation and denial of an area's greatness. In the process, the established place-myths of self-sufficiency are further weakened, and labourist appeals to local autonomy look increasingly romantic and outmoded.

Local political autonomy

Local councils remained suspicious about the tourism option. On the one hand, the dominant local political culture was committed, as we have seen, to preserving the traditional occupational base of the Valleys. On the other hand, Rhondda Borough Council's ability to secure replacement manufacturing jobs on its own was already markedly compromised by the start of the Thatcher administration in 1979. The borough council found itself faced with no answers to the question of 'what was to be done' in the Rhondda. I have already suggested that the industrial heritage option presented itself as a magical solution. It could provide safekeeping for the old traditions, whilst at the same time tapping into the new entrepreneurial public funding philosophy of the Welsh Office and the Conservative government. Eventually, as chapter 6 will describe, Rhondda Borough Council became convinced that its mining heritage could be put to good economic use as part of the tourist trail.

However, as geographers have noted, assent to the tourism, heritage and enterprise agenda has profound consequences for the local political sphere itself. Goodwin (1993) describes how a similar labourist political culture in Sheffield first tried hard to fight steel closures in the early 1980s, but then found itself unable to provide alternative employment. The entrenchment of the Conservative Party's hold on power as the 1980s progressed eventually brought about a 'dramatic rethink', in which 'it was recognised that private sector resources were essential to any future regeneration' (1993: 152). From then on, public–private partnership was to replace confrontation, and image became a crucial resource for place-marketing. The dereliction of the Don Valley was replaced by the 'domed palaces of leisure' of the huge Meadowhall shopping centre. In the process, the council had to cede power to the Sheffield Urban Development Corporation, whose establishment was a condition of central funding for regeneration.

Similarly, as we shall see in chapter 6, when the Rhondda began chasing large sums of money for the heritage project under the aegis of the Welsh Office, political control over the project was taken out of the hands of Rhondda Borough Council and transferred to a consortium dominated by the Welsh Development Agency and the county council. Thus, local areas are forced to both trade upon and transform their local identities in the rebranding game. In the Rhondda, a local labourist identity, which had held on to its political hegemony despite the disappearance of the coal industry largely because of the lack of successful alternatives and the absence of cultural realignment, found itself in the 1980s invited to market that identity in terms of the heritage-tourism option. The paradox is that, in the process, this very identity is made redundant through being publicly displayed as heritage, as are its claims to provide locally derived and locally controlled solutions. The potential problem with heritage, and one which will be explored in successive chapters, is that, in the process of servicing the rebranding of locality, heritage may reduce the identity it puts on display to a commodified cliché.

2

New vernacular heritage: wider cultural and economic contexts

1. The new heritage

Heritage is part of a burgeoning new culture of display, in which a variety of different *sites* are transformed into *sights* to capitalize on new forms of cultural consumption. In addition to the local context explored in the last chapter, therefore, heritage needs to be placed in wider contexts. Indeed, that local context has itself shifted in response to wider transformations at a UK political and cultural level, particularly during the enterprise-focused years of the 1980s and 1990s. These wider transformations include successive UK governments' embrace of urban entrepreneurialism (section 3, below), but also encompass changes in patterns of consumption in the UK and beyond in the technologically advanced, industrialized West. There is, in particular, a turn towards more vernacular, experience-centred forms of cultural consumption, a context without which it is impossible to explain the emergence of what I call the 'new heritage'. Out of these contexts has sprung the professional knowledge that constitutes the 'heritage industry' (chapter 8) and its characteristic recommendations for a leisure-orientated and accessible heritage 'product'. The context of Rhondda heritage needs to be mapped in the light of these wider transformations in cultural consumption if we are to avoid seeing the Rhondda as an island cut off from 'outside' influences.

Heritage everywhere?

The multiplicity and diversity of heritage museums in Britain today is unprecedented. Each offers a glimpse of a unique and singular event, place, time-period or way of life. Visitors can take a trip to Flambards Village Theme Park, with its reconstructions of a

'Victorian Village' and 'Britain in the Blitz', or learn 'The Story of
Carlisle's Place in Turbulent Border History' at the Tullie House
City Museum. We can find out how cider was traditionally made at
the Hereford Cider Museum Trust, discover Dover's historic past
at the White Cliffs Experience and see the industrial heritage of
Leicestershire at Snibston Discovery Park. Many attractions are
representations of particular places and form part of the tourism
and leisure strategies of particular localities. I shall be exploring
the reasons behind this boom in local heritage attractions during the
course of this chapter

In Wales, visitors can learn how canals were built and used at the
Canal Exhibition Centre in Llangollen, Clwyd, visit the Sygun
Copper Mine at Beddgelert, see how the Celts lived at Celtica,
Gwynedd, or hear the story of mining communities at Big Pit and
the Rhondda Heritage Park in the south Wales Valleys. They can
also explore the houses and buildings of rural (and, to a lesser
extent, industrial) Wales at the open-air Museum of Welsh Life at
St Fagans, near Cardiff. Public funding for museums in Wales has
been increasing year on year. Welsh Office funding of the branches
of the National Museums and Galleries of Wales and its grant-in-
aid to the Council of Museums in Wales increased by £5 million
between 1985 and 1995 to £13.240 million, and local government
support for museums and galleries nearly doubled from £4.1 million
in 1989 to £7.7 million in 1995 (Casey, 1995).

Two caveats need to be added, however, to any claim that
heritage is expanding so unrelentingly that we are in danger of
becoming a 'nation of museum attendants' – although it might have
looked that way in the 1980s (Francis, 1981). First of all, heritage is
not a new phenomenon. As David Lowenthal (1985, 1998) points
out, and as the many studies of the nineteenth-century explosion in
tourism testify, historical landscapes, cityscapes and buildings have
long been consecrated as 'attractions' and 'sights' on a tourist trail.
Secondly, it would be wrong to characterize the past two decades as
a period of relentless and vigorous growth for the museum and
heritage sector. Although the visibility and range of heritage attractions has undoubtedly increased, the sector as a whole has been
buffeted by wider shifts in regional policy in the UK. During the
1980s, as the UK Conservative government abandoned Keynesian
principles of state-assisted funding for public services, and increasingly curtailed the financial autonomy of local government, many

small, local, publicly funded museums could no longer survive. Almost half of the museums registered with DOMUS, the museum statistics digest, are run by local authorities, but there has, recently, been a general squeeze on public-sector funding for museums resulting in budget shortfalls for many (Selwood et al., 1995).

Although nearly all the major studies of heritage repeat the claim that, in the UK, a museum opens every fortnight (Hewison, 1987; Urry, 1990; Walsh, 1992), we have few reliable figures on closures. Whilst overall visits to museums in 1990 registered the largest yearly increase (of 6 per cent) since 1977, the average number of visitors per museum declined from 72,000 to 48,000 between 1978 and 1988, as the number of museums grew – from 716 to 1,222 (Eckstein and Feist, 1991). Indeed, there was a general slump in visitor attendance at national museums in the early 1990s, linked to the general recession in tourism, although there was evidence of a pick-up as the decade wore on (Selwood et al., 1995). Though a large proportion of today's museums have opened since 1980 (43 per cent of the total according to British Tourist Authority figures cited in Selwood et al., 1995), it is difficult to discover how many have closed in the same period.

Rather than talking about a heritage boom *per se*, it is perhaps more appropriate to examine what it is that is new about heritage today. Museums, of course, constitute only one category of heritage attraction. The offically accepted definition of a museum is as 'an institution which collects, documents, preserves, exhibits and interprets material evidence and associated information for the public benefit' (Selwood et al., 1995: 30). There are many new heritage developments that do not meet this definition, including the spread of city centre theming and waterfront developments which contain heritage displays (Urry, 1990). This book concentrates on institutions which interpret a particular heritage but which do not necessarily have a formal collecting or preservation role. The changing visitor experience and interpretative approach of this new generation of 'heritage museums' constitutes the subject matter of this book. The next section will discuss these changes in terms of two parallel trends: towards the increasing use of simulation techniques on the one hand, and towards an increasingly vernacular principle of display on the other. In the light of these key shifts in the nature of the heritage experience, it makes more sense to talk of a 'new heritage' rather than a heritage boom *per se*.

Museums of the senses

What is heritage? In its broadest sense, heritage refers to all preserved or inherited artefacts, buildings and landscapes from the past. When juxtaposed with the term 'museum', however, heritage assumes a more specific meaning, denoting an institution which operates via a particular mode of historical display. Heritage typically favours the construction of simulated environments over the collection museum's static display of artefacts. The principle of simulation is designed to encourage a more interactive and hands-on visitor experience than that offered by the traditional museum. Design consultants for the Rhondda Heritage Park, for example, described their plans thus:

> We are proposing a new kind of visitor attraction, at least so far as Britain is concerned. It will not be a museum, but an *experience centre*. The distinction is an important one. In a museum – even one as lively as, say, Beamish – the basis is a collection of genuine objects ... However, we see the RHP as depicting the past, not through the display of original objects, but through the visitor's *senses*. Original buildings or exhibits are useful in this process, but maybe they are not necessarily essential to it. Like the museum, we seek to present the authentic; but the *authentic experiences*, not the *authentic objects*.
>
> (John Brown & Co. et al., 1989: 6; my italics)

The emphasis on experiences rather than objects is characteristic of heritage, and indicative of a broader UK trend away from traditional museum forms of display during the 1980s and 1990s. This trend has been inspired by, and replicated in, new heritage projects in Australasia, the USA and other (particularly northern) European countries. The collection museum's reliance on the scientific categorization of artefacts is rejected in favour of a new mode of contextualized display, which draws in many ways on the characteristics of the folk museums, such as St Fagans. Various technologies of *interpretation* are employed to ensure that objects are situated within three-dimensional environments, that these environments are replete with people and that visitors interact with them through sight, sound, touch and – increasingly – smell and taste, too (Hooper-Greenhill, 1994; Light, 1995). The Rhondda Heritage Park epitomizes this trend, as the above quotation illustrates.

The heritage experience seeks to establish a lively, 'living history' environment within which visitors can exercise all their senses, rather than simply gazing at glass cases. Instead of having visitors surveyed by uniformed museum staff, heritage museums often employ 'demonstrators' dressed in period costume, who are encouraged to interact with visitors and elicit questions and conversation. The demonstrators are part of the whole experience and are intended to make artefacts and buildings seem more real. Objects are picked up, handled and used in their 'actual' environments. It is the human and social context that is brought to the fore, rather than the objects themselves. Indeed, as Hewison (1989) notes, many of these heritage centres are really 'museums without collections' since they often lack formal collecting or preservation policies.

Vernacular heritage

Heritage is certainly not a new phenomenon. However, traditional heritage fare up until fairly recently consisted mainly of important public buildings and monuments: historic remains and excavations, cathedrals and abbeys, castles and museums, historic streets and villages, civic halls and buildings of state. Aristocratic private residences, such as stately homes and country houses, were also deemed part of 'the nation's heritage' as, too, were the homes of famous people. Today, on the other hand, heritage has expanded into the ordinary domains of human life. In place of grandeur, wealth and power, it is now centred on the everyday and the idiosyncratic. The emphasis on people, discussed above, points to the vernacular aspiration that underlies the heritage phenomenon: the aim is to offer 'ordinary people now' the chance to encounter and learn about 'ordinary people then'.

The objects of the tourist gaze have thereby multiplied, from the traditional 'auratic' mode in which rare and original historic artefacts hold centre stage (cf. Benjamin, 1973), to the vernacular mode, in which the familiar, mundane world of 'the people' is displayed through reconstructed backdrops and settings. For Urry (1995), this represents a 'democratisation of the tourist gaze', in that the state's patrimony – in the form of castles, country estates, cathedrals, and so forth – no longer has monopoly over 'our heritage' (see also Samuel, 1994). Neither is the idea of 'the people's heritage' confined to the essentially rural and 'quaint' vision of the folk museum. One of the major beneficiaries of this vernacular mode has been industrial heritage. In Wales alone, industrial heritage attractions set up over the past two decades include the Llechwedd Slate Caverns at Blaenau Ffestiniog; Big Pit Museum at Blaenavon, Sygun Copper Mine at Beddgelert, Cefn Coed Colliery Museum at Crynant, Neath, the Welsh Slate Museum at Llanberis, the Rhondda Heritage Park and no fewer than seven narrow-gauge railways (see Edwards and Llurdes, 1996).

New forms of vernacular visitor experience, however, are not limited to industrial heritage sites. Visitors to Llancaiach Fawr, for example, in south Wales, find themselves entering a Tudor manor house, once the home of a well-to-do seventeenth-century family, and stepping into a living history simulation:

> History comes alive at Llancaiach Fawr. The stone walls of this fine Tudor Manor House contain a vivid image of the seventeenth century as it might have been. From the moment that visitors enter the formal gardens, they are surrounded by the sights, smells and sounds of the past. Stewards dressed in historical costume wait to guide them on their journey into history. In every respect it should be an unforgettable experience.
>
> (visitor brochure)

Here, aristocratic culture is translated into the vernacular. Instead of the traditional trudge around sectioned-off rooms, visitors interact directly with the servants and stewards of the great house. The Pritchards themselves are 'out' when visitors 'call', and their absence allows visitors the freedom to roam the house themselves and to meet the servants. This gives visitors access to the backstairs life of the house: the preparation of food, the buying of produce, the keeping of accounts, and all the various skills and crafts which serviced the household's needs. Indeed, it is the servants' lives which constitute the main focus of interest: the Pritchards themselves fade into the background. Every effort is made to banish the vestiges of a formal museum environment. Participation, conversation, and an easy familiarity with the 'servants' are encouraged – and the latter do not seem to be monitoring visitors' behaviour in the traditional way but rather treating them with courtesy and deference, as if they had a lower social status than the visitors themselves.

Heritage's claim to offer access to the vernacular realm is reflected in wider contemporary trends in cultural display, in which the previously taken-for-granted emphasis on the 'high', 'official' cultural realm is challenged (although not necessarily, it must be added, dethroned). For Featherstone, this reflects a situation in which older attempts to define a national 'common culture' through key authoritative institutions such as the BBC are displaced by voices celebrating the diversity of 'uncommon cultures' (1991: 141). This is a phenomenon which has variously been defined as cultural democratization, de-differentiation and declassification (see Bauman, 1992; and Lash, 1990, for an extended discussion). Whether de-differentiation describes real changes in socio-cultural values, or merely reflects the new design-led aesthetics of the late twentieth century is a moot point. What is more important is to note its current status as the standard and expected norm in cultural display.

These trends can be dated back primarily to the 1960s, a decade in which the 'history from below' movement began to take shape. At the time a minority and 'progressive' cause, its claims, according to Raphael Samuel (1998), are echoed in the current consensus against 'drum-and-trumpet history' (in spite of the Conservative government's attempts in the 1980s to return to a focus on victories and conquests in the national history curriculum). The progressive history of the 1960s embodied a rejection of both Empire and Nation as the traditional frameworks for history teaching. Instead, history should be 'either intensely local or global': either 'Grandmother's Washing Day' or 'Building an Arawak Hut' (Samuel, 1998: 83). Heritage in the UK, in many ways, has followed suit: celebrating the most parochial and quotidian of local lifestyles as well as the diversity of 'other' cultures, through eschewing the ethnocentrism of the traditional anthropological museums. (The claim that heritage is nevertheless inherently nationalistic is an interesting one in this respect, and will be examined further in the next chapter.)

In the museum world, the new principles of display have been most clearly registered at the level of nomenclature: the word 'museum' being extended and often supplanted in an effort to grant semiotic space to competing claims. The terms 'community museum', 'local museum', 'heritage museum', 'living history museum' and, in a more defiant vein, 'heritage centre', have all emerged as alternatives. Even labels more usually associated with theme parks are becoming increasingly accepted for heritage attractions, with tags such as 'world', 'village', 'park', 'story' and 'experience' appearing frequently. As we saw above, at one point the Rhondda Heritage Park was to be called an 'Experience Centre', so determined were its consultants to banish the term 'museum'. Such developments increasingly blur the lines between theme parks and museums. This book employs the term 'heritage museum' as a general means of referring to the new breed of vernacular, interactive museums, while the term 'collection museum' refers to those unreconstructed (mainly national, but also local) museums which have remained with the glass-case, scientific paradigm of display (cf. Bennett, 1995).

The new museology

Studying the subtexts through which these new heritage museums construct particular visions of the past is one of the concerns of 'the new museology' (Vergo, 1989). This term has been the source of some confusion in the UK. As Boylan (1990) points out, the European usage of the term focuses on particular new forms of museum representation, notably the 'community museum' and the 'eco-museum' (see chapter 4), whilst Vergo's eponymous edited collection rather refers to the critical study of the ideological purposes of museums. Both, however, reflect a climate in which the cultural assumptions that inform traditional museum practice are being questioned.

Much of the impetus for new museology's concern with representativeness has come from the post-colonial critiques of ethnography and anthropology over the last two decades. There has been a concern with the restoration of cultural artefacts taken from indigenous peoples by colonizing nations in the nineteenth century, and a self-conscious anxiety about the museum's authority to represent the 'other' (see Bal, 1996). Although much of the anxiety has been centred on ethnographic museums which display 'other' cultures, especially those of the developing world, it is arguable that the proliferation of heritage museums displaying local Western cultures has in part been a response to similar concerns. They, too, reflect a concern to be more inclusive, representative and populist than traditional collection museums that exhibit more élite forms of knowledge. This is reflected in the vernacular trend that I have been describing.

From glass cases to leisure spaces

The new heritage is not just confined to new institutions with new names. Established museums, too, have felt the need to respond to the challenges of interactive interpretation and vernacularization. The larger national museums have had to adjust to a new economic climate in which they have had to broaden their appeal in order to justify public subsidy, and they have been joined by scores of smaller attractions which have themselves grown out of that climate. New fiscal conditions have forced museums to compete for visitors by making direct appeals to the public. There have been three principal strategies adopted. Museums now employ personnel to concentrate on marketing and merchandising, in order to reach out to new sections of the population; they have begun to diversify into leisure spaces for different kinds of consumption, rather than relying on the exhibitions alone; and they have adopted new techniques of display and interpretation, in order to enliven and open up exhibitions to a wider popular appeal.

One of the major consequences has been an increasing willingness to adopt lessons from theme parks. For instance, rather than dedicating the museum's space to exhibitions alone, museum buildings may now include craft demonstrations, 'event' rooms, auditoriums, performing arts spaces, shops, coffee bars and restaurants. In addition, museums are redesigning their display areas to reflect 'themes' rather than chronologically or scientifically categorized collections. The National Maritime Museum at Greenwich, for example, has just opened twelve new themed galleries, which attempt to replace the older emphasis on displaying ships as evidence of British naval achievements with a more multi-faceted examination of shipping as a global commercial, scientific and military trade. The following excerpts from the museum's online publicity texts illustrate the new focus on contexts, people and interactivity:[1]

> The new National Maritime Museum aims to carry [its] messages in a powerful way to a mainstream rather than specialist public, taking big themes and presenting them in a broad, international and contemporary context ... We believe that the sea is a key part of shaping British identity, and that by presenting the collections through a modern frame of reference some of the recent agonising on national identity may be more understandable. Traditionalists may be uncomfortable. Where are the reassuring, massed displays, consistent reminders of British

supremacy, when the biggest and best ships carried British naval power, trade and irresistible traditions to that part of the world upon which the sun never set? The answer must be, that if they were ever there, those values were never a reality for a large part of the population and will never be accepted by the citizens of the next century.

One of the galleries, 'All Hands', is aimed primarily at children and illustrates the new approach well:

All Hands displays sea skills and technology used in the past and the present. The first part of the gallery focuses on people. Featuring a Viking, a Tudor explorer, a mid-shipman, a Victorian shipbuilder and a twentieth-century yachtswoman, *All Hands* explains our changing relationship with the sea. In addition to the magnificent model of the 74-gun ship HMS *Cornwallis* (built in 1813), *All Hands* includes interactive exhibits on diving, propulsion, gunnery, cargo-handling and signaling, with an activity room used for workshops and events.

The focus on identifiable human characters and on interactive exhibits is a key contemporary feature of the new heritage, as is the emphasis on themes and contexts. Not surprisingly, there was considerable controversy when the new galleries were opened.

2. Contexts of the new heritage

Restructuring the tourist gaze

These developments need to be placed in the context of wider transformations in the 'tourist gaze' (Urry, 1990, 1992). The public, it seems, has an increasing desire for and access to a diversity of tourist sites, and, at least in the case of the new service class, enjoys more leisure time and spending money than at any time before. As a result the objects deemed worthy of the tourist gaze have diversified. Urry argues that different tourist sites invite different types of tourist gaze, ranging from the romantic (searching out aesthetic sights for solitary contemplation) and the anthropological (pursuing ethnographic details about 'ways of life') to the collective (which shares its ambit with others and looks for familiar, crowded environments). Different kinds of heritage attraction attract different gazes, but the anthropological one is undoubtedly predominant in the case of ethnographic heritage centres.

Spectacle and display have become the organizing principles of tourism ventures. With the decline of mass tourism, where vast numbers of people took their annual break at the same time and in the same (often seaside) destinations, tourism patterns in the 1980s became increasingly fragmented into different cultural experiences. Up until the 1980s, tourism was supposed to have little to do with culture (Rojek, 1993). Now, however, they clearly overlap. Tourism attractions are focused on the experiential: destinations in which tourists can 'sample' different socio-cultural realities (Craik, 1997). Tourism is increasingly seen as an opportunity to acquire what Bourdieu (1984) calls 'cultural capital'. In the case of heritage, however, culture is defined in the more democratic and popular terms of 'local colour', for instance, or popular tradition, rather than high art. Tourism offers 'customised excursions into other cultures and places' (Craik, 1997: 121), and tourists leave with the merchandising and souvenirs that epitomize and evidence the cultural identity they have 'visited'.

Contemporary tourism is an ambivalent mix of the individualized and the standardized, the particular and the generalized, and there is some debate over which predominates (Ritzer and Liska, 1997). While Urry (1990) argues that tourism choices, for example, for flexible and individually tailored experiences as opposed to pack-aged itineraries, depend on the class-based socio-cultural resources and aspirations of the social subject, Ritzer (1996) highlights the increasingly managed, rationalized and McDonaldized nature of tourism as a globalized industry. In his argument, these choices are merely a product of lifestyle marketing. While experimentation and cultural 'sampling' may access all kinds of 'exotic' experiences which would not previously have counted as tourist attractions, these are increasingly provided within calculating business systems which seek to maximize profit, predictability and control. Yet the tourist experience is not solely defined by its economic functions. The question of how heritage negotiates the interface between the social meanings of consumption and the economic meanings of production is one of the major issues that analysis needs to confront. Heritage offers encounters with the past that are, argu-ably, both highly standardized yet also unpredictable – as later chapters will show.

Cultural consumption and heritage

The particular appeal of heritage is clearly closely interlinked with the trend towards a diversified yet highly managed cultural tourism, in that it offers to satisfy the desire for local colour within sites that are nevertheless safe and organized. But what impels the desire itself, and what other objects does it seek out? In order to understand heritage as a social practice, it is necessary to examine more closely the wider social contexts which shape these new developments in the tourist gaze. To do this, we need to examine patterns of contemporary cultural consumption. New forms of tourist organization pick up on and reinforce developments that are already emergent in wider cultural and socio-economic relations: they do not on their own create these new values. I shall look at socio-economic factors in the final section of this chapter, in discussing how heritage has been co-opted into economic regeneration schemes in ex-industrial areas. First, however, I explore two fields of cultural transformation which offer a way in to understanding the wider popularity of heritage, and upon which local tourism and leisure planners and entrepreneurs can draw. These are, respectively, a new valorization of the past and a related revalorization of place.

The turn to the past

Heritage can be seen as just one of many forms in which the past is displayed and consumed in contemporary society, and thereby as a manifestation of a more general fascination with historical representation. Raphael Samuel, the late British social historian, suggests that we now live in an 'expanding historical culture' in which the 'work of inquiry and retrieval is being progressively extended into all kinds of spheres that would have been thought unworthy of notice in the past' (1994: 25). The German literary critic, Andreas Huyssen, likewise diagnoses a pervasive 'museal sensibility' in contemporary society, and argues that the museum – 'a key paradigm of contemporary cultural activities' – is itself spilling over into other areas of cultural life. He argues that the practice of consuming, recording, preserving, recreating and recovering past forms is no longer limited to the built, visible space of the museum or the heritage centre, but is symptomatic of a contemporary 'memory boom of unprecedented proportions' (1995: 5).

This phenomenon is often discussed in terms of debates around nostalgia and what has become known as 'retro culture'. There is, certainly, plentiful evidence that heritage attractions of all kinds are burgeoning, and that the range of retro forms of consumption is increasing. In one sense, the 'turn to the past' could be seen as evidence of a worrying retreat into endless and complacent memorializing, which forecloses on the possibility of active and critical engagement with the present. On the other hand, it could be interpreted as the effect of a contemporary logic of temporal experimentation, in which time becomes subject to new kinds of playful representation – with heritage being simply one such manifestation. In what follows I aim to indicate the contours of debates over the nature and implications of historical consumption in contemporary society.

Nostalgia, conservatism and retreatism

Nostalgia is notoriously difficult to define. Most simply, it means a 'yearning for yesterday' (Davis, 1979), in which 'then' is seen as preferable to 'now'. Nostalgia is founded on a preoccupation with loss – with what was or might have been, rather than what is or will be (Tannock, 1995). Turner identifies four dimensions of loss in what he terms 'the nostalgic paradigm': the loss of a golden age; the loss of values and moral certainty; the loss of meaningful social relationships; the loss of authenticity or simplicity (1987: 150–1). Turner does not, however, conclude that nostalgia is inevitably conservative. Instead, he suggests that it 'may lay the foundations for a radical critique of the modern as a departure from authenticity' (1987: 154). Wilson (1997), too, argues that nostalgia provides important means of confronting and understanding the dislocations of ever-changing urban space.

Many commentators, however, have seen nostalgia as inherently right wing (see, for example, Ascherson, 1987). This view is probably not unconnected with the fact that retro consumption became especially prolific and visible during the years of the 1980s Conservative governments in the UK and the Reagan administrations in the USA. For Robert Hewison, a major critic of heritage whose specific complaints about the 'heritage industry' will be examined in the next chapter, nostalgia is inevitably politically conservative. Although he accepts that nostalgia is 'an important agency in adjustment to crisis' and 'a social emollient' (1989: 47), he argues that in the guise of heritage it encourages cultural stagnation and reaction.

Nostalgia is also seen as symptomatic of a contemporary political apathy and a failure of the critical spirit. For Fredric Jameson (1984), the present is characterized by a postmodern breakdown in historical representation, for which the 'nostalgic mode' becomes a too-ready substitute. The turn to the past is a *retreat* – from the 'crisis of historicity' that characterizes the condition of postmodernity, in which the meta-narratives for making sense of history have been undermined (Jameson, 1984: 68). In this account, museum society is a refuge from the maelstrom of postmodernity: the more we endlessly recycle the past in commodity culture, the less we are able to gain a handle on the real relations that structure our lives (see also Harvey, 1989a).

Similar echoes of retreatism occur in Patrick Wright's account, which characterizes modern life as profoundly problematic for individuals to assimilate as it involves all kinds of bewildering changes and dislocations. Heritage has proliferated because the 'destabilising demands of social transformation' (Wright, 1985: 17) have accelerated in late modernity. Thus nostalgia allows a kind of redemption of the losses of modernity, and an easy means of protecting people from apprehending them as such. The more stressful the present, the more we turn to the past for solace, and the more we imagine it as a simpler, easier, more certain or more comforting place.

Such retreatism arguments may seem compelling. Yet they do not do much more than propose a familiar term – escapism – as an explanation for the heritage boom. They thus take it as axiomatic that the present is characterized by particularly intense experiences of dislocation and alienation, which thereby explain the phenomenon of nostalgia. This argument is rejected by David Lowenthal (1998), however, who documents the long history of both nostalgia and the popular apprehension of intense social change. He points out that people have lamented the loss of familiar landscapes, artefacts and buildings since the French Revolution first ushered in the major social upheavals of modernity.

Given its longevity, it would seem that nostalgia cannot on its own account for the recent explosion of heritage throughout Western Europe, the USA and Australia. If nostalgia is to be defined as the backward-looking apprehension of loss and decline, it cannot offer much insight into the phenomenon of new heritage forms. To assume that gazing on the past is a negative activity that betrays an inability to engage with the present is to neglect the ways in which the past is very much a product of the present. New ways of representing the past are created and popularized in the present, and can thus tell us a good deal about the social preoccupations of today. We thus need to do more than simply invoke the mantra of society's obsession with the past. In the following section, other possible explanations are offered as to why the past should seem so attractive to us now, and why our engagement with it should take the particular forms it does.

The past in modernity

The turn to the past can fruitfully be interpreted not as a retreat from the present but as stimulated *by* the present. In this perspective, the heritage gaze is not a gaze on the past but a gaze which is thoroughly rooted in the present. It is the highly visual, mobile and technologized culture of late modernity which allows the past to be represented in forms which simulate it so effectively (through cinema, television, photography, video and computer games). Thus, our desire for the past is a manifestation of contemporary forms of representation which have been conditioned by the mobile gaze of media culture. The popularity of the past does not, perhaps, rest on a yearning for yesterday, but on the desire to explore a simulated past from the vantage point of a present-day voyeur, consumer or visitor.

Desiring the past does not necessarily mean a desire to return there. J. B. Thompson (1995), for instance, suggests that the popularity of cultural tradition should not be interpreted as out of synch with modernity but stimulated *by* modernity. Modern technologies allow tradition to be disembedded from the constraints of obligatory, situated and localized interaction, and to be 're-moored' in new and diverse contexts – within, for example, the multiple forms of urban spectacle (1995: 183–191). Thus, traditions can be consumed and experienced without the constraints of authority and obligation within which they first developed. Spectacles of the past grant access to history without the dead weight of actually living it. The pleasure of heritage may derive more from the experience of gazing on a fully elaborated reality, that can nevertheless be switched off, than from any desire to bring the past back.

In a similar argument, Sandberg (1995) notes the 'in-betweenness' of the heritage gaze, in which the visitor's gaze is free to wander over many sights/sites whilst the object of the gaze is fixed, static and homogeneous (the 'folk' way of life, or the 'mining community'). Sandberg argues that the gaze on the past 'common folk' which is catered for at folk museums should not, therefore, be interpreted as nostalgia for that past. He examines the accounts of visitors to early Swedish folk museums at the turn of the century, and suggests:

> Spectators were more often intrigued by the in-betweenness of the folk museums, by the ways in which they both managed the losses of modernity – the weakened connections between body and culture – and celebrated the powers it endowed on spectators – powers of mobility, invisibility, panopticism. The availability of 'watchable pictures' of folk culture, taken together with the sense that one could encounter 'reality itself', was an appealing combination for modern, urban spectators, one which eventually led spectators to prefer the representational project to the 'real thing'.
>
> (Sandberg, 1995: 333)

In this sense, the early folk museum offers a type of experience which anticipates that offered by the cinema, television, and other visually mediated forms of representation. The early open-air museums did little more than offer static and wooden *tableaux*; the new heritage, on the other hand, blends the three-dimensional advantages of simulated environments with the new multimedia technologies of communication to produce simulacra which allow the past to be consumed through all of the senses. Television, from this perspective, helps to create the desire for something it cannot satisfy: the experience of walking *through* past environments, handling three-dimensional objects and 'stepping into' the spectacle itself. The gaze on the past is not, therefore, a compensation for the lack of authenticity in modernity, but is stimulated by modernity's emphasis on the sensory replicability of people, places and times. Huyssen argues that, in this sense, 'instead of being separate from modernisation, the museum functions as its privileged cultural agent' (1995: 33).

Vernacular heritage in the late twentieth century is both similar to and different from the Scandinavian folk museum at the moment of industrialization. It, too, preserves and displays an ordinary and working-class world, but at the later historical juncture of deindustrialization, globalization and a highly mediated and technologized visual culture. If modernity is about flux and constant change (Berman, 1983), part of the appeal of heritage plausibly lies in its simulation of a fixed and unchanging world – not because visitors really want to return there, but because they can juxtapose both worlds from a privileged vantage point. The heritage sites of today represent the industrial communities of yesterday: miners, steel-workers, slate quarrymen, canal workers and so on. Like the Scandinavian folk museum, they invite a tourist gaze which seeks out spectacles of ordinary and familiar ways of life, but those which are no longer the obligatory ways of life. They stage the vanishing of the familiar, but only through the familiar having already become strange.

Time travel and the (post) modern subject

The 'in-between-ness' of the gaze on the past is akin to the fantasy of time travel. It both craves instant access to the past as 'other', and values the preservation of that past in the present. Lash and Urry (1994) argue that late modernity is characterized by two new senses of time: the instantaneous 'computime' of nanoseconds and microelectronic switching, and the 'glacial evolutionary time' of popular scientific discourse (a widespread awareness of the environment, the planet and the species, for example). Instantaneous time allows people to experience different cultures and timescales at the flick of a switch or the click of a mouse, while evolutionary ('glacial') time is firmly opposed to the destruction of environments, histories and places.

The new temporal relations of modernity invest time with a significance and fascination that stimulates the desire for sites that experiment with temporal representation. Instantaneous time commodifies history into subjective fragments uprooted from the slow narratives of their historical contexts. Glacial time encourages rather the opposite movement, in that, here, history is understood in its long-term contexts, stretching far into the past and into the future (Urry, 1994: 141). Heritage can be seen as a product of both senses of time, in that, whilst it fragments, manages and commodifies the past, it also preserves it and stages its slow passing. Thus, both heritage and its opposite – 'futurist' culture, such as science fiction films – stage our appreciation of time as a long stretching journey, which can nevertheless be 'experienced' instantaneously through technology and the mobility of contemporary consumption. The turn to the past, then, can be seen, most profitably in my view, as *part of* contemporary popular culture, rather than as an anti-modern, alienating strategy.

The turn to place

However, the view that heritage is a means of appropriating the past through consumption can only take us so far in understanding the phenomenon of the new heritage. Heritage is not merely a simulation of temporal mobility but also offers the experience of *spatial* mobility. Different heritage centres offer different spatialized performances of the past, rather than simply pastness *per se*. If visitors choose to visit heritage museums rather than contenting themselves with Disneyland, they are seeking something other than the mere spectacle of the 'old days'. Instead, what heritage museums offer is the history of a *particular* place or lifestyle. They tell 'the story' of Wigan, the Black Country, Dover or the Rhondda, of coalmining, crofting, canal work or fishing. This aspect of heritage is overlooked in the debates over nostalgia and time travel, which focus only on heritage as a forum for the representation of time.

Place is a central organizing concept in the new heritage museums. If we consider some of the UK heritage museums that have received critical attention in recent debates on heritage, we can clearly see that they all claim to represent the 'story of a place': Beamish Open Air Museum in the north-east of England, and the People's Palace in Glasgow (Bennett, 1995); the Ironbridge Gorge Museum in Shropshire (West, 1988); Albert Dock in Liverpool (Mellor, 1991); the Wigan Pier Heritage Centre (Hewison, 1987; Davies, 1988), Aros on the Isle of Skye (Macdonald, 1997); the People's Story in Edinburgh (Hooper-Greenhill, 1992). In addition, one might mention heritage centres such as the White Cliffs of Dover Experience, the Oxford Story or the Black Country Living History Museum. These are, above all, representations of small, local places encapsulating particular 'ways of life'. It is surprising, in this light, that the relationship between museums and place has largely been theorized at the level of the nation (cf. Wright, 1985; Delaney, 1992), and in discussions of colonial and post-colonial representation (for example, Coombes, 1992).

It is at the level of locality, rather, that heritage's representation of 'place' and 'community' needs to be further interrogated (cf. Fyfe and Ross, 1996, discussing community in relation to residents' views of local heritage in Stoke-on-Trent). Many newer heritage museums have explicitly been set up in order to display aspects of local identity, often as part of local economic regeneration strategies, in which the marketing of place is a crucial factor. It is this context which has formed the impetus for many of the new museums and heritage centres, as we shall explore below (see Corner and Harvey, 1991; Robins, 1991). Concepts of locality, place, community and local identity are central to understanding such initiatives. The ways in which heritage museums pick up on and reproduce particular place-myths will be the subject of chapters 4 and 5.

Images of community, in particular, are omnipresent at local heritage museums. They reflect a reinvigoration of the community ideal within Western cultural forms since the 1960s, which has been noted by many theorists (see Morris, 1996; Chaney, 1993; Bauman, 1991). Bauman, for example, sees the present period as the 'age of community', characterized by 'the lust for community, the search for community, the invention of community, imagining community' (1991: 246). The cultural appeal of community has been bolstered by a more general 'turn to place', in which the specific characters of localities take on both economic significance, in the context of a global/local nexus of place competition (Harvey, 1989a, b; Robins, 1991), and social significance, as a means of summoning up local political allegiances and as a cipher through which class, gender and other identities can be asserted in the local civic sphere (Massey 1995a, b; Bagguley et al., 1990).

For many writers, the idealization of place is a retreat from the time–space dislocations of globalized culture, 'the search for secure moorings in a shifting world' (Harvey, 1989a: 302). In this can be heard echoes of the retreatism discussed above in relation to critiques of retro-culture. Other writers, however, drawing on the framework of late/post-modernity and mobility, emphasize the mediated nature of place cultures and draw attention to the ways in which late modernity stimulates the fascination with visualized, virtual places. Featherstone (1993) points to the increasing accessibility of images of specific places through globalized communications, which bring proliferating and diverse local cultures into everyone's sitting-room. One might also mention here Maffesoli's (1995) thesis of the rise of 'neo-tribes', in which human collectivity is increasingly organized around lifestyles and symbolic attachments. Gazing on simulated communities in heritage may afford similar opportunities to experience 'virtual' communities.

In a related argument, David Chaney points to the ways in which television itself invites its audience into an 'abstract' collective, which imagines new forms of community with participants that are physically absent and unknown. Thus, the new, mediated ideal of community consists of 'privatised participation in communal forms' (Chaney, 1993: 177). We could argue, indeed, that 'community' is increasingly idealized *because* it is imagined in these dislocated forms, with heritage culture providing the material and thus seemingly authentic staging of its solidity, three-dimensionality, and thereby its 'reality'. In this sense, the turn to place is a cultural aspiration rather than reflecting any real strengthening of local social relations.

3. Heritage, localities and economic regeneration

There is, then, a body of work which identifies a turn to the past and a turn to place as key features of contemporary mediated society. However, to return to the debates around cultural expression versus market manipulation mentioned earlier, we also need to visit the other side of the heritage problematic – the question of its entanglement in relations of production and socio-economic markets. There is no doubt that heritage is both a polyvalent site for cultural consumption as well as a more unambivalent economic commodity for various strategies of economic regeneration and place promotion. This section turns to an examination of the contexts in which these wider consumption values have been incorporated into policies for local economic development. In other words, I shall consider to what use or range of uses local agencies of governance and business have put the new popularity of the past and place and the new expansion in cultural consumption.

Urban entrepreneurialism in the 1980s

It was particularly in the 1980s that numerous new heritage initiatives began to appear in Britain's localities, a period which coincides with many of the wider cultural changes discussed above. Bianchini (1993) describes how the role of culture in local urban planning policy has changed over the last three decades. The 1970s were dominated by an increase in cultural planning in most European cities, spurred by left programmes of community participation, widening access to the arts, the democratization of public space and the revitalization of urban cityscapes. Publicly funded heritage projects in the UK such as Beamish Hall reflected these ideals of public access (Johnson and Thomas, 1992). Cultural amenities were seen as part of a public service that should be initiated and resourced by public funds and bodies.

In the 1980s and 1990s, however, 'the language of subsidy was gradually replaced by the language of investment' (Bianchini, 1993: 13). The 1980s was the decade of increasing urban entrepreneurialism, competitiveness and privatization in local economic development (cf. Harvey, 1989b; Sadler, 1993), and it was also the decade when the 'new heritage' boom began. A swathe of heritage projects, though still often set up and subsidized by local government, were now inserted into newly marketized local economic development strategies for urban regeneration, place promotion and tourism (Ward, 1994). Although heritage projects are often far from being free-market enterprises, in that many are funded – initially at least – through public-sector grants and subsidies, the rhetoric, priorities and strategies of the market increasingly provide their rationale and managerial direction (McGuigan, 1999).

Public funding is justified on the grounds of the social and economic benefits that tourism ventures are supposed to generate: the local provision of employment, wealth generation and environmental improvement. Public funding is also directed at extracting 'leverage'; that is, public money is used to lure in private investment (Bianchini and Schwengel, 1991). It is intended to help ventures achieve success in the market by meeting initial capital

costs – such as land purchase and reclamation, building refurbishment and product design – to get visitor numbers and spend established. The aim is to provide an attractive prospect for eventual
private investment and 'partnership' by fashioning heritage into a
marketable asset.

The local, the global and the 'presentation of self'

It may, at first, seem paradoxical that local, small-scale heritage
ventures became such a key target of economic development, just
when the intensification of economic globalization was instituting
new 'flows' of standardized goods and commodities across vast
distances (Castells, 1989; Appadurai, 1990). One might have
thought that the globalization of commodity markets, which since
the end of the 1970s has been destroying the regional productive
specialization of the UK, would work to obliterate both the
currency of locally specific images and the potency of locally
planned solutions to the wider dislocations of deindustrialization
and restructuring. Although Wales until the beginning of the 1980s
was spatially divided along industrial lines (steel in the south;
coalmining in the Valleys; slate quarrying in the north), these strong
productive identities were increasingly weakened throughout the
1980s and 1990s. And yet these are precisely the decades in which
those identities become newly affirmed, displayed and profited from
through local heritage ventures.

It has also been recognized, however, that globalization is
accompanied by the creation of new competitive nuclei of local
production and consumption (Massey, 1984; Cooke, 1989). It is
argued that the need to find new markets and to cut costs as
companies face new global competition means that local variations
(in regulation, institutional control, wage levels, communications,
land price, quality of life, image and so on) become more rather
than less important (Harvey, 1989b). Localities, made up of 'layers'
of processes of investment and disinvestment over a period of time,
offer quite particular local economic markets in specific locales.
Although it is important not to exaggerate the agency and
autonomy of local areas, as Massey (1991) notes, it is clear that
local agencies of governance have considerable gains to make and
losses to face, depending on how far they can manage and market
these local qualities for the purposes of new inward investment.

Increasingly, the particular resources and attractions that local areas can offer capital are configured as *representational* challenges. Each locality is catapulted into a competition to market those qualities that will allow it to gain a competitive edge over its rivals. Harvey (1989b) describes how since the beginnings of the current period of reorganization and readjustment in capitalist economies in the 1970s, nation-state governments have increasingly withdrawn from the attempt to provide local areas with buffers against the resultant deindustrialization, structural unemployment and fiscal austerity which has hit local regions so hard. This has resulted in a rise in 'urban entrepreneurialism', in which local government has abandoned the earlier style of 'managerialist' governance in favour of 'civic boosterism' on a more intense scale than ever before.

Harvey further notes that, of the options open to local governments for increasing their area's stakes in the market-place, those strategies which can attract consumer spending that can be relatively limited to the area in question are seen as providing the best returns. This means trying to lure in lucrative activities which will produce local spending: attracting key control and command functions (such as TV networks, government administration centres and so on), gentrification strategies, waterfront and other property-based redevelopment projects, shopping centres, urban spectacles, entertainment and tourism. Heritage, of course, is high on the list of such local 'assets' (Corner and Harvey, 1991; Zukin, 1991, 1995). Different areas attempt to corner different sections of the market. Sheffield, for instance, has tried to specialize in retail developments, popular culture and international sports provision (Goodwin, 1993). The 'presentation of self' becomes all important, and aspects of local identity – such as heritage – that can help to define this image as well as generating local spend and revenue are co-opted into an expanding market of local signs and images.

Local government, regeneration and heritage

It should be noted that the phenomenon of place-promotion is not a new one (Barke and Harrop, 1994; Ward, 1994). It is, however, clear that the business of place promotion has become much more market-driven and competitive due to the disappearance of local production monopolies and the reduction of centrally funded and locally administered regional aid. In the early 1980s, local governments located in areas that were being rapidly blighted by deindustrialization, and in which vast areas of ex-industrial land were becoming derelict, found themselves unprepared to deal with the situation (Fretter, 1993). Economic development became increasingly a matter of emphasizing the differences (which may in reality be slight) between one region and the next, and the careful nurturing of assets tailored to the demands of funding bodies (both private and public) and venture capital enterprises.

Ex-industrial towns are seeking, therefore, to capitalize on the reputation of their industrial heritage, particularly in order to promote tourism (Barke and Harrop, 1994). The gains of integrating conservation with economic planning include establishing that the area has 'historic worth'. Bradford has been quite a success story in this regard. However, there are many pitfalls to using heritage for place promotion. An obvious problem is that there is not only one market for 'the product'. Local authorities have a responsibility simultaneously to outside public funders, outside private investors, local residents and local welfare agencies, to name just a few of the faultlines. Local identity is co-opted differently along these different axes of communication. While the message to outside funders might require emphasizing the neediness of an area in order to win competitive grants for urban development, the message to local welfare agencies must be that those needs are well provided for, whilst the one presented in glossy brochures to the outside investor should project an image of vigorous growth and financial health.

The ambivalent place of heritage in this complex network of relations has been noted by Robins (1991). He describes the North-East's uneasy relation to its cultural icon Andy Capp, during a period when Newcastle was trying to recover from economic devastation:

> In the new global arena, it is necessary, then, simultaneously to minimise and maximise cultural forms ... In this part of the country, it is over the symbolic body of Andy Capp that the two logics contest. 'Andy Capp is dead – Newcastle is alive' – that is the message of enterprise ... If the spirit of enterprise wants to kill off Andy Capp, there is, however, a counter-spirit that keeps him alive. The region's industrial past is its burden, but it is also its inheritance. It is clear that history can be made to pay ... But if heritage is to be marketed, it becomes difficult to avoid the reality that the Northeast was once a region of heavy engineering, shipbuilding and coal mining.
>
> (Robins, 1991: 39–40)

The concept of place or community as an identifiable 'product' becomes meaningless in such a situation, and the contested nature of local heritage is exposed. The case of Andy Capp illustrates that the process of constructing place-images and identities is not merely a top–down one. These identities may be profoundly contested by various local groups, some of whom may be in a position to prevent their gaining complete hegemony. In the case of restructuring Lancaster, for example, the solutions proposed for its future economic direction became the site of intense controversy (Bagguley et al., 1990). Conventionalized specifications of the city as 'traditional community' were not uniformly shared by the whole population: while the service class in Lancaster attempted to mobilize the 'auratic' heritage image of the city (that is, one which emphasized its unique cultural qualities – see Benjamin, 1973), other groups pursued very different agendas.

A similar example of local contestation is provided by Jess and Massey (1995) in their analysis of conflict in the Wye Valley over the conversion of a traditional farm into a tourist attraction. With long-term residents in favour and incomers (mainly artists and writers) against, it provides a good example of the differing values attached to place by different social groups. Furthermore, appeals made to local distinctiveness and community can end up in exclusionary tactics to separate one 'community' from another. They can be used to justify new entrepreneurial property practices which hive off sections of urban space into zones, and in the process deplete available publicly accessible space. Zukin (1995), for example, argues that urban development is increasingly organized around the concept of security, which is transforming public social space into gentrified, privatized, secure enclaves and overmanaged leisure sites. Urban entrepreneurialism may mean that local authorities collude in a strategy of 'pulling up the drawbridge' to keep social problems well away from the gaze of key 'clients'.

Studies such as these indicate that both the cultural and economic dimensions of heritage need to be kept in view, and not artificially hived off into separate areas of inquiry. Whilst the new heritage may appear to be the result of new patterns of cultural consumption, it is also difficult to disentangle these from the economic contexts of production that stimulate the creation of new lifestyle-orientated markets. It is clear that, although the new heritage is not merely an economic strategy imposed by agencies of governance and marketization, nor should it be seen straightforwardly as the expression of local cultural identities or reconfigured temporal–spatial consciousness. Whether it is ultimately a depthless, postmodern form of playing with cultural identifications, or whether it represents a more politically engaged invigoration of historical consciousness remains a matter of debate. Certainly, Raphael Samuel's often persuasive argument against the 'heritage baiters' (1994) tends to neglect the marketized and governmental relations within which heritage projects are developed. At the same time, Harvey's pessimistic treatment of heritage as merely 'bread and circuses' (1989b) is not tuned into the various ways in which the motivations of heritage consumption overspill a single classification. The debates and controversies that these issues have provoked will be the subject of the next chapter.

3

Heritage debates

Heritage, this book argues, is an ambivalent mixture of the authentic and the manufactured. Much of the discussion so far has focused on its manufactured aspects, in that the local and wider contexts of its production have been the major focus. There is a conventional distinction made, however, between seeing heritage as an expression of top–down, class, market or governmental realignments and as an expression of bottom–up popular consciousness. These contrasts have been discussed within the literature that has become known as the 'heritage debate' (Lumley, 1994). The present chapter will trace the contours of these arguments more fully and will attempt in the process to sketch out a new direction for the study of heritage which might open up fresh perspectives beyond the rather limited terms of this debate.

1. History versus heritage

Heritage, it has been claimed (Hewison, 1987), is 'bogus history'. Heritage has often been counterposed to history, in the sense that it is held to lack the objective, critical stance of the latter. David Lowenthal, for example, distinguishes two kinds of historiographical practice: the enterprise of 'history', which 'explores and explains pasts grown ever more opaque over time', and that of heritage, which 'clarifies pasts so as to infuse them with present purposes' (1998: p. xv). In this argument, history is dedicated to making forgotten pasts understandable, while heritage aims to fashion the past into forms that serve current needs. The suggestion is that history is more objective and less self-serving, since there are no 'present purposes' in its practices. Concern about the ability of heritage to represent the past accurately is also attributed to its characteristic visual modes of representation, which, it is argued, reduce the past to that which can be seen, felt and heard: 'it is hard to convey a legal system in visual terms, but law is no less central to our historical understanding because of that' (Jordanova, 1989: 26).

Hewison, too, wants to uphold a distinction between the proper pursuit of 'history' and the suspect practice of 'heritage'. He acknowledges that 'the impulse to preserve the past is part of the impulse to preserve the self' and that 'without knowing where we have been, it is difficult to know where we are going' (1987: 47). However, as it is expressed by 'the heritage industry', he argues, this impulse is distorted into commercialized and shallow simulations of the past. In his book *The Heritage Industry* (1987), the classic statement of the anti-heritage position, Hewison examines a range of different manifestations of heritage, which he terms 'the imprisoning walls upon which we project a superficial image of a false past', a 'shallow screen that intervenes between our present lives, and our history' where 'the past becomes more homogeneous than the present, it becomes simply "yesteryear"' so that 'the result is a devaluation of significance, an impoverishment of meaning' (Hewison, 1987: 135–8). Heritage, he argues, works in the interests of conservatism and political authoritarianism, for it ensures that the populace, busy smiling on the past, has its back turned to the politics of the present.

Heritage and nationalism

Heritage has frequently been defined as synonymous with nostalgia. Many accounts of nostalgia emphasize the ways in which it has been deployed in élite discourses to legitimate the power of the nation-state. Nairn (1988), for example, identifies the period in which Britain's colonialist global domination first came under threat (roughly 1880 through to the mid-1920s) as the age of a new 'wilful' nostalgia, in which national identities and traditions were appropriated and 'invented' by the British state in order to characterize colonized societies as backward and simple (see also Robertson, 1990; Hobsbawm and Ranger, 1983). Samuel (1998), too, points out that nationalist fervour was most vociferously promoted in the age of Britain's withering colonial base, and that the nation's 'heritage' was exploited freely in attempts to shore up the national psyche.

Patrick Wright (1985) adopts a similar analytic framework in focusing on the ways in which populist heritage came to buttress appeals to nationhood under Thatcherism in the 1980s. These appeals, he argues, overcome the disenchantment of everyday life by offering a shopping list of attributes that *incorporate* the vernacular realm rather than holding aloof from it. Thus, as 'national identity' expands to include coal mines and tenements, it more effectively – and more insidiously – brings 'the nation' into alignment with 'the people' (see also Billig, 1995, on 'banal nationalism'). 'Heritagization', then is a hegemonic strategy for securing allegiance to the national imaginary, in which 'Britishness' is defined through ideological values of tradition, conservatism, family values. Wright's thesis is that heritage appeared on the agenda of policy-makers and entrepreneurs at roughly the same time as the Thatcherite administrations started to mobilize images of 'our traditional culture' in the 1980s. For Wright, the heritage boom is evidence of a political hegemony which trades on old cultural securities to substitute for the economic insecurities of deindustrializing Britain.

Heritage and politics

Wright's later work on heritage (1992), however, recognizes that the term covers a vast array of different social practices – from metal detecting to canal restoration – and points out that many such efforts are directed at democratic ideals of popular access to history. Much of the concern excited by the term 'heritage' derives from the ambiguous connotations of its self-consciously populist image. Heritage museums, as opposed to traditional collection museums, make appeals to the popular domain of everyday life, rather than to the élite domain of specialist knowledge. This appearance of the past on the popular stage seems to attract particular critical concern; in David Lowenthal's words, it 'excites partisan extremes' (1998: p. xiv). This is because heritage is seen to be deeply embroiled in the determination of ordinary people's political consciousness. We have already seen in chapter 2 how pervasive is the fear that heritage merely offers a politically conservative and nostalgic interpretation of the past, papering over dissent and conflicts and replacing them with a rosy view of harmony. This has been a major concern of left historians, both in Wales and beyond.

In these debates, the representation of the past is seen as a political practice. Underlying them is a conviction that the cultivation of a proper sense of history is of vital importance in the formation of popular political consciousness. The dangers of heritage, therefore, lie in its perceived ability to distort history and thereby to misinform or mystify the visitors who gaze upon it. This is tied up with left projects for forging class consciousness and political allegiances of various kinds, always alert to the ideological aspects of history-making. This is essentially Patrick Wright's position. In his 1985 diagnosis of heritage as irretrievably subservient to nationalist sentiment, Wright seeks to identify another, more politically radical kind of engagement with the past which would reclaim its 'critical and subversive potential' (1985: 26). He is not, however, hopeful of finding it while heritage succeeds so effectively in capturing the past for the service of the nation.

These questions become all the more pressing when the heritage under investigation is a contested one. In the case of Wales, and also of other proto-national formations such as Scotland, heritage is frequently shrouded in controversy. Faultlines are drawn over the question of what constitutes the identity and heritage of Wales, and what qualifies to be recognized as Welsh heritage (see chapter 4). These are profoundly political questions, which have considerable import for the ways in which appeals to national feeling are mediated in the public sphere. In addition, there is the matter of how adequately that heritage is judged to be expressed at particular sites, which may stand accused of failing to tell the right story in the right way. Concerns about the trivialization, romanticization or depoliticization of history can readily stir up local sensibilities and become mired in local political conflicts, especially where there are contested claims to community and belonging. Chapters 6 and 7 will explore in depth the local debates and concerns in the Rhondda which emerged through the faultlines of heritage in the 1980s.

Heritage from above versus heritage from below

In a very different approach to Wright's and Hewison's, Raphael Samuel (1994) stresses that 'heritage mania' is not a symptom of decline or some worrying, neo-conservative cultural coup; on the contrary its emergence in the late twentieth century is symptomatic of the collapse of the cultural two-class divide and the blurring of the high/low-culture opposition. Whereas the trappings of tradition and heritage used to be the preserve of the upper class, now they have become appropriated by everyone. In the process, Samuel argues, history's metamorphosis into populist iconographics dismays the intellectuals, who would secretly prefer history to remain safely unassailable within the walls of the British Museum. In Samuel's view, far from being 'Thatcherism in period dress' (1994: 291), heritage is harnessed by different political interests at different times, showing itself as a hybrid form that finds expression in a myriad of ways.

Samuel is attuned to the popular, ground-level enthusiasm for history ('Clio's invisible hands') – a generalized urge to rescue and preserve the rubble lying in the wake of capitalist redevelopment. It is a perspective that sees history as a diffuse and universal social form of knowledge which is invigorating and enlightening in ways that text-based history is often not. Both Hewison and Wright are far more pessimistic, on the other hand, keeping their sights on the ideological agency of the state and corporate culture. For them, the power to define the past is located in the top–down strategies of planners, policy-makers and commercial developers, rather than in the bottom–up activities of Samuel's invisible hordes of history enthusiasts. Thus, we have a debate that focuses on the ideological functions of heritage: on the one hand, a belief in the multiple popular determinations of historical consciousness; on the other, a conviction that this is structured by public forms of display harnessed to dominant political interests.

Heritage and marketization

The political-ideological commentary discussed above and emanating in the main from historians and literary critics represents one strand of discussion in the heritage debate. Another is provided by critiques centring on the marketization of heritage, which have come more typically from the disciplines of human geography and sociology. These have been focused on the embroilment of heritage in local planning and development contexts. The last chapter showed how heritage has emerged as a central strategy in countless urban redevelopment schemes across the UK. Local and regional planning strategies now depend centrally on mobilizing and capitalizing on culture, and heritage provides a ready storehouse of narratives and symbols for tourism-orientated redevelopment initiatives (Zukin, 1991, 1995). The 'sign value' of heritage in symbolic economies has therefore been central to arguments highlighting the commodified relations of heritage production and consumption.

Different heritage projects make different cultural appeals, of course, and it is important to recognize these differences rather than lumping all instances of heritage together. However, the kind of heritage museum which is explicitly conceived as a tourist attraction and designed to aid local economic regeneration tends to deliver a fairly standard package of amenities and interpretative approaches. Thus, even though they may communicate quite distinctive messages about history, and sit within a particular network of localized social and political relations, heritage attractions of this kind typically use the same tried and tested techniques: professionally produced *tableaux*, often designed by the same set of consultants, audio-visual shows, walk-through historical sets and reconstructed buildings, rides of various kinds or walking itineraries, restaurants, cafes and the inevitable gift shop selling local souvenirs alongside pots of preserves and items of craftwork. This amounts to a heritage model which aims to deliver a familiar and predictable kind of visitor experience, and one that is quite different from the traditional collection museum (Macdonald, 1997).

Some of these heritage attractions are funded publicly under local councils' enterprise schemes or regeneration initiatives. Others are a mixture of commercial investment and public funds. As we shall see with the Rhondda case-study in later chapters, even where public funding is provided, few of these projects are carried out in-house. Instead, professional consultancy firms are contracted to assemble the displays. It is this commercial element of heritage which differentiates it from public museums, whose displays are created by curators rather than professional interpreters (although we have seen that the line between traditional museums and heritage museums is becoming increasingly indistinct). The fact that heritage interpretation has become a professionalized industry induces fears that heritage attractions are merely standardized commodities trading on generalized formulas, and fuels arguments that they should be viewed as industrial products rather than sites for the mediation of historical knowledge.

Worries about the marketization and commercialization of heritage represent a powerful strand of critique in the heritage debate.

In David Harvey's (1989a) perspective, for instance, the turn to the past is a type of 'bread and circuses' strategy, in which people are fed nostalgic cultural forms as organized spectacles, and which function as commodity forms in commercial markets. The emphasis here is on the ways in which heritage identities can be used to market localities and to shift vast amounts of consumer goods – from houses to dress fashion to domestic artefacts – in the name of historical 'authenticity'. Harvey shows how, in the process of promoting heritage, local democratic government can be undermined through the creation of unaccountable quangos – such as urban development corporations and other agencies that usurp the business of economic governance from locally elected councils (see also Goodwin, 1993). Sadler (1993), likewise, documents the ways in which cultural marketization serves to obscure alternative ways of defining, organizing and funding cultural representation, and to construct powerful agencies for buttressing the political hegemony of free-market urban policy.

Doreen Massey (1994) extends this critique by documenting the social ramifications of the top–down promotion of particular placed heritage identities: in the redevelopment of London's docklands, for example, the equation of the area's identity with an essentialist image of the white working-class East End provided a potent rallying cry for a backlash organized around racist, anti-Asian appeals. Her critique of organized heritage ventures focuses on their public elaboration of essentialist identities, which 'relies on a view of there having been one past of this place, one story to tell' (1994: 114). The alternative involves acknowledging the insertion of places within wider spatial divisions of labour and a nexus of multiple cultural identities germane to their historical formation (see also Massey, 1995a, b). Against these tendencies towards the public consecration of essentialist place-identities, Massey (1993) wants to rescue 'a progressive sense of place' which would allow conflicting and diverse heritage stories to be recognized and acclaimed.

A related concern focuses on the cultural standardization inherent in place promotion. Holcomb notes its role in sustaining an 'international aesthetic' organized around 'eclectic conformity', a 'fragmented palimpsest of past times and distant spaces' and a 'commodified ethnic culture and sanitised classlessness' (1993: 142). The notion of 'eclectic conformity' is a suggestive one, capturing that sense in which standardization means not homogeneity but an endlessly reproduced series of thematic variations (an analysis which is reminiscent of the 'culture industry' thesis developed by members of the Frankfurt School – see Adorno and Horkheimer 1979; Marcuse, 1968). Thus, heritage becomes merely another measure of the 'aestheticisation of everyday life' (Featherstone, 1991), based upon recognizable themes that can easily be flagged in promotional brochures. The argument here is that the commodification of heritage can end up stifling cultural diversity and inviting local people to identify with only the most stereotyped and facile images of civic culture. Thus, the local public realm can itself be reduced to a series of commodified themes, which has the effect of entrenching and redefining the divides between social groups on aesthetic and stylistic grounds (see Bourdieu's arguments on social distinction, 1984).

While the potential of heritage to be represented in essentialist terms and exploited in opening up and maintaining social divisions has to be recognized, there is a danger, also, that cultural forms such as heritage are simply dismissed as the products of markets and powerful political discourse. This is a conclusion which risks losing sight of the complex ways in which the economic and the cultural are bound up together (Jacobs, 1994). Heritage representations are potentially both standardized and localized. On the one hand, they are shaped by the demands of economic development agencies and the tourist industry for visitor-friendly 'products' through which accessible and affirmative stories can be told; on the other, heritage's distinctive claim is to tell the story of a particular place, and it must thus be centrally concerned with providing locally recognizable, particular historical accounts.

Herein lies an important distinction between the heritage museum and the theme park, in that the latter does not claim to have the locally authenticating function that heritage does. The theme park makes reference to only the most familiar, mythic and widely recognized stories and legends, in order to evoke 'the feel of the past'. The heritage museum, on the other hand, has as its mission the telling of a story that marks out this place from that one, or this way of life from that one. In this sense, whether or not that attempt is successful, heritage is characterized by its promise of bringing together both local particularities and generalized images. It is important to examine how these dual functions 'meet' within any one instance of heritage rather than to assume from the outset that the particular has been eclipsed. This book thereby sets itself the task of exploring how, and with what consequences, local understandings of history are shaped and moulded into the public forms that attract the tourist gaze.

2. Beyond the heritage debate: leisure, reminiscence, identity

We have seen, so far, how critiques of heritage focus on its supposed power to effect ideological distortions in popular historical and political consciousness, as well as its role in heightening social divisions by reducing cultural values to localized, essentialized and commodified stereotypes. In both of these dimensions of critique, it is assumed that cultural representations play a powerful role in shaping social attitudes and behaviour. Such a *cultural effects model* has, however, itself been criticized by sociologists concerned that it overstates the ability of cultural forms to determine social behaviour, and also that it accords too significant a role to textually mediated ideology (for example, Abercrombie et al., 1980). Such critiques have been germane, too, in key recent debates in cultural and media studies, which have contested the structuralist assumption that media texts determine popular consciousness through the ideological nature of cultural representation. An alternative tradition has focused instead on the ability of audiences actively to decode and reinterpret media discourse rather than to be subjectively positioned by textual forms (see Morley, 1992, for an overview of these debates).

These shifts in social and cultural theory have inaugurated a new attention to the nature of visitor interpretation in heritage sites. There is still, however, a paucity of research into how visitors actually interact with heritage representations. As John Urry (1996) has pointed out, it is unclear to what extent visitor interactions should be understood as active 'readings' or decodings, and therefore analysed as sites for the communication of cultural-ideological messages, or whether they should be approached as activities of reminiscence and leisure-gazing, and therefore seen as part of a more general terrain for cultural consumption and the expression of social identities. Part of this uncertainty, I suggest, comes from the difficulty of categorizing the representational status of heritage museums. In providing both fully elaborated historiographical texts which the visitor will 'read' (such as audio-visual shows, artefactual and wall displays and sound commentaries) alongside more diffuse forms of representation which rather invite a 'wandering', sight-seeing or performative kind of interaction (such as buildings, sets, open-air landscaping and *tableaux*), heritage museums blur the boundaries between texts and environments. As a result, the kinds of interaction they stimulate are complex and not easily classified.

There are many media through which 'the past' is imagined, and these should not be hived off into separate areas of enquiry. Nor should the extent to which heritage attractions are consumed in terms of elaborated messages be overstated. As tourist and leisure attractions, they constitute a day out for fun and relaxation rather than necessarily imprinting a lasting and coherent interpretation of history in the minds of their visitors. Mellor (1991), for instance, argues of Liverpool's Albert Dock reconstruction that this site is in fact, just that – a *site/sight*. It is an object of the pleasure-taking but not overly interested gaze of the day-tripper, who is more concerned with shopping, wandering around aimlessly and en-gaging in personal reminiscences than in receiving any *message* from the displays of Liverpool's past. In this sense, argues Mellor, theorists who wring their hands in dismay at the ideological damage done to the nation's critical spirit along the heritage arcades are in fact missing their crucial function, which is that of leisure.

Although such a perspective provides a useful corrective to assumptions that heritage texts profoundly alter the historical consciousness of their audiences, it nevertheless risks subsuming heritage into a general theory of consumption. Against this, the argument of this book is that heritage attractions need to be analysed as distinct cultural forms, even though they share many features with other historical and leisure-orientated experiences (including television and film). This is because, as we have seen, they occupy a special position within the nexus of local social relations as well as offering a characteristic type of visitor experience. Both the specific appeals and forms of heritage as well as its location in wider contexts of historical communication need to be brought into the picture.

Heritage museums offer an array of challenges to the researcher. As Crang (1994) argues, heritage should not be made into a 'transcendent signifier' and fixed into a unitary identity. Instead, we should try to grasp the processes through which visitors 'animate' heritage, rather than seeing it as a set of values that can be pinned down in advance through an analysis that is purely theoretical. It is thus important to pay attention to the performativity of heritage: the ways in which visitors, texts and environments interact to produce historical knowledge. Heritage involves visitors in encounters with artefacts, landscapes, buildings, audio-visuals, tour guides, animated displays, rides, walk-through reconstructed environments and so forth. The ways in which the past assumes a shape and a form in visitors' minds during these different kinds of encounters has not, so far, received adequate empirical investigation.

Recent calls have been made, however, for ethnographic research into heritage visiting as a social practice (Urry, 1996; Dicks, 1997a, 2000). This involves attending to the visit as part of people's more general engagements with the past within the context of their location in wider socio-cultural formations, such as class and household relations. Fyfe and Ross (1996), for example, argue that the motivations of both visitors and non-visitors need to be studied in the context of their everyday lives, paying particular attention to their interactions with local history in different forms, as well as the extent to which they define themselves as museum-goers. They draw on the theoretical framework provided by Bourdieu (1984), which sees museum visiting as part of a wider system of distinctions which classifies culture into differentiated social-capital values. This critique offers an important corrective to market-research-style enquiry into 'who visits', by widening the scope of analysis into locality-based ethnography (for further discussion of visiting, see chapter 9).

To gain an understanding of how visitors/audiences make sense of different forms of communication about the past, we need to look at how signs of the past (whether material, graphic or filmic) acquire meaning in particular contexts (in glass cases, on television screens or in heritage museums). As Urry (1996) points out, we need a more developed theory of *reminiscence*. Practices of popular historical understanding need to be theorized both on a psychological, affective level, in the construction of personal identities and memories, as well as on an ideological, cultural-communicative level in terms of the reproduction of particular discourses about the past and its relation to the present. Looking at heritage in relation to social identities, in particular, can map how it mediates historical knowledge in the form of personal biographies, memories and emotional attachments to places and times. Macdonald suggests, for example, that heritage offers the potential for local cultural and social appropriation, and that therefore heritage 'can be a way of telling the people's story, and of helping to make sure that it will be heard' (1997: 175). Such an approach allows us to gain an insight into the mutual interdependence of 'private' and 'public' images of the past.

3. A new approach to heritage

Further work is needed, then, on how visitors actually engage with the forms of the past that heritage offers them. What expectations and knowledge do visitors bring to the site when they visit, and what images and stories do they carry away with them after the visit is over? This is a question that concerns the relationships between heritage and other domains of historical knowledge. It suggests two kinds of enquiry: that of intertextuality, discourse and collective memory, and that of reminiscence, identity and personal biography. In the first, we could ask how the knowledge gleaned by visitors from heritage encounters can be related to public discourses of the past mediated through television, film and radio, schools, colleges, books and magazines. The second concerns how visitors make sense of this knowledge in relation to their own biographical experiences, personal memories and conversations about these with other people. I do not intend these two dimensions to be seen as separate – the public sphere and the private sphere. On the contrary, the interesting questions for the understanding of heritage issue from the dialectic between them. Thus, heritage is both a public myth-making display-case as well as a private, identity-conferring arena. Its significance lies precisely in this dual quality.

The heritage debate has too often been conducted in abstract terms with little or no detailed reference to such questions. Similarly, there has been a lack of detailed research into how particular heritage sites have developed. Of course, there is much of interest to be debated at a theoretical level about the various kinds of appeals that heritage seeks to make. However, before we conclude that heritage 'is' one kind of phenomenon or another, it makes sense to assemble some knowledge about existing heritage sites which can shed light on how they came into existence and how they mediate historical understanding.

Heritage as communication

In order to understand how heritage generates an understanding of history, it is necessary to investigate how visitors make sense of its exhibitions and displays. These kinds of questions relate very closely to a central concern of media studies, which is the development of theories for understanding the ways in which television, print and film communicate. As in the historians' debate over heritage, there have been differing perspectives in media studies on how the 'effects' of the media should be understood: whether, for example, the power of media messages is to be found in their language and images, in audiences' active interpretations, or in the institutions and political economy of media organizations. These are long-running debates, which need not concern us here. However, the principle that underlies them – that representations are sites of communication and that the mechanisms and effects of that communication require careful study and theorization – is an insight which has much to offer the heritage debate.

The heritage museum, then, is a space within which public communication takes place between exhibitions and visitors. In presenting the history of something (a local area, a craft, an industry and so on) meanings are mobilized (through images, objects, buildings or narratives) which are orientated to an audience. The business of the heritage centre, like television, is to translate particular subject-matters into forms that can be accessed by an unknown quantity of unspecified and absent others (cf. J. B. Thompson, 1995). This is reflected in several recent calls for heritage and museums to be theorized as public communication, using methods drawn from media and communication studies (Lumley, 1988; Silverstone, 1988, 1989, 1994; Hooper-Greenhill, 1995; Macdonald, 1995; Fyfe and Ross, 1996).

In approaching heritage as communication, we need to recognize that this communication is embedded in the social contexts in which heritage is produced and consumed. Thus, production (the putting together of the exhibitions), texts (the exhibitions themselves: slide shows, audio-visuals, *tableaux*, etc.) and consumption (the active interpretation of texts by visitors) are all aspects which determine how heritage communicates. Heritage may be seen, in Roger Silverstone's words, as 'a process in which the apparently discrete elements of production, representation and response are understood as dynamically interconnected' (1988: 232). If heritage is to be seen as a social practice, production and consumption must be understood as linked processes, enabling analysis to consider both how heritage texts are developed and also how visitors respond to them. This approach provides a fruitful way of focusing attention on three sites of analysis: production, text and consumption.

Beyond the museum walls: heritage as a social practice

However, the question remains of how these three realms are defined. If they are understood as bounded by the museum walls, we begin to see the pitfalls of an insufficiently social model of communication. Too often, in museum studies, the social and cultural contexts of heritage are left out of the picture. In Hooper-Greenhill's (1994) approach, for example, what curators (and other exhibition designers) create is understood to constitute the 'source' of the message, what visitors do is called 'reception' and the ways in which visitors and designers respond to the message in successive feedback loops accounts for the production of meaning. Silverstone, too, though calling for an integrated analysis of 'production, representation and response' (1988: 232), nevertheless appears to limit the realm of 'production' to the decisions, negotiations and actions of produc*ers*. Production, one often finds, is equated with the practices of exhibition design, professional interpretation and curatorship, and consumption confined to the immediate responses of visitors to these 'messages'.

Both production and consumption, however, are more complicated than this. The field of production, for example, is not exhausted by the activities that characterize curation or exhibition design. Instead, it takes place within the structures of funding, control, management and so on that characterize the museum/ heritage site as institution. Further, the institution itself is situated within wider networks of social and economic relations. These may include relations between the heritage site and local business and enterprise agencies, local history societies and enthusiasts, central, regional and local agencies of governance, relevant heritage-orientated organizations (the Tourist Board, the National Council for Museums, the conservation quangos such as English Heritage or CADW). These relations are often conflictual, resulting in 'reconstruction struggles' over how the locality is to manage its resources and specializations (Bagguley et al., 1990: 146). The museum's walls around the displays and exhibitions inside do not keep the real world out.[1]

In addition, the production process is crossed through with wider *cultural* relations. In the next two chapters we will be looking at the range of public images and symbols, stories and narratives, which are part of the cultural currency of how we talk about the past: images of 'the way we were', of mining communities, of heavy industry, of 'the Valleys', 'Wales', and other imagined communities. These popular understandings furnish heritage production with all kinds of shorthand cultural appeals that visitors will readily recognize. Since the producer of the heritage text does not create these meanings, the individual curator, exhibition designer or audio-visual producer cannot be seen as their author. In this sense, heritage texts are permeated by wider historical discourses, and by the echoes of other texts which mobilize signs of the past (cf. Barthes, 1977, and 'intertextuality'). What may seem to be the raw material of heritage – the local histories and anecdotes, the place-myths and images of localities – turn out in fact to be thoroughly cooked. In chapters 5 and 8, we will look at how these wider cultural discourses which organize the stock of images and stories we think of as 'the past' can be identified in the exhibitions which claim to present us with 'the Rhondda'.

Consumption, too, is a complex area. There are all kinds of questions concerning consumption that are central to the communication process but which go beyond the immediate interactions of visitor and exhibition within the space of the heritage site itself (Fyfe and Ross, 1996). Studies of 'reception' need to acknowledge that visitors do not arrive in the exhibition space as blank slates ready to be written on by the text, but themselves are part of cultures in which those wider cultural discourses circulate. Visitors may already have – consciously or unconsciously – quite fixed notions of what a mining community consists of, or what 'the old days' were like. In addition, consumption should be understood as a social practice: sociological analysis has considered the particular ways in which the tourist gaze is structured by different modes of looking, and organized within class/gender relations and regimes of taste and distinction (Bourdieu, 1984; Urry, 1990). In the light of all these considerations, we cannot see heritage meanings as originating within, or being confined to, the designer/text/visitor triad.

Encoding and decoding the heritage text

This discussion has highlighted the deficiencies of those critiques of heritage which rest on a priori assumptions about the historical meanings it generates. Thus, we cannot say, for example, that the commercial relations which structure the development of a particular heritage site will determine what messages its visitors will assimilate. In the same way as other forms of media such as historical television programmes communicate quite complex and varying messages about the past, heritage is the forum for different forms of historical representation and interpretation. On the other hand, one would not want to claim that there is no specifiable relationship between the conditions of production of a heritage centre and the kinds of texts that it will display, and thus the range of interpretations that visitors will make. What is needed is a theoretical framework that allows production, text and consumption to be linked together in ways that do not assume simplistic cause-and-effect relations between them.

In order to understand these relations between production, text and consumption, it is useful to think of communication in terms of a circuit of encoding and decoding. Stuart Hall (1980) proposed an influential theoretical model of encoding and decoding in relation to television, which can fruitfully be applied to heritage communication (see Dicks, 1997a, 2000). Following this model, the conditions and processes of production of a heritage centre are *articulated to* (rather than determine) the form and nature of the exhibitions and displays within. The model of articulation, derived from Gramscian hegemony theory, seeks to capture the sense in which different practices are brought into ideological alignment with each other. In the case of heritage, the various practices that constitute heritage production are positioned within public discourses about the past which also inform the creative decisions made by designers and the readings made by visitors.

Heritage displays are not, therefore, 'authored' by their designers. In so far as they generate meaning, they do so by mobilizing and echoing signs and discourses about the past, history, imagined communities and so forth that are in general cultural circulation. In this sense, they are intertextual (Barthes, 1977). Further, however, they are necessarily organized according to certain principles of representation. For instance, many displays have a narrative structure which does not originate in an individual act of creation but which belongs to a much wider 'grammar' of narrative conventions. Images, too, communicate through iconic signs which have become naturalized into a 'language'. Heritage interpreters necessarily work within these wider conventions (as chapter 8 will show). The meanings of the displays thus do not originate within the processes and conditions of production itself, but are re-presented and reconfigured through the practices of encoding and decoding.

Similarly, if we turn to decoding, we can see that heritage texts do not have meaning in and of themselves. Instead, meaning is generated through the encounter between readers (visitors) and texts. Visitors, as we have already seen, bring their own active processes of interpretation to bear on what they see and hear in the heritage centre. Clearly, the text exerts some degree of determination over what kind of meanings the visitor will make of it. Some displays may be very didactic; others will be more open. However, the encoding/decoding model suggests that all texts work to 'prefer' a particular kind of reading (Hall, 1980). Thus, heritage texts will structure the history presented in such a way that a particular set of interpretations is encouraged. The extent to which visitors reproduce this 'preferred reading' (as opposed to making aberrant readings) will in turn depend on the cultural map within which visitors are situated (Morley, 1992). For example, if they have access to quite radical discourses of history, perhaps through politics, study or through work experiences, visitors will bring those frameworks of knowledge to bear upon the interpretative encounter with heritage.

By thinking of heritage as social communication, which involves a circuit of encoding and decoding situated within a social context, it is possible to begin to map the various social, cultural and economic relations which govern the production of 'messages about the past' at heritage centres. Specifying these relations, unfortunately, involves the analyst in a potentially boundless task, since it is impossible to describe all the relevant relations of production and consumption – still less to identify the provenance of discourses about the past. However, by attending to the economic, social and cultural relations within which heritage texts are encoded and decoded, it is possible to arrive at a fuller understanding of heritage as a social practice. This book attempts to follow through such a project by examining the ways in which heritage is both produced and consumed.

4. The multiple faces of heritage

Heritage has been debated with two broad sets of concerns in mind. First, it has been discussed as a symptom of our obsession with 'the past'. In this perspective, it is assumed that what heritage visitors are seeking is a generalized experience of 'the old days'. This may be condemned as a wallowing in nostalgia, or defended as a symptom of postmodern temporal mobility: the temporal *flaneur*. Second, it is discussed as a phenomenon in its own right, and viewed as a source of 'bad history' – false, simplistic messages about a past that is shorn of critical reflection or complexity. I argue that both of these perspectives, which are closely related to each other, neglect an important dimension of heritage, which is that it is not just about historiographical adequacy – it is not just pastness that heritage displays. Instead, heritage conveys particular messages about particular times and places, and is bound up with the display of collective cultural identity. In this perspective, heritage constructs a sense of Welshness, Rhondda-ness, etc. It is part of the terrain within which we imagine community.

Of course, the adequacy of historiographical representation is important to the project of imagining community, too. Which version of the community's past ends up on display is crucial to the public communication of the community's cultural identity. What we need to examine is how the 'preferring' of one historiography over another comes about, and how particular stories of the past get to be in the heritage park. By taking an 'imagined communities' perspective, we can appreciate that every version of the past is tied up in particular cultural and political agendas. What appears to be a simplistic or romanticized narrative may be the outcome of quite complex contestation 'on the ground'. What appears in the 'show' needs to be traced back through the threads of this contestation, so that the cultural context of heritage's identity claims can be better understood. All historical representation is caught up in cultural distinctions that imagine communities in one way or another. So the interesting question about heritage is not 'How does it represent history?' but 'What does it tell us about the particular articulation of local identity which is represented in particular sites?'

II. IMAGINED COMMUNITIES

4

Wales in a glass case

Heritage does not only represent the past; it is also a powerful means of defining place. By representing people in geographically located communities such as nations, regions and localities, it sets up homologies between peoples and territories (Dicks and Van Loon, 1999). The discussion in the present chapter will draw on the concept of the 'imagined community' (Anderson, 1991), and will thus focus on the place-authenticating claims of heritage. Although Anderson's account discusses the general potential of narrative and iconography to imagine collectivity, it is also clear that these collectivities can be imagined in various ways, with variously conceived boundaries. Rather than seeing heritage as a simple reflection of cultural realignments, this chapter focuses on the potential of heritage actively to construct different visions of collectivity. The previous chapter showed that the role of heritage in constructing collective imaginations has frequently been viewed as a distorting mirror, but the discussion here will focus on the different angles through which the lens of the past refracts a variety of place-identities.

Heritage museums elevate the unique identity claims of particular places, even though they may often rely on generalizing tropes to do so. Thus, instead of focusing on general worries about the 'emptying out' of history (cf. Jameson, 1991), it is more useful to consider how heritage 'fills in' history by elaborating it through particular images. Heritage's claims to represent 'the people of place x and time y' are especially significant: examining their contours can tell us a good deal about the faultlines and preoccupations of different national and subnational 'island stories' (Samuel, 1998).

1. Heritage and Welsh identity

The public display of the past has been crucial to the development of new regionalist, ethnic and proto-nationalist formations (cf. McCrone et al., 1995). Whilst heritage can be set to work in constructing patriotic sentiment and bolstering the national myths and legends of powerful nation-states, it is also germane to the self-assertion of marginalized or peripheralized 'imagined communities' (Anderson, 1991). The claiming of common 'roots' in the past, especially if these are deemed to have been stifled by a colonizing or dominant central power, injects a powerful energizing force into nascent, proto-national collectivities (cf. Dicks and Van Loon, 1999).

In non-state political communities such as Wales, the generation of collective images and narratives has been a primary means of publicly asserting, as well as denying, the coherence of the nation-in-waiting (see, for example, Gruffudd's account of heritage as national identity, 1995). This process may – arguably – be intensified with the advent of (albeit partial) self-government in Wales. History is a central arena within which claims about the meaning of 'Welshness' can be publicly aired, debated and contested. The past is thereby deployed in the public affirmation of identities which are struggling to establish themselves as key to the idea of the nation. This points to a possible difference between how a preoccupation with the past is to be understood in Wales, Scotland and Northern Ireland, as opposed to England. It is arguable that the nostalgia paradigm is less convincing as an explanation for the preoccupation with history in areas which are defined, and/or define themselves, as marginalized, peripheralized or colonized. Public displays of Englishness, on the other hand, court the accusation of a self-satisfied indulgence in memories of a glorious past.

It is noteworthy, indeed, that many of the heritage critiques examined in chapter 3 have been directed at English heritage sites and agencies, which they accuse of promoting jingoistic and conservative interpretations of the past. By focusing negatively on the connotations of élite and hegemonic forms of national heritage, such analyses neglect the ways in which heritage contributes to a positive affirmation of *vernacular* identity for localities, regions and other subnational collectivities. Horne (1984), for instance, notes the ways in which the heritage of the peasantry has been used in attempts to establish the unique cultural traditions of new nations struggling against imperial occupiers. In Scotland, Northern Ireland and Wales, heritage necessarily acknowledges, and may often seek to highlight, the marginalized position of a vernacular identity struggling to assert itself against the centre (see Macdonald, 1997). There is, potentially at least, a sense in which it opens up spaces for representations that offer critical reflections on élite power-formations. This is a potential that future chapters will explore, in discussing the Rhondda Heritage Park.

Imagining community

Benedict Anderson (1991) has provided a fascinating account of how the 'mapping' of the nation through museums and censuses made a fertile breeding ground for anti-colonial nationalist movements in the eighteenth and nineteenth centuries. He argues that nations are actively constructed communities, in which the face-to-face mode of human interaction has been displaced by an *imaginary* collectivity, disseminated by print-media such as the novel and the newspaper. This collectivity, cultivated through public sites of mediation such as heritage, enables community members to take each other's existence for granted and to imagine amongst themselves a commonality – however vaguely apprehended – of identity. This impression is produced through various narrative forms (from novels to maps and museums), which disseminate the idea of a shared temporal and spatial unity. The members of imagined communities are engaged in different spheres of life and will meet face to face only a handful of the other members; yet through these sites of mediation 'they' can think of themselves as sharing the same past, present and future within a unitary collective identity.

Drawing on Anderson's theorization of imagined communities, Shields (1991) develops the concept of 'social spatialization' to refer to the processes through which space is socially produced through discourses (metaphors, images, 'popular etymologies', and the like) which ascribe particular associations to particular places. Thus, Brighton becomes associated in popular culture with illicit weekend pleasure; the north of Canada, on the other hand, is canonized as the land of wilderness. Shields argues, further, that social spatialization does not merely offer discursive frameworks for imagining places, but that these imaginations themselves become directive, and affect planning decisions and policies. In this way, particular places come to specialize in particular experiences and connotations, from which it is difficult to escape (see also T. Hall, 1997).

However, Shields also shows that place-myths are never fixed, because 'contradictions are always being encountered and old notions abandoned' (1991:65). This points to the contested and shifting nature of collective representations, a subject which Anderson neglects. The public affirmation of one version of collective identity simultaneously works to silence others, and yet also – paradoxically – to open up a space for those excluded voices to clamour for attention (Dicks and Van Loon, 1999). Place-identities can be the subject of dispute amongst various local groups, who may try to contest their use in urban redevelopment strategies. In the case of restructuring Lancaster in the 1980s, for example, attempts to define Lancaster's future, post-industrial identity were the site of intense local controversy (Bagguley et al., 1990; see also Jess and Massey, 1995, on conflict in the Wye Valley, and various examples of 'dissonant heritage' documented by Tunbridge and Ashworth, 1996).

In Wales, too, different visions of identity deploy different versions of the past. No fewer than eight of the sixteen chapters in the collection on Welsh identity edited by Tony Curtis (1986), *Wales: The Imagined Nation*, are centrally concerned with how Wales has been imagined in the past, showing the concern over the uses to which the past is put. As P. Morgan notes, 'it is not only a matter of keeping the legends alive, but also keeping alive through legends' (1986:20). The collection sifts through the shadows cast by older national myths, images and symbols which have sought to claim one kind of particular identity or another for Wales and its regions. In what follows, these faultlines are explored further, showing how the past is continually invited to provide the symbolic public regalia for particular versions of the locality, the region and the nation.

Nationalism and rural/urban images of Wales

There has been a long-standing and almost caricatured split between the rural and urban imaginations of Wales. Morgan (1983) shows how crucial the dissemination of rural myths and narratives have been for successive periods of Welsh nationalist sentiment since the seventeenth century. The 'Welsh spirit' was held to reside in the traditions of the mountains, song and nature, whilst the industrial southern Valleys have been seen as anglicized: not the 'true' Wales (Humphreys, 1995; Gruffudd, 1999). Price (1992), for instance, describes the Valleys' identity-shift in nationalist sentiment from the pre-industrial rural landscape admired in the writings of B. H. Malkin to the 1930s 'landscape of degradation', in which the industrial and crowded valleys are described by different writers as a 'fallen' and defiled place:

> That Glamorgan could be viewed as the whore of the family of Wales who sold herself to English industrialism and was seduced and abandoned, is too powerful an image to be ignored. It implies ... another Wales that was poor but pure. A Wales formed through the contemplative gaze and eternally visible as a site of unproblematic 'nature'.
>
> (Price, 1992: 99)

The social space of the Valleys, then, as the epitome of the 'Glamorgan whore', is represented by a strand of romantic Welsh writing as alien to the 'unsullied' social space of 'the real Wales'. This imagination clearly hitches Wales to a particular rural place-myth, upon which Welsh nationalism in the nineteenth century constructed the twin edifices of traditional Welsh identity: land and language.[1] This imagination of Wales extends beyond nationalist sentiment to include wider cultural representations. Humphreys (1995: 137) points, for instance, to the different status of Welsh landscape painters: those who, like John Piper, depict Snowdonia and the 'wilderness' are recognized as Welsh artists; those who create images of the Valleys, like George Chapman, are known as Rhondda artists (see also Jones, 1986).

The community of communities?

In the twentieth century nationalism had to modernize its cultural appeals and widen its symbolic scope. As Kahn (1984) points out, an important suturing function was provided by the image of community. Nationalist discourse has frequently appealed to this ideal in attempts to unite Wales around a cohesive identity, one which furnished more modern and less romanticized connotations than the nineteenth-century celebration of the *gwerin* (see below). One of Plaid Cymru's most influential modern activists, Saunders Lewis, described the ideal Welsh nation as a 'community of communities', in which the widespread Nonconformist traditions could bring together the collectivist and working-class-based meaning of community in the south and the folk meaning it articulated in the rural 'heartland' (Kahn, 1984: 22). It is an image which projects Wales as a classless, united community of 'the people' – marking it out from the socially divided and class-ridden identity of England.

Attempts to unite Welsh identity around a distinctive ideal of community which includes both the urban-industrial and the rural versions have continued, however, to look shaky, and in the 1980s and 1990s, according to some, to fall apart (Giggs and Pattie, 1992; Adamson, 1996). The question of what constitutes Welsh identity has been reactivated with the revival of the Welsh language, and the corresponding problematic status of the largely (but not exclusively) English-speaking Valleys. The shifting appeals to Welsh identity made by Plaid Cymru illustrate this instability. Adamson's (1996) thesis is that recent inward-migration to central rural Wales has contributed to a dissolution of the rural/urban, mountains/Valleys hybrid identity which was forged within the party through the vague and binding concept of community. He argues that Plaid Cymru has mobilized two opposing imaginations of community as if they were one and the same:

> The concept of community employed by Plaid Cymru has never been defined and it has retained an open meaning which allows individuals to insert their own sense of community into party rhetoric. Two dominant conceptions of community have existed. The first is a sense of rural community with an emphasis on kinship, neighbourhood and identifiable patterns of language, culture and religion. The second is a sense of industrial community, associated with coal and steel production, with networks of mutual aid, traditions of working-class politics and labourism. As long as the meaning of the term community was not defined, all sections of the Party could feel loyalty to a concept of decentralist socialism founded in communities ... A farmer on the Llŷn peninsula could feel as committed to the concept as a miner from Maerdy.
>
> (Adamson, 1996: 41)

The current protracted crisis of economic and cultural restructuring in both rural and urban Wales has resulted, according to Adamson, in the final dissolution of this hybrid ideal of the community of Wales. Both the rural and urban identities have been shattered by new experiences of economic and social dislocation under conditions of disorganized capitalism (Lash and Urry, 1987), and by new allegiances and shifts in the local political sphere, particularly in the period coinciding with devolution (Thomas, 1999). There is some evidence, for example, that a tripartite cultural and economic division of Wales is now emerging, consisting of Welsh Wales, Valleys Wales and British Wales (Roberts, 1999), and which is articulated to the rural/urban divide but not entirely congruent with it.

Such fragmentation does not, however, dissipate the heritage impulse. By contrast, it could be argued that it is the breaking down of traditional monopolies on cultural representation (exercised via state, church and party-political patronage) that has provided the immediate context for the heritage boom of the last two decades. We saw, for example, in chapter 1 how a cultural tradition that was hegemonic in the Valleys, namely labourism, began to crumble in the 1980s under the weight of the failure either to sustain or to replace the economic productive base upon which it was built. Heritage, it could be argued, is a kind of dual-pronged response to a dislocation that is both economic and cultural, promising economic regeneration as well as cultural reinvigoration. Such dislocation throws up a variety of affirmative images: from élite tradition (in the case of castles, manor houses and cathedrals), to labourist tradition (in the case of mining and industrial heritage) and folk tradition (in the case of rural and 'Celtic' heritage). In publicly displaying these different identities as memories rather than actualities, heritage exposes the faultlines of Welsh historical identity as well as foregrounding the absence of a unifying or established national identity in the present day.

As a result, heritage is enmeshed in a tangle of contrasting images which continue to ensnare attempts to define what Wales *is* by mythologizing what it *was*. Such disjunctures contribute, in no small measure, to the controversial and contested position of heritage in Wales today, a heritage which is nonetheless burgeoning and diversifying all the time. This point serves to underline the fact that heritage proliferates in conditions not of secure, complacent, hegemonic cultural identity, but of fragmented, contested and competing historical identifications. By examining the forms it takes, and the ways in which it echoes the faultlines that characterize other forms of public historical representation – such as the popular media or academic historiography – it is possible to understand heritage as a positive forcefield in the interplay of collective representations. This can be illustrated if we turn, now, to the question of

Welsh historiography and museography; a terrain in which many of these key controversies have risen to the surface.

2. The folk-heritage tradition

Heritage and tourism in Wales have, until recently, largely reflected the deeply rooted rural/urban split imaginations of Wales discussed above (see also Gruffudd, 1999; Humphreys, 1995). It was in Wales that the UK's first open-air folk museum was founded, and this folk-heritage identity provided, for many decades, the flip side of the Welsh heritage 'establishment' – as represented by castles, churches and cathedrals on the one hand and empty landscapes and wildernesses on the other. This folk tradition has been seen, romantically, as constituting the 'real' heritage of Wales, something that represented the lives of 'ordinary people' as opposed to lords, princes and bishops. The following quotation shows clearly the preferred status accorded to the folk heritage:

> In Wales there are a number of attractions that illustrate the image-making potential of tourism, and together they tell two important parts of Wales's story. The castles and industrial heritage museums tell a story of conquest and exploitation – the material aspects of domination by England. The folk museums, by contrast, highlight the cultural distinctiveness of Wales; they help to establish in the mind of the tourist that Wales has its own identity, based in a rich and ancient culture that is different from that of England.
>
> (Pitchford, 1994: 4)

Here, the history of Wales is divided into two: the native Wales and the Wales imposed from the outside. What is interesting about this account is that – along with castles – the industrial heritage of Wales is cast as the alien import, an outcome of 'conquest and exploitation', whereas Wales's 'own identity' and 'cultural distinctiveness' lies in its folk traditions. The folk heritage is positioned as the 'true' identity, revealed in its purity once the trappings of the Anglican colonizers have been cleared away. This indicates the uneasy position that industrial heritage occupies in this commonplace imagination of Wales, and shows how this imagination seeks to use heritage to draw a clear border between Wales and England.

The folk, the gwerin *and the people*

The folk-heritage tradition, with its aim of preserving and interpreting rural farming life, was established early in Wales. The Welsh
Folk Museum, opened in 1948, followed the principles of the
Scandinavian open-air museum at Skansen, opened in 1891, which
aimed to replace the traditional focus on objects and curios with a
whole, reconstructed environment displaying the life of 'the folk'.
Constructed in the grounds of St Fagans Castle, which had been
donated to the museum by the earl of Plymouth, the Welsh Folk
Museum established an open-air setting for reconstructed rural
buildings displaying craft and farming traditions. Iorwerth Peate, its
founding curator, wanted 'not to create a museum which preserved
the dead past under glass but one which uses the past to link up
with the present' and thus 'to show clearly the unity of all life and
of all human activity, yesterday, today and tomorrow' (Peate,
1948: 13). There is a dual emphasis here: on 'folk' as an inclusive
term, embracing the whole of 'our culture', and on a Welsh national
identity expressed as 'the Welsh way of life' (1948: 57). He was
insistent that only the Welsh could interpret Wales correctly, and
that, therefore, the museum attendants had to be Welsh-speaking.[2]

Although they seem anachronistic today, folk museums were
conceived as a revolutionary new approach to the interpretation of
history. The great Victorian and Edwardian national collection
museums (for example, the Natural History Museum, the Science
Museum, the Victoria and Albert Museum, the National Museum
of Wales) were consciously opposed to the display of 'spectacle'.
They defined themselves in opposition to the preceding fairs,
carnival shows and cabinets of curiosities where the objective was
to induce wonder and surprise through the display of assorted
exotic curios. Instead, they removed objects to laboratory conditions, situating them in standardized glass cases to display the
scientific principles of classification and specialization (Bennett,
1995). The folk museum, on the other hand, reintroduced the
emphasis on spectacle, although differently from the earlier cabinets
of curiosities. It put on display a whole recreated environment,
rather than disembodied (and displaced) objects. The spectacular
principle became that of ethnographic display – of a people situated
in an environment, rather than of things exhibited in containers.
The idea was to make history accessible, through having visitors

actually walk within it. Visually laid out in buildings, artefacts, *tableaux vivants* and costumed scenes, the past was exposed for everyone freely to explore its minutest corners.

The folk museum claimed a more vernacular reach than the traditional museum, both in what it put on display, and in the visitors it hoped to attract. It laid claim to a gaze not on the 'other' of the curiosities and wonders of the early museums, nor on the 'other' of the science museum's expert knowledge, but on the *self* – the everyday knowledge and the ordinary experiences of 'the people of Wales'. Peate expressed the hope that 'to it will come school-children for tuition, architects, artists and craftsmen for inspiration, country men and women "to cross the bridge of memories", colliers and quarrymen to view anew their wider heritage and townsfolk to discover the permanence of Welsh life' (1948: 61). Thus, the aim was not to display élite forms of knowledge, but to educate people about *their own* culture, a culture that was framed explicitly as Welsh. Whilst the collection museums confronted visitors with expert, scientific and specialist knowledge, Peate wanted visitors to recover the everyday knowledge that their grandparents had. He hoped thereby to inspire the reinvigoration of rural Welsh communities, not as aestheticized objects of the tourist gaze but as models for localist, utopian alternatives to the tyranny of in-dustrialism (Gruffudd, 1995).

The folk-heritage tradition itself drew on a burgeoning post-war academic and political interest in the recording of 'vanishing' lifestyles. In Wales, the classic research in the sociological tradition was carried out by Alwyn D. Rees, whose 1951 book *Life in a Welsh Countryside* was the first academic study of Welsh community life (see Owen, 1985; also Day, 1989; 1998). Chapter titles from this last work indicate its anthropological influence: The Economy, House and Hearth, Farmsteads, Family, Kindred, Religion. In 1960, Rees published (with Elwyn Davies) a collection of studies called *Welsh Rural Communities*, which documented life in a rural village, a coastal village, a small market town and the tradition of chapel-going in a small community. His was a project of rescue ethno-graphy, involving the documentation of disappearing ways of life, in areas which were: 'relatively secluded and entirely Welsh-speaking ... which could be expected to have retained many features of the traditional way of life' (Rees and Davies, 1960, quoted in Owen, 1985: 29). These communities were peopled by the *gwerin*, the

Welsh word that straddles the terms 'people' and 'folk', who were popularly seen, Gruffudd (1999: 151) points out, as 'rural, Non-conformist, moralized and Welsh-speaking; an idea that would be used in opposition to Anglicisation and to the imposition of an urban-industrial Britishness on Wales'.[3] These have been the powerful images of organic, closed and homogeneous localities which, as Graham Day shows in his discussion of the Welsh rural community studies tradition, have shaped the perception of Wales as a 'community of communities' – even though the realities of local social life in rural Wales are considerably more complex and nuanced than such a categorization allows (Day, 1998).

The Valleys mining community

The industrial slate and coalmining localities, though themselves greatly depleted by the 1950s, were neglected in this lament for Wales's vanishing 'heartland'. This is not to say, however, that they were silenced. Williams (1985) argues, in fact, that Wales has been characterized by two competing discourses of place – the rural *gwerin* and the industrial working class. The latter tradition, centred on the labourist imagination discussed in the first chapter and epitomized by the ideal of the archetypal mining community (cf. Bulmer, 1975), had – particularly since the 1930s – begun to popularize through film and novels the industrial, proletarian ideal of community (Stead, 1986). The Valleys, in this alternative tradition, were synonymous with 'coal, community, nonconformity (of many kinds), trade unionism, self-education, democracy and socialism' (Francis, 1990). This was an alternative set of meanings for imagining community in Wales, and one which lamented the loss of solidarity, political activism and mutual aid that the decline of the coalmining industrial base was seen to herald. However, the hold on the canonical version of Welshness established by the folk traditions made it difficult for this alternative, proletarian tradition to lay claim to Welsh national identity. It was a tradition that rather looked to a class-based, non-nationalist vision of collectivity.

Gareth Rees describes how such a vision of community was used as a basis for local political campaigning in 1970s and 1980s south Wales in relation to local political campaigns against, notably, school milk cuts and in order to oppose pit closures: 'We've taken a hundred years to build these communities; you can't kill them over night', proclaimed the Chairman of Deep Duffryn local mining lodge threatened with closure in 1978 (quoted in Rees, 1985: 399). During the miners' strike of 1984–5, the campaign's appeal to occupational and community survival as against one based solely on wages, jobs and work conditions marked the dispute out from the industrial strikes of the 1970s. Drawing parallels between the 1984–5 strike and the General Strike of 1926, Gilbert concludes that the community appeal (in south Wales, if not in Nottinghamshire) of the later dispute was a direct inheritance from 1926: 'the strike was simultaneously a defence of "community" and a rediscovery of its possibilities' (1992: 3).

This appeal to community is made in response to the *local* impacts of wider economic change, and the attempt to organize resistance on the local level (this was the case throughout many UK coalfield localities during 1984–5). Rees (1985) argues that the mobilization of community in the south Wales coalfields was the result of various political and economic pressures that have forced a distinctive, local and place-based response to restructuring. The NUM in south Wales played a locally based campaigning role throughout the 1970s and 1980s, necessitated by the spatial unevenness and local specificity of the NCB's industrial restructuring. It was also prompted by the decreasing possibilities of purely workplace-orientated political action and the resultant diffusion of protest throughout the pit villages, which was organized around neighbourhood networks, especially women's groups.

However, it is doubtful that the appeal to community could have been made so forcefully and vociferously in south Wales had it simply reflected an economically and politically motivated strategic localism. As Rees also points out, it also drew upon an already familiar, diffuse and elaborated set of images depicting the 'traditional coalfield community' (1985: 394 see also Strangleman et al., 1999). Community itself offers a repertoire of positive images which are readily recognizable, of which the mining community is conventionally held to offer one of the most potent. Throughout the 1980s and 1990s, we have seen a growing tendency for political campaigns to summon up images of community, neighbourhood, home and the particularity of place, rather than to depend on purely class-based or doctrinaire appeals.

Community studies

The documentation and celebration of working-class community was not confined to post-war Wales. It was an imagination that also impelled the explosion of community studies in the UK in the 1950s and 1960s, produced against a backdrop in which it was claimed that the transformation of the social order was signalling community's eclipse. A large number of studies appeared which asserted the continuing, although threatened, salience of community identifications in working-class occupational localities (Crow and Allan, 1994). These studies ranged from Young and Willmott's *Family and Kinship in East London* (1957), whose half a million copies sold make it the most widely read sociological book in Britain, to Jackson's *Working Class Community* (1968), documenting a range of 'working class traditions', Dennis et al.'s (1969) classic account of a Yorkshire mining village, *Coal is our Life*, to Tunstall's (1962) study of fishing communities called *The Fishermen*.

In many ways, the folk and industrial imaginations of community share similar characteristics in the post-war ethnographic imagination. The local social life under investigation was overwhelmingly that of the working class, whether in urban industrial or rural farming occupations. The strong anthropological instinct behind them is plain in the choice of occupations 'in decline' – independent fishing, coalmining and small-scale agriculture. The 'traditional way of life' was understood to characterize the 'traditional working class', under threat because the class system itself was claimed to be breaking apart in post-war 'affluent' Britain (Critcher, 1979). Although the folk studies eschewed the imagery of class, so central to the industrial-labourist traditions, both types of community study attempted to shore up an ideal of vernacular collectivity, epitomized in the twin images of the people and the folk. We shall see how these images were played out in the context of Welsh heritage below.

Abandoning the folk

The folk-heritage tradition in Wales was subject to increasing criticism from the 1960s onwards. Increasingly, Peate's vision of a Wales united around a classless, harmonious folk identity, which patently drew on long-standing and romantic notions of the *gwerin*, came under attack. It was criticized both by a new generation of left historians interested in the industrial and proletarian traditions (see below), and also by a new wave of museum professionals and curators who were concerned to present a more 'objective' and less romanticized view of Welsh life. When Geraint Jenkins took over the position of curator at the Folk Museum in 1987 he was critical of its idiosyncratic preservation of assorted rural buildings, which, in his view, merely replicated the curiosity-driven approach of the early, 'unscientific' curio museums (Jenkins, 1986). By concentrating on the 'quaint' customs of rural labourers and farmers, many of Wales's new museums were painting a skewed and unbalanced vision of Welsh heritage:

> We have to unravel the many strands that contribute to the overall personality and character of a community. We cannot select and isolate one or two elements that may take our fancy and forget the remainder, when the purpose of our work is to present an authentic and comprehensive picture of community life.
>
> (1986: 7)

Jenkins was concerned that artefacts selected for preservation were unrepresentative and lacking in historical legitimacy. As a result of a romantic and nostalgic refusal to let old buildings decline, there had been a haphazard and unscholarly quest to preserve at any cost. This had resulted from the Folk Museum's exclusive concern with rural, as opposed to industrial, Wales.

From the late 1980s, the Folk Museum underwent a change of direction and began to seek a wider range of buildings, including industrial acquisitions such as the Rhyd-y-car miners' cottages in 1987 and the Oakdale Miners' Institute. In 1995, it changed its name to the Museum of Welsh Life. Jenkins's argument was for a more dispassionate and professional practice of heritage 'interpretation', which would regulate and curtail the burgeoning of small attractions and museums that lacked curatorial expertise:

> Many of these collections presented to the general public are merely cabinets of curiosities that have little relevance to the life of the people who visit them ... There is, after all, a vast difference between a 'collection of bygones' and a true ethnological collection developed as the result of scholarly research and presented with scholarly interpretation.

Far too many museums in Britain today merely provide a nostalgic peepshow into a largely fictitious past.

(Jenkins, 1989: 123)

In the scientistic perspective which is proposed here, heritage is about education, and not about attractions. The miseries of the past must be displayed alongside its compensations. Heritage must further the cause of study and knowledge; not the provision of spectacles or experiences. Authenticity and selectivity are key principles in this argument. As a result, the construct of 'the folk' or the *gwerin* is simply unrepresentative and romantic, seeking to deny the fact that the aristocrat, the shopkeeper and the labourer are all equally a part of Wales's heritage.

The new industrial Welsh heritage

The new focus on the inclusivity of heritage and the turn away from its folk connotations helped to usher in a period of expansion for industrial heritage attractions in Wales. CADW, for example, which is charged with conserving buildings that are culturally signifi-cant for Welsh heritage, has reflected this shift. Recent efforts have been centred on broadening the definition of what constitutes heri-tage, away from the traditional reliance on castles, churches and manor houses. Increasingly, this means including the industrial his-tory of Wales, so that 'chapels, colliery buildings, Victorian schools and hospitals and canal structures are included in the lists along with farm buildings, terraced housing and telephone boxes' (McLees, 1997). It has also meant overcoming the traditional polarity of con-serving high-status public buildings on the one hand and promot-ing the landscapes of mystical and folk Wales on the other. Welsh heritage has thus sought to distance itself from the images of popu-lar tourism inherited from the nineteenth century and enshrined in an iconographic portraiture of women in Welsh shawls and stove-pipe hats (cf. Brewer, 1999).

Welsh labour historiography

The new professionalized approach to heritage, however, has itself been subjected to criticism from the group of left social historians that came to the fore in Wales in the 1970s and 1980s. As Patrick Hannan observes, in the 1950s there was 'scarcely a textbook to be found on the subject of Welsh history' (1999: 151). By the 1970s, however, a flourishing new Welsh social history was being produced by a new generation of Welsh labour historians, Kenneth O. Morgan, Dai Smith, John Davies, Hywel Francis among them, who were inspired by the 'history from below' movement of the 1960s. The labour history journal, *Llafur*, was founded in 1972, dedicated to the study of Welsh industrial and political social movements. This enthusiasm reflected a period in which, in Dai Smith's words, 'there was still a sense in which you could alter contemporary political activity' (quoted in Hannan, 1999: 153). It also kickstarted enthusiasm within BBC Wales and HTV for Welsh social history, producing the series based on Dai Smith's book, *Wales! Wales?* in 1984.

As Humphreys (1995) points out, the 1970s and 1980s saw an interrogation of what constituted Welsh identity, with Dai Smith's book and Gwyn A. Williams's *When was Wales?* (1985) adding a question mark to the idea of the Welsh nation. One of the targets this new generation of social historians had in their sights was the folk-heritage tradition. As Dai Smith makes clear in the revised edition of *Wales! Wales?* which he published in 1999 as *Wales: A Question for History*, the new Welsh historiography was founded on the principle that it was the twin processes of industrialization and urbanization and the anglophone and working-class traditions that were responsible for forging the distinctive identity of Wales as a modern nation. This perspective was directly counterposed to the trappings of established Welsh heritage tourism which had insisted on its essentially rural, mystical and Welsh-language identity, epitomized in the imagery of daffodils, song and druids. For the new labour historians, the folk tradition was an anachronistic and romantic irrelevance.

Hywel Francis, in berating the early 1980s heritage boom in Wales for turning its people into a 'nation of museum attendants', is scathing about the Folk Museum:

> It's all about Welsh dance, music, costume, barns, crafts, coracles, carts and idyllic sterilised whitewashed cottages. But no word, as far as I can see, about land-ownership and social control except revealingly (?) in

the first sentence of its guidebook where the Earl of Plymouth's 'generosity' is acknowledged in giving and selling land and property to the museum!

(Francis, 1981: no page nos.)

This was written, of course, before the museum's belated embrace of Wales's industrial traditions. Yet Francis is equally dismissive of the burgeoning industrial heritage sector in Wales. His criticism rests on the perceived failure of Welsh industrial heritage to do justice to the social and political struggles of working people, and its obsession instead with 'those puffing machines at the Industrial and Maritime Museum'.

It was Raymond Williams who drew attention to the opposition between the terms 'the folk' and 'the people' in his novel *The Volunteers* (1978), the former referring to a rural and cosy past, the latter to a vibrant, unsettling and political present. For the socialist historians of the 1970s and 1980s, it was through the political construct of 'the people' that Welsh heritage should find its true expression. In this perspective, Jenkins's vision of inclusivity remains tied to outmoded constructions of Wales as a united 'community'. Dai Smith, for example, whilst welcoming the new direction taken by the museum under Jenkins's curatorship, identifies in it a reluctance to countenance the display of conflict or dissension. Instead, he sees a continuing reliance on visions of 'wholeness, and harmony, and community, and distinctiveness, and togetherness, and uniqueness' (1990–1: 5). What Smith wants to showcase instead is the vibrant popular culture of the Welsh working class, acknowledging, and not conveniently forgetting, that much of this culture is thoroughly modern, anglophone, American-derived and not unique to Wales:

[St Fagans is] a view of the past that speaks of non-conformity, and not of Roman Catholicism, of Welsh Language dialects, and not of English tongues, of miners' institutes, but not particularly of Odeons or Plazas; it can accommodate Llanelli RFC but not Everton AFC; it speaks about Welsh taverns, but not of red-brick public houses; it speaks of craftsmanship but not of labour-saving dynamite ...

(1990–1: 5)

This is a perspective which rejects the 'olde-worlde' appeal of heritage and which argues, instead, for a ground-level reflection of 'ordinary people's ordinary lives'. The heritage centre that is the subject of later chapters, the Rhondda Heritage Park, is tightly entangled in the threads of this debate, not least because Dai Smith was engaged as the principal script-writer of its audio-visual narratives. Heritage thus registers, in a particularly stark manner, some of the ongoing debates over the political character of Welsh identity.

Collective representations and 'political' heritage

This politicized dimension of heritage is always lurking under the surface, fuelling dissension and conflict over how 'the people' are to be represented. Once heritage abandons its traditional preoccupation with the material culture of a social and political élite, the question of how it imagines the 'ordinary people' comes more clearly to the fore. Are 'they' to be thought of as a collective identity, united around shared moral or political values, as in the notion of imagined communities and national identifications? Or are 'they' to be deconstructed, and imagined rather as a constellation of fragmented and conflicting identities? If the former, how is this collectivity to be identified, if it is not to be reduced to a folk, with all the connotations of moral fixity, romanticism, social immobility and political abeyance implied by that label? If the latter, how can fragmentation be represented? If heritage's task is to paint multiple pictures of plural identities, how are these to be defined, and how are the relationships among them to be envisaged? In the process, what happens to the possibility of asserting any level of *placed* collectivity at all, from the national plane down to the local?

Answering these questions requires coming to terms with a theory of representation. The logic of collective representation, it has been argued (for example, Barthes, 1977), draws boundaries around subjects and thereby seeks to repress difference. In the moment of acknowledging one more subdivision, a further assertion of identity is effected, seeking in turn to contain further splittings. This means that any project of collective representation rests on unstable categorizations, which are always subject to further contestation and realignment. This is the case whether the collectivity is imagined as a folk, a people, a community or a 'community of communities'. Thus, any attempt to define an 'inclusive' heritage, one that allows a thousand flowers to bloom and celebrates difference, always operates through asserting identity, or sameness, at one level or another. In the light of these impossible resolutions, the question of heritage's truthfulness, representativeness or objectivity has to be bracketed off – at least with regard to the representation of 'the people's identity'. In the final section of this chapter these difficulties are further illuminated by considering at a more theoretical level the vexed question of community identity, and the role of heritage in seeking to represent it.

3. The community-heritage tradition

We have already seen how the ideal of community provided a certain strand of nationalist thinking in Wales with a convenient catch-all image through which to unite the diverse cultures of Wales into one tradition. The ideal of community thus seeks to straddle both of the collective imaginations under discussion here, namely the folk community and the people's community. However, as we have also seen, both of these imaginations tend to slide into each other, as they rely on the nostalgic apprehension of loss – for a way of life based on shared values and interests. Recent developments in museology and heritage interpretation have sought to avoid the anthropological connotations of classic ethnographic represen-tation by proposing the establishment of clearer links between museums and the present-day localities in which they are located.

The 'community museum'

The 'community museum' movement, also known as the 'eco-museum' movement and 'new museology',[4] has attempted to insti-gate a more democratic, locally representative understanding of community. Its proponents argue that:

> the true limits of the museum should not be the boundary walls of the museum building and its grounds: they should be the whole of a defined geographical territory, which might be a small village at one extreme, or a whole country in the case of a national museum ... In traditional museums the driving force and control is the expert staff and their wishes, while in 'new museology' it is the community, its collective memory and will.
>
> (Boylan, 1990: 33)

This manifesto indicates two significant aspects of the community museum ideal: that representing community is coterminous with representing place (a 'defined geographical territory') and that the museum should seek to build active and reciprocal relations with this place (beyond its 'boundary walls'). It proposes, in the process, two understandings of the term 'representation': that of displaying the past, and that of giving expression to local people's voices.

There is, however, little reflexivity evident in this definition of community: it is taken as an already-constituted territory (defined geographically), which is then simply represented or mirrored by the museum. This mirroring aspiration suggests that the anthropological view of the people in 'their' environment continues to inform the eco-museum imagination, since it fails to interrogate how community is itself produced through sites of mediation such as the museum. Community is reified into a place 'out there', and becomes something that displays can therefore be 'about'. Against this view, it is necessary to recognize that the museum's 'raw' material is always-already cooked: it consists of already-circulating mythologies of local people, their past and their place. We need to consider how the already crowded and contested social space into which the museum seeks to reach (and which it also seeks to put on display) answers back, or at the very least offers points of resistance and/or accommodation to, such definitions (see chapter 7).

Although writers on new museology may question how to access the community, and how to represent it adequately, there is rarely a sustained attempt to consider whether and how 'the local community' is itself constructed through cultural representations. In the professional museums literature, there is often a taken-for-granted notion of a particular place's heritage, as if that place were a given (for example, Browne's 1994 discussion of 'Ireland's heritage'; see also Binks, 1989). This is a perspective which has been subjected to throughgoing sociological critiques in recent years, which have pointed out that the assertion of community depends on already-constituted mythologies of place (Shields, 1991), and on public practices involving regimes of power/knowledge that seek to imagine a bounded 'we' identity (Bhabha, 1990; Anderson, 1991; Billig, 1995; see also Dicks and Van Loon 1999). In this sense, we need to consider how heritage itself reproduces particular place-myths and identities.

Reconciling community and difference

The problems of putting community on display are many, not least the danger of re-creating a homogenized and idealized vision that ends up in the same ideological quagmire as the folk ideal. The problem occurs when community is taken as a descriptor of real social relations rather than recognized as a product of collective imaginations. For some theorists, the easy way in which community is co-opted into exclusionary tactics merely exposes its retrogressive and reactionary real face. Young (1990) has pointed to the ways in which the community ideal privileges face-to-face social relations, particularly in its left-utopian versions. Instead of recognizing that all social relations are mediated culturally, it constructs an ideal of immediate here-and-now social contact, which attempts to collapse the temporal and spatial distancing that is an inevitable, and for Young desirable, part of contemporary life. In the process, difference is obliterated, in favour of a return to coherent, authentic and unitary social identities. Thus community is ultimately predicated on the drawing of boundaries around the self and the demarcation of the other.

Similarly, Zygmunt Bauman has pointed to the 'retrospective unity' that community asserts by mobilizing images of what we have lost. Community always lies just beyond reach, in a past characterized by a unity the present has allowed to slip away:

> Tonnies-style communities fall apart the moment they know of themselves as communities. They vanish (if they have not evaporated before) once we say 'how nice to be in a community'. From that moment on, community is not a secure settlement: it is all hard work and uphill struggle; a constantly receding horizon of the never-ending road; anything but natural and cosy. We console ourselves and summon our wilting determination by invoking the magic formula of 'tradition' – trying hard to forget that tradition lives only by being recapitulated, by being construed as *heritage*; that it appears, if at all, only at the end, never at the beginning of agreement; that its retrospective unity is but a function of the density of today's communal cloud ...
>
> (1992: 138)

Morris, similarly, observes that community is constituted as traditional only at the point of its dissolution. When historical change forces collectivities to shed tradition (as in the end of labourism in the Rhondda), the past becomes merely an opposition to the present/future and is thus 'frozen' as a repository of the 'old' traditions – in short, retraditionalized (Morris, 1996). Calls to return to community therefore actually mean a return to *what was constituted as community* (and frozen as such) during the moment of change or modernization. Thus, when deindustrializing areas seek to identify and market themselves as possessing the traditions of community, they are applying the heritage lens of the present to refract the traditions of the past. Community-heritage is constructed at the moment of its dissolution through the temporal break of deindustrialization. Thus, heritage images of the Rhondda are both traces of previous representations and the expression of current concerns and anxieties (for example, over the loss of identity that deindustrialization brings).

There are, therefore, problems inherent in the project of putting community on display. One of the questions that the rest of the book explores is the tension between 'community' as expression of multiple vernacular identities, and as homogenizing representation of 'the folk', 'the people of the valley' or 'the people of place x'. The democratizing mission which appears to reside in the aspirations of 'new museology' to represent the whole local social body sets itself a complex and challenging task in trying to engage, in meaningful ways, with the totality and the multivocality of people-in-place. Obstacles to such an achievement are many, not least the ready battery of images and representations that reproduces community as a bounded and homogenized social and geographical entity.

Such totalizing representations of community operate through tropes, ready-made narratives and facile metaphors. They can all too easily obliterate difference and smother conflicting voices, and they can have very little connection to the specificities or realities of particular places. Although a polyvalent and multivocal articulation of community may seek to avoid them, there are considerable pressures within exhibitionary practice to produce museal forms that can be easily assimilated to (what are considered to be) visitors' *existing* cultural repertoires, rather than to challenge these and thereby risk confusion (see Silverstone, 1988, 1994). Thus, by activating familiar images of community, museums, in accordance with their new vernacular aspirations, can more readily tap into the language and imagery of popular discourse. The temptation to deploy easily recognizable, stock images is thus a difficult one to resist.

Romancing the coal

The dangers of romanticizing and mythologizing community are clearly present in the case of the south Wales Valleys. It is an area which has been particularly subjected to a process of cultural mythification, ascribing to it images of the archetypal mining community. Chapter 1 showed how such images were central to the local labourist political culture in the Rhondda, built on the ideals of hard graft, the family wage and community spirit. Many of these values have become associated with a hackneyed and sugary idealization of 'the people's' community. In *How Real is My Valley?* (1994), John Evans takes the heritage industry to task for endlessly recycling only those images of the south Wales Valleys that accord with those from the John Ford film *How Green was My Valley*. The Rhondda Heritage Park is one of the museums that Evans has in mind when he makes this critique.

However, this critique, which is undoubtedly justified on a number of levels, leaves certain issues unresolved. Given that the coalmining traditions of the Valleys deserve their fair share of heritage interpretation, should this be executed in a way that studiously avoids any of the available stock symbols? Or is it a question of how those instantly recognizable images and tropes – the community spirit, union solidarity, terraced housing, women in shawls, tin baths, the pit hooter – can be set to work in narratives that construct more complex and challenging meanings, rather than the romanticized stereotypes that Evans fears? These are questions about the 'how' of interpretation rather than the 'what', and as such are not easily resolved.

If we are to conclude that every representation of community necessarily depends on a logic of identity that is constraining and reactionary, there is no space left to explore the potentially positive aspects of collective representation. Earlier, a distinction was drawn between 'folk' and 'people' versions of the community ideal. The former is constructed through an anthropological imagination that seeks to document community as a way of life. It sees community as anachronistic and exotic, out of kilter with advanced Western society – a 'vanishing other' to be preserved through various projects of rescue ethnography such as the folk museum. The 'people' community ideal, on the other hand, though sharing elements of this backward-looking gaze, is more amenable to political mobilization. When inserted into political discourse, this version imagines community as a resource for future-oriented collective action. The aspiration in the political usage is for organizing communal forms of resistance, protest or self-provisioning held to be enabled by local allegiances afforded by community. It calls for the founding, or the refounding, of the 'good community' as a utopian ideal. It therefore has a future-looking rather than a purely backward-looking orientation (see Dicks, 1999). It appears most visibly in communitarian arguments, but has also figured importantly in socialist campaigns and programmes organized around various forms of working-class activism – particularly in coalfield cultures (cf. Rees, 1997; Kamenka, 1982).

This political vision of community has been especially salient in attempts to reassert the vibrancy and distinctiveness of the south Wales Valleys 'way of life', as we saw in chapter 1. Although heritage may seem to signal an eclipse of hope in the continued relevance of such images, it also puts them on public display and consecrates them as descriptors of local identity. By picking up on labourist inflections of the 'good community' as well as trading on stock images of 'the vanishing other', heritage in the Rhondda potentially mobilizes both the anthropological and the political meanings of community. It therefore offers a public showcase for identifications which have potential political and utopian articulations. In this sense, it is too easy to dismiss heritage as inevitably nostalgic and merely retrospective; rather, we should examine how these competing paradigms are resolved within particular heritage forms. The next chapter will examine how the Rhondda is defined at the Rhondda Heritage Park, by illustrating how traces of the imaginations discussed above are registered in its historiographical scenes and narratives.

In conclusion, we need to return to a central argument of this book, that these generalized appeals (of community, the past, the vernacular and so on) can only be turned into the built forms of heritage within specific local spaces and times. Visitors to heritage museums may both seek and find only a cosy reflection of vanishing community. Nevertheless, the heritage site has to engage with history that is already written and rewritten, and already contested, down through the years – reproduced through local social and cultural relations as they change and shape new economic and political conditions. Thus, the outcomes of heritage initiatives cannot be assumed in advance, and nor can their form be taken for granted. Instead, there is a continual interplay of generalized and particularized influences, producing heritage as a cultural intersection rather than a destination. While homogenizing images of the vanishing other and standardized practices of professional heritage interpretation (see chapter 8) work to translate the multivocality of local life into accessible and perhaps hackneyed images, this may still be accomplished through utopian representations that have a certain local political 'authenticity'.

Furthermore, as physical places that can be bodily accessed, local heritage sites contain all sorts of limitations on pure 'Disneyfication', because their built structures cannot simply be reinvented. A colliery cannot, for instance, be easily turned into a Wild West theme park.[5] In addition, as we shall be exploring in chapter 7, they have a range of sitting personnel attached to them. Most local heritage sites – almost by definition – have a long history of a prior use in a former incarnation. Whether it is the old mill, the canal, the farm buildings, the dockside, even the reclaimed waste-tip, there are potentially numbers of locally situated interested parties who have particular claims on the space, built or symbolic, which the heritage centre appropriates (cf. Bagguley et al., 1990; Urry, 1995). There are, therefore, various aspects of heritage which suggest that the simple activation of myths, tropes, commonplaces and other blurred images viewed 'from the hill' do not necessarily subsume its available meanings, or can at least be supplemented by alternative accounts.

5

The Black Gold community

The ideal of the archetypal mining community has long furnished an entrenched blueprint of collective life in the south
Wales Valleys. The values encapsulated by this ideal have been
both socio-cultural, based on human communion and a coherent,
shared culture, as well as political, centred on class-identity and
collective action. The former include values such as neighbourli-
ness, togetherness, mutual aid, community spirit, close-knittedness,
choral singing and chapel-going, and the latter embrace qualities of
solidarity, democracy, socialism, self-education, collectivism, activism, trade unionism. They provide recognizable frames of meaning for public discussions and representations of the area and its
inhabitants. This constructs a discursive domain within which
local identity is commonly articulated, even though the ideal is
often summoned up only in the moment of acknowledging its loss.
A combination of these ideals, as this chapter will explore, lies at the
heart of the vision of the Rhondda displayed at the Rhondda
Heritage Park.

Whether these qualities of community life can actually be found
in the area or its history is not under discussion here: attempts to
identify and describe actually-existing communities are fraught with
theoretical and empirical problems. What is more significant for our
present purposes is that the popular purchase of these qualities
suggests that local cultural identity has conventionally been defined
along the axis of community. In fact, these two categories of commonality reflect two related discourses of community identity. The
first is community as shared human values, founded on the common experience of living in a particular place and sharing similar
occupational and working lifestyles; the second is community as
shared collective interests, rooted in a consciousness of solidarity
and the potential for collective action. One might also identify a
third discourse of community (which heritage resolutely ignores),

encapsulated in images of a 'community of deprivation' and which
has often provided the terms within which 'the Valleys' are
imagined in certain metropolitan myths of a backward Valleys
hinterland.[1]

The essential point is that the representation of community
involves implying, however indirectly, the *source* of the unifying identity – whether this is imagined as a shared moral identity
(a unity of values emanating from the 'spirit' of people-in-place),
or a shared political identity (a unity of interests built upon shared
social and economic position). I suggest that the dual representation of a place-based moral unity on the one hand and a class-
based political unity on the other is a tension underlying vernacular
industrial heritage representation. This chapter will explore how, as
do many other popular cultural representations of collectivity,
heritage hitches the two visions together.

First, in framing shared collective interests within a place-based,
moral unity, heritage contains the political implications of historical
collective representation within specific spatio-temporal boundaries, obscuring their wider reach. Heritage continually suggests
that the relevance of such collective images are confined to a particular time and place. Second, and conversely, the cosy assertion of
moral unity is also, in its turn, disturbed by heritage's simultaneous
evocation of shared collective interests and action. Since that
experience is rooted, in the case of coalmining and other proletarian, industrial occupations, in a shared class position, the heritage
text can hardly fail to flag class in one way or another. Contra the
assumptions of the heritage critics (chapter 3), it would require quite
a feat of re-presentation to silence the class discourse altogether.

It should be acknowledged, nevertheless, as Bommes and Wright
(1982) argue, that heritage can showcase class only to depoliticize it
by re-presenting it as 'the people's humble contribution to the
nation'. This danger certainly needs to be recognized in discussions
of vernacular industrial heritage. On the other hand, as Macdonald's (1997) analysis shows, heritage can also offer celebratory
narratives of collective action and working-class culture. In drawing attention to the political basis of collective action, it can potentially activate a more inclusive, cosmopolitan sense of community
that may establish connections between the heritage-place and its
visitors' lives. Different heritage museums utilize different strategies of representing collective identities and interests. In this sense,

vernacular heritage is rather an ambivalent historical form, in that its outcomes cannot be assumed in advance. It can both erect a temporal, spatial and moral boundary around working-class experience (the moral community) as well as potentially breaching that boundary by invoking images of a wider, activist, class-based unity (the political community). This chapter will explore the faultlines of this ambivalence further, by examining the representation of community at the Rhondda Heritage Park.

1. The archetypal mining community

The moral, place-based and the political, class-based discourses of community are reflected in two traditions of social scientific discourse, the socio-political vision of community (what I have termed elsewhere – see Dicks, 1999 – 'the good community') and the socio-anthropological vision (the community of the 'vanishing other'). These designations do not describe actually existing communities, nor are they mutually exclusive by any means. Rather they involve two major power/knowledge formations, based on two distinct foci of aspiration. The first aspires to document forms of *collective action* – the potential for organizing communal forms of resistance, protest or self-provisioning, held to stem from the local allegiances afforded by community. This usage has a future orientation, based on community's potential to offer utopian solutions to political problems. The second aspires to document a particular *way of life* encapsulating common human lifestyles and values, and which is particularly related to bounded geographical areas. In this usage, the aspiration may be purely backward-looking, in that this way of life is often (but not invariably) felt to be epitomized in past times and in past places – a way of life which is associated with traditional societies, eclipsed or threatened by contemporary social and economic change.

The image of the mining community blends elements of the political usage of 'the good community' with aspects of the 'vanishing other'. This becomes clear in influential sociological treatments of the mining community. Sociology and social history have long been interested in the determinants of collective political action (see, for example, Harrison, 1978). In the 1970s, explanations moved away from the earlier focus on occupational culture, that is, on identifying shared work experiences as the prime determinant of political activism, to a wider, culturalist focus on a shared way of life. It also reflected a move from focusing on the objective socio-economic position of community members to their subjective experience of community (see, for example, Williamson, 1982). It was this shared cultural experience, rather than class or occupational position alone, which, it was argued, determined the propensity of groups to take collective action. This shared way of life was theorized through the construct of community, which aligned class-interests derived from the Marxian concept of 'relation to the means of production' with sociological and culturalist foci on subjective values and ways of life. In the process, the *place-bound* qualities of community came to be more clearly emphasized, due to the focus on local human interactions and key local social institutions.

Bulmer offers the classic discussion of the archetypal mining community from within this framework. He argues that extra-labour-market relations are central to the dynamics of miners' political behaviour and criticizes approaches which isolate occupational solidarity from its embeddedness in local community structures:

> By putting conflict based on class at the heart of the analysis, attention is directed away from the local social relations of Gemeinschaft which also characterise mining communities. Occupational solidarity and communal sociability, moreover, are distinct phenomena, and the over-riding emphasis on the former is not warranted on logical grounds.
>
> (Bulmer, 1975: 67)

Thus, it is not just the social relations of work which are seen as determining, but their immersion in a wider form of sociality: community. This sociological model of the mining community urges consideration of both 'subjective orientations' and 'structurally-distinctive features of work and community' (p. 77). This produces an 'ideal type':

> The traditional mining community is characterised by the prevalence of *communal social relationships* among miners and their families which are *multiplex* in form. The social ties of work, leisure, family, neighbourhood and friendship overlap to form *close-knit* and interlocking *locally based collectivities* of actors. The solidarity of the community

is strengthened not only by these features themselves but by a *shared history* of living and working in *one place* over a *long period of time.* From this pattern derives the *mutual aid* characteristic in adversity and through this pattern is reinforced the *inward-looking focus* on the locality, derived from occupational *homogeneity* and social and geographical *isolation* from the rest of society. Meaningful social interaction is confined almost exclusively to the locality.

(Bulmer, 1975: 87–8; italics added)

This, then, is the classic statement of the archetypal mining community.[2] The notion of the mining community as a world apart (geographically isolated) is a point of considerable emphasis. In fact, there are certain resonances here with the 1950s thesis of the isolated single-occupation community (Kerr and Siegel, 1954), even though Bulmer defines community much more broadly. The effect is to bring into discourse an academically theorized and elaborated conception of the industrial working class as experiencing a *special and other* way of life in particular bounded places. Let us try and summarize the major features of this imaginary of community:

1. *Solidarity* (acting on the basis of collective interests, or affective bonds). Members are alleged to share the same interests, or to put collective interests before individual ones. This solidarity is understood to be both objective (it is in the interests of the collective), and subjective (the collective feels it is in their interests).

2. *Shared values, norms and meanings* (collective traditions, a shared culture, a communal moral code). This implies cultural homogeneity and the existence of a consensus or a harmony of values.

3. *Constraints and limitations* (membership is not a matter of volition but circumstance; residents are thrown together due to the labour market). There is little social or geographical mobility. This distinguishes the idea of 'community' from those reformulations that define it purely by interest alone (as in the 'gay community', the 'church community' and so on). Latter-day communitarians (for example, Amitai Etzioni and his followers) reject this aspect of community and argue that community in the contemporary social world can be achieved on the basis of free choice.

4. *Collective action* (shared political culture, the possibility of collective mobilization). The community can act in 'its own' interest, independently from other communities, or from 'outside' society. As we have seen, different types of community are held to display different degrees of collective activism (Gilbert, 1992).

5. *Historical identity* (tradition, intergenerational continuity, a shared history). The community involves a particular form of temporality: a 'longue durée', a timeless stretching back and stretching forward (Calhoun, 1983). This means that traditions are inherited and reproduced over generations, making change relatively slow-paced.

6. *Residuality* (the threat of eclipse and the problem of survival or revival). In classical sociology, the historical progression of human collective life is *from* community *to* society (cf. Tonnies, 1955 [1887]). So community is either on the brink of eclipse or already eclipsed. In the community studies literature of the 1950s and 1960s, community was seen as supplanted by the post-war 'affluent society'.

7. *Class identity* (industrial proletarian or rural folk images). This class identity is secured, in particular, through the association between community and common occupation (farm labouring, fishing, shipbuilding, mining). Community is seen as characterized by manual labour in either agricultural or industrial occupations.

8. *Gender segregation* (men are the breadwinners; women the homemakers). The archetypal community – particularly the industrial one – is usually represented as being marked by a strict gender division of labour.

9. *Locality* (the community is a recognizable territorial formation, and its members exhibit an attachment to place). This aspect of community has attracted considerable debate, with several sociologists insisting that place is not necessary to community (for example, Lee and Newby, 1983; Willmott, 1986). Agnew (1989) points out, however, that the local and place-based aspects of community have in fact provided a central feature of its embedded mythology. Other sociologists want to retain the placed dimension of community: Crow and Allan's (1994) overview of community studies, for example, is subtitled 'An

introduction to local social relations', and is committed to a model of community as place-based social life.

These characteristics coalesce into three distinct modes through which the specificity of community identity is configured: ways of life and shared meanings (the social and cultural), history and duration (the temporal) and locality (the spatial). The archetypal mining community is represented, in other words, through constructing a social, temporal and spatial unity. In addition, we can see that the image of the archetypal mining community is, in fact, a hybrid discourse, bearing traces of the 'good community' (in its solidarity and collective action), and the community of the 'vanishing other' (its temporal residuality, moral values and distinct place-identity). I would suggest that such an imaginary provides the representational logic for many vernacular heritage museums. In what follows, I shall look in detail at the Rhondda Heritage Park's representation of the Rhondda and examine how it engages with this repertoire of conventional images of community.

2. The Black Gold community

The Lewis Merthyr, an old Victorian colliery which finally ceased production in 1983, had by 1990 metamorphosed into the Rhondda Heritage Park – a multimedia 'living-history' evocation of the mine and its community. It has two stone-built winding houses, which used to contain the headgear and engines for winding both coal and mine-workers up and down the shafts. These winding houses are named the Bertie and the Trefor, these being the names of two of the children of W. T. Lewis, the mine-owner. In these two buildings, visitors watch audio-visual displays which tell the story of the Rhondda and the Lewis Merthyr colliery. There is another audio-visual show in the old colliery fan-house just across the pityard.

The fan-house has a waiting area where there are extensive wall displays. These offer visitors a name for the entity upon whose heritage they are gazing: the 'Black Gold Community'. One of the pictures, entitled, 'A Growing Community', is accompanied by the following text:

For over 100 years the two valleys of the Rhondda have been home to a community which owed its existence to coal. Almost every family was directly or indirectly dependent on coal for survival. They have shared times of great joy and sorrow and often suffered poverty which would have crushed lesser communities. Now sadly, the pits of the Rhondda stand idle. Eventually, the scars left by a once great industry will heal, but the story of coal will be etched in the memories of its people forever ...

Today, the community, though closely knit, will always extend a warm welcome to visitors, perhaps because their own fathers were the recipients of just such a welcome when they first arrived with hearts full of optimism, eager to join the vast army toiling underground, in an effort to satisfy the world's insatiable appetite for steam, warmth and fuel.

The Rhondda Heritage Park (RHP) presents, then, the story of a community – the Black Gold community. The exhibitions comprise walk-through reconstructed shops and a miners' cottage, three audio-visual multimedia presentations in the old colliery build-ings, a guided tour underground culminating in a thrill ride to the 'surface', and various displays and mining artefacts around the colliery yard, all of which aspire to tell the story of community. Thus, the history of a people-in-place is displayed within the confines of what was once just a place of work, but which now contains and displays much more than this – the 'community of the Rhondda' itself.

The space, time and social life of the Rhondda

There are three audio-visual shows for visitors to watch at the Rhondda Heritage Park, and they form a tour known as *Black Gold*. It is this tour, rather than the underground experience, which constructs an imagined community of the Rhondda, and which forms the basis of the analysis presented in this chapter. Visitors watch the first show in the Bertie winding house and then they join the tour underground. When they resurface, they rejoin *Black Gold* in the fan-house, and finally go on to the Trefor winding house to complete the entire itinerary. Each of the three audio-visual present-ations mobilizes a particular dimension of community mythology: place (Bertie), social life (fan-house) and work (Trefor). Through the weaving together of elements from both the community of the 'vanishing other' and the 'good community', the story of the

Rhondda becomes the story of the archetypal mining community, as we shall see below. However, I also want to argue that it works at a deeper and more particular level than simply as a rehearsal of familiar community mythology. It also provides links to some of the locally specific conditions and relations that we have been exploring in previous chapters, and particularly to those concerns and cultural dislocations which are triggered by the crisis of local identity during the slow course of deindustrialization. What follows is an analysis of how these various generalizing and particularizing linkages are produced (Appendix 1 contains a full breakdown of the *Black Gold* story-lines).

3. Representing the Black Gold community

On the one hand, the texts of *Black Gold* rely on mobilizing the general, mythic qualities of community that we have been exploring. They draw on meta-narratives – some sociological/historical, some more commonsensical and ideological – that make the heritage story resonate far beyond the boundaries of a particular local history. Thus, the story of the growth of the mining industry is presented as a story of modernization and urbanization; the Depression and industrial decline are explained in terms of global transformations; the nature of the industry is described through the trope of comradeship-through-adversity; the relations between men and women reproduce the commonplace of women as the long-suffering guardians of the domestic realm. Each story, then, is told through the lens of a wider, mythic story. *Black Gold* thus actively recycles the wider mythology of community, which allows the heritage texts to be recognized and readily comprehended by the tourist gaze. Thus the particularities of local history are translated into the generalities of mythology (see Barthes, 1973).

On the other hand, although the stories are framed as abstract mythic narratives, they also present stories of the everyday. They organize the past into 'affective tales' that bring 'abstract stories and everyday experience together' (Crang, 1994: 345). In the process, they provide a considerable mass of detail and commentary which gives them a specific, locally authenticating content. Simply to point to the resonances and similarities between *Black Gold* and other heritage representations of community is to end up, as some studies do, with an analysis that sees heritage only in terms of its general features (for example, West, 1988). Instead, I argue that heritage is characterized by a tension between the general evocation of community, and more detailed accounts of history which have a particular local resonance. The contrasting of A. J. Cook (the miner's leader) and W. T. Lewis (the coal-owner), for instance, ties the story into local frameworks of knowledge in which these figures have particular connotations. The description of the miners' institutes and libraries gives a specific Valleys inflection to the wider archetypes of mining culture. In particular, the detailed description of the colliery as a workplace offers an insight into the varied nuances and particularities of mining as an occupation. Through such details, popular commonplaces – the myth of manual labour as the antithesis of books and learning, or the image of miners as a lumpen, homogeneous 'mass' – are challenged by the provision of 'inside' information relating to *this* place and *this* industry.

The spirit of place

W. T. Lewis, the colliery-owner, proclaims at one point in the first multimedia show, 'Make no mistake, we have made the name Rhondda and of Lewis Merthyr ring out around a world that needs coal as it needs oxygen itself: we are the future!' The Rhondda's global fame is constantly reiterated, and its coal represented as 'the best in the world'. Thus, Rhondda's coal is 'its own': a territorial attribute, defining the boundary of life 'between these enfolding hills'. An organic and symbiotic relationship is set up between the people, the colliery and the Valleys landscape: 'Rhondda ... made its mark. And it's marked its people. Indelibly.' The precise identity of this 'it' is left unclear, but it is distinguished from 'people', thus suggesting an almost spiritual entity residing in the Rhondda-as-place. The texts thereby attribute a historical agency to place, endowing it with the power to act and to change, in tandem with 'its' people. In this way, the Rhondda takes on a self-contained and bounded place-identity.

The local 'here' of the Rhondda is opposed to the distant 'there' of elsewhere. As Bryn Rees, the local Lewis Merthyr miner-narrator, relates, 'I was born around 'ere, just down the road'. 'There', on the other hand, is 'the new docks at Cardiff', where the coal is exported to 'the coal bunkers of the Empire'. 'There' is the city, the seaside, the world beyond the Valleys. Although Rhondda's connections to this 'wider world' are emphasized, these are always posited as connections *between* one territorial formation and another, so that the sense of a unique place-identity is heightened rather than dissolved. Not only is 'here' sharply distinguished from 'there', but 'here', it is claimed, gives rise to 'there'. 'Here' is where the coal was discovered, the coal which went on to fuel an imperial navy and to reach 'the coal bunkers of the world'. Thus the Rhondda becomes the epicentre of wider forces, rather than being their product. By returning again and again to the specificity of *this* place, the narratives assign a spatial explanation to social forces. Hence the story is the 'story of the Rhondda' rather than the 'story of the mining industry' or the 'story of Victorian industrial relations'. The Rhondda becomes the place where it all began.

Rhondda thus assumes the attributes of a protagonist on the stage of world history, and appropriates a central role within that history. This is a centrality which is not recognized in hegemonic UK national narratives. Areas such as the Rhondda have been consigned to the periphery in the national imagination of 'Great Britain' and the Empire. They have not been accorded due recognition for having provided the raw materials for the UK's industrial expansion, or been compensated for the loss of life thereby endured. Yet the narrative at the RHP is at pains to point out, in contrast, that the Rhondda was not peripheral, but was at the hub of the vast network of Empire that depended on its coal:

> If you want to know what put the 'Great' in Great Britain, you don't have to look much further than Rhondda coal. In those days you couldn't do anything, from crossing the Atlantic to running a railway or a factory, without coal. And Rhondda steam coal was the best in the world for that. Rhondda was world famous for it.[3]

This excess of self-aggrandizement cannot be understood outside the fact of Rhondda's essential peripherality and marginalization in the 'golden age' of Empire. In this sense, the RHP works similarly to the celebratory fictions of proto-nations that emerge as the inevitable corollary to colonialism and exploitation by larger powers.

Indeed, the RHP's claiming of fame is not based on confident and positive assertions of power, as is the case with the triumphant nation-state through its capital-city-based collections in national museums (cf. Anderson, 1991). It is instead founded on an insistence of the recognition of something *lost*, something that has gone unacknowledged by the centre (whether London or Cardiff), which benefited from the Rhondda's labour and exertions. By insisting on its past fame and importance, the narrative is delivering a reproach to the centre for abandoning the Rhondda to decline and decay, and for its appropriation of the 'Greatness' all for itself. It does so through articulating this sense of loss, bitterness and even anger to a dominant discourse of national pride and Greatness. In this sense, the RHP works hegemonically to hitch the miners' story to imperial territory/history, where Rhondda can have its own long-overdue share of the Greatness.

The spirit of the people

What unites the 'people of the Rhondda'? In *Black Gold*, they appear, above all, as special: energetic, self-provisioning, resilient, solidary and disciplined. Whereas the place-affirming rhetoric claims that 'coal made the Rhondda', the people-affirming strategy counters with 'but Rhondda means much more than coal'. Although what unites the 'people of the Rhondda' is their common experience of living and working at or near the colliery – as Bryn Rees says: 'the colliery just dominated our lives' – the texts also claim that this unique identity comes to have a life of its own, independently of the mines. When the collieries close, the common culture lives on; although the industry dies, the people's character endures. In this way, community is not rendered dependent on the quirks of history, but on an essential character that inheres in people, place and time.

According to *Black Gold*, the Rhondda character comprises resilience, communality, cosmopolitanism, energy, self-reliance and orderliness. But by far the most elaborated of these is the quality of energy. The Rhondda people are, above all else, an active, energetic, busy, vital people. *Black Gold* elevates these qualities into a 'vital legacy' which nothing can exterminate. In fact, so determined is this insistence on vitality and activism, it is as if the narration were acting as a rejoinder to those who might harbour different images of Rhondda people. In south Wales, the long years of industrial decline in the Valleys have resulted in a sedimented metropolitan-centred myth which caricatures Valleys people as 'backward', out of touch, traditional. Such images belong to a 'deprived community' discourse which is at odds with the celebratory visions of the 'good community' or the 'vanishing other'. In *Black Gold*, this present-day spectre of decay, deprivation and depopulation is kept at bay. Thus, the texts implicitly take issue with a conventional viewpoint that sees miners as an unskilled mass, and mining communities as dead-end, defeated or dependent.

In this sense, *Black Gold* reproduces many of the images of labourist cultural identity, by challenging New Right rhetoric caricaturing industrial, collectivist working-class communities as backward, unenterprising and dependent. Thus, the narrative does not merely mobilize myths, but performs social and political acts too, by offering a rejoinder to the spectre of the 'ghost town', *and* by advertising the people of the Rhondda as dynamic and future-orientated. This type of specific address links the text in with the contexts in which it has been constructed. It points both to labour-ist themes of self-provisioning, 'grit' and 'hard graft', as well as to the promotion of the region's distinctiveness and potential for reinvestment and economic renewal – thus seeking to effect the magical resolution of collectivism and entrepreneurialism that, I have argued, lies at the heart of vernacular heritage. By banishing images of the 'deprived community' discourse of community, *Black Gold* hopes to make a dent in the right-wing place-myth that seeks to consign the ex-mining Valleys to the scrapheap of the (post)modern world (chapter 1).

Just as place is marked out through a here/there logic, the people are defined through an us/them strategy. The principal character in *Black Gold*, Bryn Rees, is a miner from Lewis Merthyr Colliery, and local resident. In his narrative, the people become an 'us' just as the Rhondda is a 'here'. This strategy of having Bryn tell us the story of *his own* community has an authenticating effect: Bryn claims merely to be its spokesman or representative. His presence seems to guarantee *its* presence. It is almost as if the community were narrating itself through the personal voice of the vernacular. Par-ticular phrases establish the collective averageness of the narrator: 'Like *most lads*, I . . .'; 'All of *us boys* in the village . . .'. The union is the Fed, 'as *we* called it', and the miners' leader '*our own* A. J. Cook'. When the Depression hit, 'nothing *we* did could stop the pits closing', until the Labour government 'gave *us miners* what *we'd* first asked for in 1912'. On the other hand, 'they' are non-miners or non-locals – the outside state authorities and the coal-owners: '*they* did prove the steam coal was there'; *'they* were certainly a far cry from the streets of the Rhondda'; 'that's when *they* sent the troops in'. The people are thus marked out by a class discourse which differentiates them from 'the authorities'.

In the fan-house show, the narrator is Neil Kinnock, who is positioned as the outside, objective commentator, rather than part of the collective 'we'. His Welsh accent has a much more formal and rhetorical style, suggesting empathy and neutrality at the same time. Here, the use of 'they' assigns a common character to the 'people of the coal valleys', as in 'they marched and demonstrated'. This commonality is also achieved through the substitution of the collective subject pronoun 'they' for other subject designations: 'the *human response* was swift'; '*a community* showed ...'; '*a people* that refused ...'; '*the people* responded'; '*women and family life* had been essential'; 'sure of itself as *a place and a people*'; '*Rhondda faces* were once signalled ...'. In short, the collective identity of the people is both directly made present through Bryn's narration (the 'we' of community), and also objectively confirmed by the authoritative voice of Kinnock (the 'they' of community). Each narrator gives, respectively, subjective and objective evidence of the people's common identity.

The spirit of history

The Rhondda community is built on a temporal identity, so that it appears as a 'spirit' moving through history. As Ricoeur (1984, 1985, 1988) argues, narrative time is essential to the representation of identity. *Black Gold* relates the biography of community, telling its life from birth up to the present, and insisting that the qualities of the historic Rhondda remain in the present day. Times may change, yet the essential 'spirit of the Rhondda' remains intact. The Rhondda becomes a living organism, growing up and growing old through the vicissitudes of historical change. In its youth, the sparsely populated rural pre-mining valley is suddenly filled up with people, whose provenance is unclear. As the 'old Rhondda' is dragged from its rural sleep into the coal era, time changes gear into a new mechanical, noisy, busy age in 1855, when 'the first train of Rhondda steam coal, 38 clanking wagons of it, went bumping down the valley to the new docks at Cardiff'. Time thus seems to begin in the Rhondda at the moment of the discovery of coal. The impression is of a way of life which, once activated, will never disappear, since – even in its old age – the particular 'human world' of the Rhondda has simply matured and become consolidated: 'brawling and boisterous before 1914, sure of itself as a place and a people in the 1920s and 30s, and thereafter ever-changing. And naturally so.'

Two modes of historical time shape the *Black Gold* narratives: first, the journey of a collective 'spirit' and, second, its 'stopping off' in particular *tableaux* or scenes. These two temporal senses correspond to the objective (chronological) and the subjective (phenomenological) understandings of time that philosophers have long debated (see Adam, 1990). In the first, Bryn presents time as a succession of chronological events, related to us as facts that are lined up in a sequence through which he directs the visitor. In the first show, for instance, the historiography is narrated as a passage through time from the 1850s (the 'discovery of coal') to 1958 (the 'stopping off point'). It is as though visitors actually climbed on to that first train of Rhondda steam coal, and went bumping down time until forced to alight in 1958. On the way, we encounter various *tableaux*, slides and scenes, as if we were looking from the train window. All the time, the 'voice in the dark' of Bryn's narration conducts us through history, introducing us to various characters, facts and events as though we were on a guided tour.

In the second, subjective sense of time, a particular instant is surveyed from within in its own terms as a 'now', with its own past and future, and its own personal subnarrator. Thus, at different stages, Bryn hands the narration over to other narrators who talk from within their own present, trapped within the moment of their own illuminated *tableau vivant*. The voice of the mine-owner, W. T. Lewis, at one point, rings out from the darkness to one side of the winding house proclaiming the Rhondda's industrial might, while later the three-dimensional figures of the marquis of Bute and his architect, William Burges, are illuminated against a backdrop of Castell Coch, as a voice proclaims: 'My dear Burges, your plans for my new castle are quite exquisite, though I fear Rome and Assisi have quite spoiled me for anything else.' The visitor is invited to imagine each illuminated tableau as a 'now'. This device visualizes a narrative 'meanwhile', which proposes that although community members are spatially and socially separated, nevertheless they all share the same 'now' at any one point in 'homogeneous, empty time' (Anderson, 1991: 25). Thus the texts work through fusing the linear, chronological movement of time with an infinite number of 'stopping off points' in which the community is subjectively experienced.

However, the question mark over the current identity of the Rhondda hangs unspoken in the air. In the final show, the narrative's abrupt termination in 1958 and its silence on the last thirty years leaves us in mid-narrative. Change is represented through vocabulary that suggests natural decline and flow ('the age of Black Gold recedes'; 'the scars ... disappear'), as in the biography of the self. But the device betrays its own logic, for it conjures up the image of a frail old age and an eventual demise. The narratives explicitly substitute this image with one of an ever-expanding middle age of vigour and maturity, but in doing so they also introduce the expectation of narrative closure. Does the end of the story mean death and decline? This is the silence upon which the celebratory heritage texts of working-class culture inevitably falter.

4. The 'good community' and the 'vanishing other'

This section considers how the two discourses of community discussed at the beginning of the chapter, namely the 'good community' and the 'community of the vanishing other', figure in *Black Gold*. We can detect a rhetoric of the good community in those parts of the heritage narratives that make the case for the Rhondda in persuasive and even hyperbolic terms. As the above analysis has shown, the texts banish a putative rival set of associations for the Rhondda (enshrined in images of a 'community of deprivation'), and offer a robust defence of the Rhondda's people, landscapes and history. By pointing out its historical centrality and claiming for the Rhondda its own myth of origins (in the discovery of steam coal), by insisting on its people's enduring energy and resilience, by representing time as an organic and evolving journey onwards through the ebb and flow of history, the texts imagine the Rhondda as an activist community, a player in a 'forward march' into a utopian future of emancipation. From this perspective, the RHP proposes a very hopeful, humanist-socialist vision of working-class solidarity within local close-knit communities. It is a vision that has stirred the imaginations of many writers both in the socialist tradition (E. P. Thompson, Richard Hoggart, Raymond Williams) and in the communitarian tradition (Amitai Etzioni and his followers).[4]

The community of the vanishing other, by contrast, is conjured up through the quasi-anthropological insistence on the symbiosis between people and *their* environments, within *their* time, so that they become the 'the people of the Rhondda'. An 'extended ethnographic present' is constructed, giving a timeless character to the people which inheres in their social patterns and in the landscapes of their habitat (Clifford, 1997; Marcus 1994; Fabian, 1983). Community as the vanishing other is special and distinct, with its own time, its own place, its own people. It seeks to attract a nostalgic rather than a utopian gaze, as it denies the continuities between then and now, here and there, them and us.

Whilst the political vision offers a forward-looking image of solidarity, activism, cosmopolitanism and resistance, the anthropological discourse endows the Rhondda with qualities of tradition, small-worldliness, containment, high moral codes, immobility. Whereas the tropes of time travel insist that history is a continuing and unfolding journey, the texts simultaneously summon up a narrative end-point, a point at which the lights go on and the visitor can say 'that was then and this is now'. Although we are invited to share the subjective worlds of the *tableaux vivants*, we pass them by as the narrative leads us on. The narrators urge us to appreciate the vitality of local culture, but by squeezing it into the enclosed world of community we are offered only the position of the outsider looking in.

The problem lies with the logic of representing community. Both types of community representation rely on the drawing of boundaries (temporal, spatial and social), through which *this* community is sharply distinguished from *that* one. Both in this sense are distanced – they are views from the hill (Dicks, 1999). Both all too readily slide into each other. Images of 'the good community' often end up relying on images of the 'vanishing other', since they need to impute common and homogenizing characteristics to social subjects. This means that, while the Rhondda's vitality and diversity is summoned up in one moment, its homogeneity and singularity is emphasized the next. Both types of discourse turn complex social relations into visions of unity and self-sameness which are bounded in space and time. This is why, historically, there has been a chequered relationship between the left and the community ideal, many fearing that it offers only nostalgic, place-based rather than class-based identifications.[5]

5. The Rhondda and the Welsh nation

As we have seen, the RHP does not, by any means, present a hegemonic legitimization of capitalist relations, nor a cosy inventory of national sentiment (as the heritage critics might suspect). Nor does it present a banal, any-place version of 'Community World'. It does feature antagonisms and struggles; it does offer a locally recognizable historiography. Collective identity, however, is symbolized through the claims and silences of the representations: what is and what is not 'the Rhondda'. In fact, the *Black Gold Community* represents a particular historical narrative that seeks to claim for the south Wales Valleys a collective identity which is labourist and transnational in character. *Black Gold's* depiction of community, which celebrates the virtues of hard manual labour and comradeship, which acknowledges the inequities of a traditional gender division of labour whilst insinuating its inevitability, which celebrates a local culture of self-improvement and individual achievement along with traditional socialist principles of collectivism, welfarism, support for nationalization and so on, is perfectly in line with the local labourist political culture discussed in chapter 1. It is, above all else, a narrative which banishes most of the images traditionally associated with the Wales of Welsh nationalism: land, language, song, wilderness, romanticism (Morgan, 1983). It is also – unsurprisingly, given that Dai Smith was its main scriptwriter – a narrative that has more in common with left history and politics than with nationalist sentiment.

Black Gold's labourist narrative of history occupies an uneasy position within the field of hegemonic images of the Welsh nation, as we saw in the last chapter. In offering the story of the 'people of the Rhondda' as a story of the heroism of ordinary working-class people in the face of exploitation and indifference, it might potentially have sought to claim a righteous, self-affirming identity for Wales, through positioning the mine-owners and politicians as English colonialists and invaders. Yet the texts steadfastly resist any such connotation. The England/Wales opposition is never mentioned. Indeed, the language of the 'four nations', in this case England and Wales, is entirely absent from *Black Gold*. The only national imagery it mobilizes is that of 'Great Britain' and the 'Empire'. These are invoked not to suggest the colonization of Wales, but as a means of challenging the official, hegemonic account of where their 'greatness' originated and to install Rhondda coal at their heart instead.

Thus, 'Great Britain' and 'Empire' become the centre against which the Rhondda is defined, alongside the affluent metropolis – the city of Cardiff (stripped of its connotations as capital of Wales). On the subject of the Welsh nation, *Black Gold* is almost entirely silent. It thus refuses to contribute to nationalist narratives predicated on a strong demarcation between the identities of England and Wales. The one mention of Wales in the three audio-visual shows – far from elaborating a distinctive anti-English or anti-British identity for Wales – actually brings the construct of the 'Welsh Nation' into alignment with that of the British Empire. The Rhondda is positioned as the rightful epicentre of the Empire *and* of Wales – and no contradiction is asserted between these two identities. Here is W. T. Lewis:

> The Welsh Nation owes to coal the prosperity that has provided us with a university, with fine civic buildings and mighty ports. Coal has made Cardiff into a veritable Welsh Chicago. The coal bunkers of the Empire, from the Cape to Aden, from Bombay to Port Said, are stocked with coal from the Rhondda, with coal that has come up, in endless streams, from this very colliery.[6]

Here, the (single) mention of Wales makes the claim that it is to coal – not to anything else – that the 'Welsh Nation' owes its true identity. In the process, it hitches this identity to a British imperial one, seeming to claim Wales's place at the heart of the Empire. Indeed, the narratives flag up what the Empire and Wales *share*: a debt of gratitude to the miners of the Rhondda.

The speech of W. T. Lewis, however, is framed in the narrative through the official, grand tones of clipped RP English, and in this sense, given the moral authority and authenticity reserved for the Valleys accent in the scripts, his contribution appears as pompous speechifying. He lacks the authoritative, story-telling relationship with the audience set up through the intimate, conversational and direct address of Bryn Rees, the collier. Thus, the attempt to invoke images of Empire is represented ironically, as a comment on the mine-owner's pretensions. In this sense, the historical narratives of *Black Gold* reproduce a historiography which is not out of synch with local labourist values, a tradition which has been founded on anti-imperial, anglophone and non-Welsh-nationalist traditions. It is based on the century-long construction of institutions to serve the needs of an industrial working class that originated both within and outside Wales (Williams, 1996). As discussed in chapters 1 and 4, attempts to promote the 'Valleys version' of Welsh identity are set against, and thus gain their lifeblood from, the hegemony of Welsh nationalist narratives. Though both types of collective identity – the labourist and the nationalist – may be losing their purchase in contemporary Welsh political culture, as Adamson (1996) claims, it would appear that the *Black Gold* version of collective identity is very much defined through these classic polarities.

Heritage and territory

Yet the idea of nation, if not of Welshness itself, still haunts the imaginary of *Black Gold*, in that it insists on defining community as a territorial identity. Indeed, its labourist narratives of working-class community are confined to a place-specific (but not a nationalist) evocation of 'Rhondda-valleyness', and squeezed into the space of subnational territory. In this sense, local, community-level heritage operates through the same territorializing modes of representation as national heritage. Local heritage *is* – potentially – an uplifting voice from the margins reclaiming an unacknowledged local identity in the face of hegemonic national and colonial myths, but it still operates through the oppositions of territorialization: here/there; centre/periphery; nation/region; national community/local community. In the process it inevitably reproduces a grid of insider/outsider relations, which in fact underlies the whole project of 'imagining communities' – be they Valleys or nations.

Other local heritage centres more explicitly flag the 'four nations' construct of community (for example, the Gaelic identity on display at the Skye heritage centre studied by Macdonald, 1997). In these cases, the locality is made to stand in for a more general narrative comprising national, anti-British imagery. Nevertheless, the similarities with the Rhondda narratives are also clear, in that all local heritage museums are centrally involved with elevating local, place-bound identity. By offering an invigorating portrayal of the unacknowledged role of local labour in the supremacy of larger, official territories (however these are defined), local heritage museums draw a territorial boundary around local history by claiming it as the 'story of place *x*'. Thus, heritage's embroilment in local identity offers a resolutely *place-based* claim to distinctiveness.

In the case of the Rhondda, this locally confined narrative presents a place-based riposte to the area's detractors and to the loss of the local industrial, productive base. This affirms the Valleys version of Wales, but also weakens the potential for linking the Rhondda into wider narratives of industrialization, deindustrialization and the crisis of capitalist restructuring. It simply restates what is (still) distinctive about *the Rhondda*. This inevitably risks sliding into essentializing and totalizing tropes of a special unitary community identity (cf. Young, 1990). Thus it could be argued that *Black Gold* homogenizes Rhondda people into a single entity. The endless photographic slides convey literal and metaphorical 'views from the hill', in which the rows of terraces and crowds of Rhondda faces conjure up a single-minded and unique human spirit bounded by the valley sides. The assertion of community thus imputes a unified value-system to local social subjects, suggesting that they act as one body.

Thus, images of the 'good community' slide into images of the 'community of the vanishing other', in that homologies are claimed between place, history and people. The utopian message that the Rhondda is modern, cosmopolitan, dynamic and energetic is short-circuited as its links and similarities with other places are simply not mentioned. Community is thus turned into nostalgia on the one hand (the community of the 'vanishing other') but also promoted as a future-orientated and dynamic place of the people (the good community). To exhibit place as community for both the tourist gaze *and* for the celebration of local vernacular identity means representing it as a contradictory mixture – simultaneously traditional and modern, industrial and post-industrial, vanishing and enduring, other and self. The Rhondda as community is seen as both dependent on the colliery yet able to survive it; a place which is both unique and mythic; its past both finished yet still present. Ultimately, I suggest, this contradictoriness runs the risk of reproducing a conventional message about history and social change: the more we change, the more we stay the same. The essential 'we' remains intact, as history unfolds around us.

On the other hand, as other chapters have shown, the rhetoric of community has served many a politically progressive cause in the local sphere. It was called into service in the 1970s labourist 'call for action' in relation to the Valleys' crisis of identity (chapter 1). It offers a potent argument against local economic and cultural dislocation. In this sense, the archetypal community myth serves both as a generally familiar commonplace recognizable to the tourist gaze, as well as a more locally specific memorial to, and potential promotion of, the specificity and vitality of place-identity. This local purchase suggests that heritage representation is not a standardized and uniform practice, constructed purely for the tourist gaze. Instead, it takes place within existing local cultural and social relations, showing that heritage exhibitions are the products of a nexus of local and wider conditions and processes. The particular processes through which the Rhondda heritage texts were conceived, designed and given shape will be the subject of the next two chapters.

III. HERITAGE, GOVERNANCE AND OWNERSHIP

6

From mine to museum: the evolution of heritage in the Rhondda

By the early 1980s, the heritage seed had already been sown in the Rhondda. Tourism, previously excluded from the industrial Valleys, was starting to be considered by local authorities as a potential source of alternative employment and local wealth generation. This was in turn spurred on by a wider ideological shift towards the promotion of leisure, consumption and enterprise culture, fostered by the New Right economic development policies of the Thatcher years and following in the wake of labourism's slow decline. Alien as such developments were to local political culture, Valleys local authorities had to adapt pragmatically to the reconfigured political relations of the 1980s against the backdrop of a continued failure to replace jobs lost in heavy industry. By the 1980s, the coalmining identity of the Valleys had so obviously become its history rather than its actuality that the continued absence of a public mining memorial in the Rhondda – with heritage being loudly trumpeted elsewhere and yet colliery after colliery bulldozed here – was glaringly exposed. What follows is an account[1] of how this heritage seed took root and developed – eventually to become the Rhondda Heritage Park.

1. Heritage in 1980s Rhondda

When Lewis Merthyr closed in 1983, only the Maerdy colliery was left working in the Rhondda. The socio-economic problems facing the area were substantial: 13.8 per cent of its economically active population were unemployed (or 'actively seeking work') in 1981

(Morris and Wilkinson, 1993), and the *Guardian* (1 November 1984) reported that 5,171 Rhondda people were chasing eighty-five vacancies in 1984. The borough's erstwhile strategy of building small ancillary factory units, in line with the orthodox emphasis on economic regeneration through manufacturing, had singularly failed to replace lost employment or halt the slow process of economic decline. These failures, together with the end of the 'social democratic consensus', the decline of labourism and the replacement of the regional aid approach of the post-war years with the UK Conservative government's promotion of local competitive markets for inward investment, combined to produce a growing sense of political, economic and social crisis in the Valleys (Rees, 1985). Change – political, ideological and social – was clearly threatening on the horizon, bringing clouds that looked distinctly unpromising for the Valleys, while the coastal belt around Cardiff was already glimpsing the rays of its new 'sunshine' industries.

Local political responses in the Valleys were necessarily channelled either into attempts to ward off change or a pragmatic acceptance of the need to adapt to new realities. In 1982, workers in the Lewis Merthyr Colliery staged a stay-down strike to resist closure, but, isolated due to the refusal of the National Union of Mineworkers to support their cause, were forced to give up. The colliery duly closed in 1983, in the midst of a politically charged but undoubtedly pessimistic atmosphere. The colliery stood empty, providing a further symbol, if one were needed, of the final end of an era. The then National Coal Board wanted to dispose of the site as soon as possible in order to discharge its responsibilities for security and maintenance, and Rhondda Borough Council faced the usual immediate pressure to proceed directly with demolition, site clearance and land reclamation.

However, some Rhondda Borough Council planners and councillors had become convinced by arguments that the old Victorian colliery should be preserved as heritage. There had, in fact, been a long-standing grassroots campaign, supported by key local politicians, and fostered by local mining history enthusiasts, for a mining museum in the Rhondda. Two figures in particular – a Bristol-based mining photographer and colliery history expert, John Cornwell, and the then branch secretary of Maerdy Lodge, Ivor England (who subsequently became a guide at the RHP), were particularly energetic in agitating for the preservation of the Lewis

Merthyr as a tribute to the mining industry. (Their story will be told in chapter 7.) At the same time, there was an increasing willingness within the council to consider pragmatically the potential role of tourism and leisure in regenerating the Rhondda. There was, thus, a meeting of two local strands of thought – a popular memorialist discourse urging the council to support a fitting tribute to the mining industry and an urban planning discourse that was beginning to recognize the potential benefits of tourism. The two cannot really be separated in explaining how the heritage museum came into being.

The heritage idea was particularly encouraged by the then leader of the council, Matty Collins. Personally committed to ensuring that the Rhondda provided a fitting memorial to its mining past, she became, in most people's accounts, the major local mover, instigator and cheerleader behind the development of the RHP until her death in 1989.[2] Support within the council for the heritage option was strengthened by the fact that it had recently lost out on a heritage project proposed for nearby Ferndale Colliery. The Coal Board had gone in and cleared the site before the necessary preparations and negotiations to preserve some of the buildings could proceed. At Lewis Merthyr, too, in 1983, the 'scrappies' were poised to go in and salvage the machinery. This was the last surviving traditional Victorian colliery in the Rhondda and hence the last chance for a mining museum.

Meanwhile, Mid Glamorgan County Council expressed scepticism about the heritage option, since it was pursuing a strategy of industrial rather than tourist-based regeneration (Mid Glamorgan County Council, 1982). In this it was still wedded to the late 1970s policy emphasis on reindustrialization through manufacturing. The county wanted to acquire and clear both the Lewis Merthyr and its sister colliery, the Tŷ Mawr, a few miles down the road and also just closed, in order to develop new industry in the Valleys and pursue its own integrated economic regeneration strategy. Both the Lewis Merthyr and the Tŷ Mawr had originally formed part of the Great Western Colliery complex. Tŷ Mawr had supplied the compression for the ventilation system at Lewis Merthyr, and all of the latter's coal had been wound up through Tŷ Mawr since the 1950s. One of its winding houses, the Hetty, was an old Victorian winding house built by W. T. Lewis, which had the same historical pedigree as the Bertie and Trefor winding houses up at Lewis Merthyr.[3] The two collieries were thus intimately connected. The county wanted to acquire both, convinced that there would in the future be a shortage of large tracts of prime, flat industrial land in the Rhondda. It had barely considered the tourism or heritage option.

This approach contrasts with that of Rhondda Borough Council, as can be seen from a 1983 report on the heritage museum's role in its local economic development strategy:

> The potential of a heritage museum on the Lewis Merthyr site lies not simply in the development of a major tourist attraction on the site itself, great though this potential is. In addition, the project is seen by the Borough Council as providing the major 'draw' to the Rhondda that will enable visitors to the South Wales valleys and Cardiff areas generally to be introduced to other attractions and features of interest elsewhere in the Rhondda.
>
> (Rhondda Borough Council, 1983: para. 3.4)

This strategy envisaged the heritage museum as the central feature of a wider tourism policy for the Rhondda as a whole. This quotation makes it clear, however, that the Tŷ Mawr colliery buildings were not included in the Rhondda's plans. Nor could they be, for Tŷ Mawr stood within the administrative boundaries of the neighbouring borough, Taff Ely. In any case, apart from the historic Hetty winding house, it was considered a modern, unattractive colliery complex with no heritage potential. It was, in fact, demolished soon after it closed.

Rhondda Borough Council were unable to proceed autonomously with their plans for a Lewis Merthyr heritage museum. The National Coal Board was asking £600,000 for what it considered prime industrial land at the colliery, and the borough could not afford the asking price. Although the Coal Board was eventually persuaded to maintain a minimal security presence on the site, it was impatient to hand over responsibility. It was clear that the Rhondda would need to access wider development funds in order to proceed with the museum. This inevitably meant bringing in both the local development agencies as well as the other interested councils. While the empty Lewis Merthyr colliery buildings continued to deteriorate physically, the Rhondda made preliminary investigations into land reclamation funding from the Welsh Development Agency (WDA).

However, enthusiasm amongst the other local agencies and councils remained uneven. The county council succeeded in purchasing the Tŷ Mawr colliery land with the support of Taff Ely Borough Council, but Rhondda Borough Council refused to allow the county to purchase Lewis Merthyr. The WDA, which was involved in these discussions in its role as principal funder for land reclamation schemes, was also sceptical about the potential for tourist and heritage solutions to deindustrialization, although there was some internal dissent over the issue. There was at the time a strand of opinion within both the WDA and the Wales Tourist Board (WTB) that museum solutions – as opposed to other leisure or business options – meant looking backwards rather then forwards.[4] In the early 1980s, the role of culture and heritage in economic development was only just beginning to be recognized in UK local planning circles, and it was frequently down to individuals to make the heritage case to sceptical colleagues. Certain influential voices within the WDA, however, were doing exactly this. In the WTB, enthusiasm at this stage was also muted, with concern centred on the fear that any new coalmining heritage project could damage existing attractions that the Board was already supporting, particularly Big Pit mining museum in Gwent.

At this early stage, Rhondda Borough Council did not, as already suggested, envisage its heritage museum needing any *long-term* involvement from the county or other councils and agencies. Plans still centred on the idea of a small mining museum, housed in the Lewis Merthyr colliery buildings and staffed by ex-miners, who would explain colliery life to visitors. This small-scale development would be confined to the south side of the Lewis Merthyr site. To the north, on the other side of the new Trehafod bypass, across the River Rhondda and the railway, lay the colliery's pithead baths, which were linked by a long, covered footbridge over to the colliery. This footbridge link was not, however, included in the plans: 'The Authority does not envisage maintaining the footbridge and split-site operation, but instead will concentrate its activities on the site containing the main colliery complex' (Rhondda Borough Council, 1983: para. 3.1). What the borough wanted was to obtain from the WDA sufficient funds to purchase the Lewis Merthyr buildings alone and begin refurbishment.

The WDA thus found itself in the unusual position of having two competing submissions for land reclamation projects at a disused colliery: one from the borough, for the heritage museum, and one from the county, for site-clearance and the construction of factory units. The WDA's response was to commission a feasibility study, which considered three land-use possibilities for the two collieries: heritage, housing or manufacturing. For the heritage part of the research, the agency engaged the services of John Brown,[5] one of the UK's leading tourism consultants, who had already worked on substantial and successful industrial heritage projects in England, such as Wigan Pier and Ironbridge Gorge. It was his section of the study that first put forward the proposal for a large-scale heritage development, modelled on Beamish Hall in the North-East. John Brown made the case for an integrated approach on both parts of the Lewis Merthyr complex – plus the Tŷ Mawr colliery site a mile down the road:

> If sufficient resources and flair are put into its development and marketing, a centre of this kind, offering an entertaining family day out, might well be able to attract substantially more visitors than the less heavily marketed Welsh Folk Museum at St. Fagan's, which receives around 250,000 annually. However, a project which does not quite make the public impact that this proposal envisages ... is in the Study Team's view much less likely to achieve such results. Timidity and compromise could be very damaging to its chances.
>
> (Welsh Development Agency, 1984: paras. 4.4.6–7)

Thus the idea of a three-site development was germinated, comprising land belonging to and controlled by the Rhondda Borough Council (Lewis Merthyr and the pithead baths), Mid Glamorgan County Council (Tŷ Mawr colliery land) and Taff Ely Borough Council, who owned a large tract of land opposite the demolished colliery known as Barry Sidings, reclaimed from the old railway sidings for coal trains to Barry Docks. Thus, with the inclusion of this extra reclaimed land, it was intended to create an integrated heritage and leisure plan for all the available ex-mining land in the area.

Diluting the mining inheritance

Within this new set of proposals, Rhondda's mining museum became just a small zone in a much larger leisure space. The feasibility study went on:

> If tourism is to be encouraged in the Rhondda, it can only be done on any scale through the creation of a major attraction ... Any new attraction has to be big enough in its appeal ... to be a complete day-out destination for substantial numbers of people in its own right.
>
> (Welsh Development Agency, 1984: 32–3)

Right from the beginning a sharp distinction was made between a small localized museum option and the intended large-scale development, which was to be 'a complete day-out destination'. It thus distanced itself from the purely memorialist urge for a commemorative museum, insisting that 'if the project had to be categorised as a museum, the most appropriate term might be a "social museum"' (1984: 29). We shall see how, later on, the term 'museum' was shunned altogether.

The proposed expansion of scale and scope was motivated by a desire to produce more than one heritage iconography, and thus to avoid reliance on a purely mining-oriented attraction. This in turn reflected a calculated desire to widen the cultural and political belonging of the project beyond a solely Rhondda-dominated ambit. Instead, two heritage images were proposed, an industrial and a rural one – a division which mirrors the rural/industrial split within the 'imagined community' of Wales discussed in chapter 4. The Tŷ Mawr site was to portray the earlier rural way of life of the valley. This site was prized because of its

> almost completely rural setting, quite exceptional in the Rhondda Valleys context, which could illustrate the time at which the beginnings of mining were superimposing themselves on a traditional rural community, and illustrating both pre-industrial life and crafts, and an early colliery ... with farm animals, rural crafts, and so on.
>
> (Welsh Development Agency, 1984: 29)

The Lewis Merthyr colliery buildings, on the other hand, would interpret the work and techniques of mining, supplemented with a complete reconstructed mining village to portray the social and cultural life of the mining community. The proposal for the multi-site development reflected an awareness of the financial benefits of a strategy offering a variety of visitor attractions, requiring movement between sites to encourage long-stay and high-spend visitor activity. It also, neatly, stitched together the twin rural and industrial community imaginations of Wales.

Competing political agendas

This feasibility study, with its emphasis on the role that the proposal could play in economic development, succeeded in convincing Mid Glamorgan County Council that the heritage idea was the preferable option. In fact, it was because this heritage proposal was packaged as a large-scale and heavyweight development that could play *the same regenerative role* as industrial units, but even more effectively, that Mid Glamorgan County Council was persuaded to come on board.[6] Rhondda Borough Council, meanwhile, were gratified to find their plans so well received and their heritage so unexpectedly and grandly promoted, but also anxious over the threatened loss of local control of the expanded project to the county and outside agencies.[7] Taff Ely Borough Council was even more ambivalent and suspicious. Most obviously, apart from the Hetty winding house, it did not own any of the cultural resources deemed to possess historical value, whilst the Rhondda had the Lewis Merthyr buildings with their impeccable industrial pedigree. Furthermore, the disused land at Barry Sidings did not immediately present itself as prime recreational material. However, Taff Ely's ambivalence really stemmed from an entrepreneurial and political competitiveness with the neighbouring Rhondda. First, its cultural commitment to the coalmining inheritance was less secure, and it did not want its identity subsumed under the Rhondda's banner of coalmining fame. Second, Valleys labourist culture was less firmly rooted here, a socially divided borough with a divided political and cultural identity.

Taff Ely straddled the Ely Valley – which is close to Cardiff, relatively affluent and suburban in character – and the Taff Valley, including Pontypridd, which is more traditionally identified with the Valleys in cultural and socio-economic terms. Taff Ely as a whole was a much wealthier borough than the Rhondda. Rhondda scored 2 out of 100, and Taff Ely 58 out of 100 on the scale of relative affluence for Welsh districts devised by Morris and Wilkinson (1993). Historically, the Ely side of the borough council resisted its identification with the Valleys and with the Rhondda, and resented money being spent on Valleys-orientated projects.[8] This also had crucial political implications, since Taff Ely – although Labour-controlled at the time – was more vulnerable to Plaid Cymru than any of the solid Labour Rhondda wards. Taff Ely's different political and social complexion was to have profound consequences for the Rhondda heritage project.

Divisions of space and politics in the Valleys

The large-scale consortium-controlled heritage plan, as opposed to the original Rhondda-only museum proposal, was called upon to do double duty. It had to both celebrate and capitalize on the fame of the coalmining identity by calling itself the 'gateway to the Rhondda', and at the same time hitch this identity to a range of other non-mining images further down towards the Ely Valley. The feasibility study proposed, as we have seen, a hybrid heritage identity that was also spatialized: the mining traditions located in the Rhondda and a set of rural images in Taff Ely intended to both display the pre-mining past as well as point to a re-greened future. This raised anxieties in the Rhondda about the dilution of local Valleys-based and labourist place-identity. The fact that the ex-mining districts of south Wales always had to struggle to imprint the 'Valleys version' of community identity on to more hegemonic images of the Welsh nation (traditionally epitomized in images of land, language and song, as chapter 4 showed) meant that political appeals in the Valleys were often built on the principle of defending a distinctive local cultural space (Rees, 1997). In relation to the development of the Rhondda Heritage Park, it is arguable that local political support for a display-case for Rhondda heritage was not unconnected to a desire to stake the place of the Valleys within a Welsh identity that had never fully reconciled itself to its coalmining industrial heritage. The feeling that 'now it's our turn to have our heritage recognized' was a major source of initial enthusiasm.

The fact that the mining inheritance was now to be incorporated into a larger patchwork of place-images threatened to decentre these local labourist identifications and to dilute this enthusiasm. As the scale and scope of the proposed project became clear, Rhondda Labour councillors became more divided in their support for it. It also meant that Taff Ely's position was further complicated. The celebrating and shoring up of the 'Valleys version' of Welsh identity through heritage helped to attract support for it amongst some local Labour councillors. Yet, since this Valleys image was closely tied to labourism, the political opponents of labourism also had a powerful reason not to support the heritage proposals. While

Taff Ely Borough Council was controlled by Labour, such dissent could be kept at the sidelines. But as Plaid Cymru strengthened its position in the borough, the accusation that Rhondda's stamp was imprinted on the heritage venture provided them with rich campaigning material against it, as we shall see below. Thus the spatial allocation of cultural resources in the feasibility study – the rural iconography to Taff Ely and the mining images to the Rhondda – further entrenched a political divide between the two councils. Both sides of the heritage hybrid had to be seen to be receiving equal attention and resources. The project's reliance on multi-agency support meant that, politically as well as culturally and economically, it was necessary to display a heritage that was not too obviously the exclusive patrimony of the Rhondda. In the light of this in-built tension, political problems in the project's development were on the horizon from the very outset.

The dilution of the Rhondda's ownership of the project's cultural resources was further aided by the standardized, packaged model of heritage brought in by John Brown[9] and the entrepreneurial, market-oriented and multiplex approach promoted in the dominant economic development rhetoric of the 1980s. In this way, heritage-enterprise can play a role in further dislodging established local political hegemonies as well as sharpening political rivalries (Harvey, 1989b). Labourism's claims to provide for local needs could not survive long under the onslaught of wider entrepreneurial governance. It was, instead, a strategy that meant emphasizing the Rhondda's dependence on outside assistance. As the study makes clear:

> The area's industrial image, the poor communications, the general lack of things to see and do (apart from 'atmosphere', which is likely at present to be appreciated by only a recondite minority) mean that any new attraction has to be big enough in its appeal to overcome these handicaps.
>
> (Welsh Development Agency, 1984: 32)

The claim to solve local 'handicaps' is a key element of the entrepreneurial reconfiguration of place. The local area is simultaneously represented as a source of rich heritage as well as backwardness, neatly justifying the need for a dose of enterprise spirit. This simultaneous promotion of local culture as both assets and handicaps is a central plank in entrepreneurial heritage discourse.

2. The development process and political contestation

By 1984, the Rhondda project had in effect become a substitute for industry and housing rather than simply a memorial to the past. It had emerged as an uneasy compromise – half marketized product, half locally authenticated memorial. In the process, the local councils and agencies involved in its promotion, funding and development began to think of it both as an economic and cultural asset and a financial and political burden. While its local memorialist underpinnings were inevitably sidelined in favour of its definition as economic resource, its significance as a site of local cultural, place-based identifications continued to haunt the project at every juncture. In this sense, it would be wrong to see the heritage project simply as an entrepreneurial product superimposed from above and divorced from local structures of feeling. On the contrary, it was the project's necessary enmeshment in local political and cultural sensibilities which ultimately defeated its entrepreneurial pretensions. The uneven contours of this developmental trajectory are traced in the account below, and further elaborated in the following chapters.

(i) 1984–1986: the launch of the project and the Gillespie Plan

In 1984, the year-long miners' strike began. With its buildings standing empty and only minimal security provision, the disused colliery was undoubtedly a symbol for local hostility towards the Coal Board. Vandalism and general deterioration quickly set in: when bits of asbestos cladding from the footbridge began to land on the highway below, the Board insisted that the borough take over as tenants of the site. Finally, in July, Rhondda Borough Council went ahead and purchased the site with development money from the WDA, putting in place the necessary security features to prevent further damage. The heritage option had been launched, and duly began its chequered career as a planning project jointly managed by three councils and two government agencies.

At this point, the various officers concerned formed the Officers Directing Group[10] to oversee the development and funding of the project. Already there was an indication of tensions to come when conflict ensued over who was to chair the group – neither borough wanted to see the county steering a project that was based in their areas, and yet each of the two boroughs was wary of the symbolic ownership of the project being claimed by the other. In the end, an officer from the WDA took the helm. This was significant, since the WDA had the strongest links with county rather than borough officers. Thus was initiated a form of control over the project which was decisively county- and WDA-led. Both the boroughs resented this, with officers from the Rhondda commenting that they felt their heritage idea had been 'taken over' by the county.[11]

The first step for the new Officers Directing Group was to secure some funds for more detailed design work to be undertaken. A successful bid to the Welsh Office eventually produced £300,000 in Urban Aid money in June 1985. This provided the project with funding to commission its major conceptual consultancy plan, the development plan of 1986 prepared by William Gillespie's.[12] This report committed the project to a more blatantly multiplex, entrepreneurial – and as it turned out – controversial course of development than the original 1984 feasibility study. While the latter had proposed a two-pronged heritage showcase (combining the mining traditions with the older rural identity), Gillespie's broadened the scope beyond heritage altogether. They proposed that historical interpretation be confined to Lewis Merthyr and to the Hetty winder. On the Barry Sidings site, a countryside recreational function was envisaged, complete with a forest centre, pony-trekking, woodland walks into the adjoining forest, an activities holiday centre and an adventure playground, so that a general outdoor pursuits and countryside leisure market could be tapped. This adventure park would even include a cable car and a dry ski-slope. The plan turned the rural heritage theme proposed by the feasibility study into a countryside recreational function, thus stitching heritage and leisure together into a multiplex whole. The influence of the 1980s Garden Festival model of development was clear.

Gillespie's wanted Tŷ Mawr and Barry Sidings sites to symbolize the future, with state-of-the-art leisure amenities, and a reconfiguration of the Valleys landscape to present 'a statement about the valleys [sic] "greening" and their changed image' (William Gillespie & Partners et al., 1986: 24). The Lewis Merthyr site, on the other hand, would represent the Rhondda's industrial past. Here, visitors were to enter the site through the pithead baths on the north side of the river, where there would be an 'events area' as well as a choral centre. This would be both a performance and a practice space for Welsh choirs and bands. Visitors would also be able to see the restored showers and locker rooms of the original baths, before crossing the long footbridge over the railway, road and river, just as the miners used to do, to arrive at the Lewis Merthyr buildings themselves. Here the winding houses would be restored and a mining village constructed, all linked down the valley to Tŷ Mawr and Barry Sidings by a steam train ride and a riverside pathway, to transport tourists from the 'past' to the 'future'.

The proposed product-mix tried, though not explicitly, to amalgamate into a unified visitor experience different cultural images drawn from heritage in the Valleys and Wales as well as a new future-oriented entrepreneurialism. The choral centre would be a space for celebrating the 'Wales in song and poetry' tradition; the Lewis Merthyr site would represent industry and community life; the Barry Sidings countryside development would express the regreened countryside aspiration; and a proposed 'mineral railway centre' at Tŷ Mawr would incorporate a link to Cardiff Bay and its hi-tech business opportunities. Historically, of course, these visions of the Rhondda and Wales have developed in competition with each other, as chapters 1 and 4 showed. Here, however, they are all determinedly sewn together in a patchwork of commodified attractions.

Gillespie's predicted a visitor attainment of 400,000 by 1991. Indeed, they surpassed the initial feasibility study in visualizing the project in the widest possible terms:

The first fundamental recommendation by the project team is that the three main site areas at Lewis Merthyr, Barry Sidings and Tŷ Mawr are inextricably linked and should all form part of a coherently developed and marketed site which should be promoted as the Rhondda Heritage Park. A site of this scale is required to allow flexibility for development in the future, and in order to establish the degree of transformation in the valley environment which provides an appropriate setting for a major tourism and leisure project. We do not consider that Lewis Merthyr or Tŷ Mawr could be made sufficiently attractive on their own to achieve the undoubted potential of a project based on Rhondda heritage and countryside.

(William Gillespie & Partners et al., 1986: 13)

The development plan, utilizing all three sites, and proposing a series of links between them, estimated a total project cost of no less than £15.49 million.

(ii) 1986–1988: the long search for funding

The multiplex strategy soon ran into difficulties. The immediate need was to secure the necessary public funding to start on the works scheduled for Phase 1. Officers had put in bids for Urban Programme grants and for PRNI money (Project of Regional or National Importance) to the Welsh Office, for a sum of £7.6 million, but a decision was still being awaited at the end of 1986. This meant that only WDA-funded land reclamation and security works could go ahead immediately. In the absence of proper funding for capital works, nothing seemed to be happening at the site, and local political uneasiness began to grow. Officers therefore decided to push for the opening of a minimal visitor attraction as soon as possible. With sensitivity forecasts showing that it could not hope to break even with fewer than 275,000 visitors per year, establishing visitor numbers early on was crucial: both in terms of generating admissions income, and to live up to the project's regenerative function in the eyes of its sponsors. However, this meant that first-stage development was to be concentrated at Lewis Merthyr, where revenue could most easily result from visitor admissions, as opposed to the Tŷ Mawr and Barry Sidings sites, where no bounded entrance-fee attraction was planned.

However, just before Christmas 1986, the footbridge that was supposed to transport visitors across the road, river and railway from the pit head baths to the Lewis Merthyr buildings was found to be unsafe. Engineers recommended demolition at the earliest opportunity. Subsequent history of the RHP was marked by repeated efforts to secure the very substantial funding required for its replacement; in the mean time, the essential link between the pithead baths and the Lewis Merthyr site was lost. The ramifications were considerable. Until money to replace it was found, visitors could not gain access to the Lewis Merthyr site. Since visitors were needed, however, as soon as possible, a decision was made to construct a temporary visitor reception centre, to be located in the old stores building at the colliery itself. This served to concentrate attention even more narrowly on the Lewis Merthyr colliery.

Then, at the same time, the project was dealt a major funding blow: the Welsh Office turned down the applications for Urban Programme funding for 1987/8. No money was left for capital development. The Welsh Office, mindful of the uncertainties posed by the forthcoming general election, refused to provide assistance for a project to which the local authorities had not fully committed themselves through to completion. In turn, the councils refused to commit any more money for capital development in the absence of Welsh Office funding. On the one hand, the Welsh Office wanted the local authorities to commit more public money; on the other, it was keen to see efforts made to attract substantial private-sector sponsorship. It was clear that the Welsh Office was suspicious of the project's management structure, where ultimate financial decision-making powers lay in the hands of a councillor-led steering group that reported back to Labour-controlled council committees.[13]

Officers were now faced with the prospect of complete rescheduling. They responded to the Welsh Office decision by commissioning various consultancy reports to strengthen the case for funding. The accumulating pile of reports merely added fuel to criticisms already circulating that the Heritage Park was, in the words of one Rhondda Borough Councillor, 'consultancy mad'.[14] Glossy studies, however, were seen by officers as the only means to convince the Welsh Office of the project's credibility. Then, in late 1987, Taff Ely Borough Council began threatening to withdraw from the project altogether. Lewis Merthyr seemed to be getting all the attention, while nothing had yet materialized at Barry Sidings or Tŷ Mawr. Gillespie's leisure proposals at the Taff Ely end had been rescheduled for much later in the project's development, and the postponement of plans for road access there meant that any benefits of the heritage project to the southern borough seemed a distant prospect.

Hostile articles were carried in local Taff Ely newspapers, where it was already clear that Plaid Cymru were committed to opposing further funding for the project: 'Councillor Clayton Jones[15] said now was the time to pull out of the project, which he called "a white elephant". To be viable, he said, the Trehafod site would have to attract more people than Caernarfon Castle' (*Llantrisant Observer*, 22 October 1987). Anxious letters and pleas flew back and forth between all the other sponsors and Taff Ely, arguing that prevarication might cost the project its support from the Welsh Office:

If the three participating LAs were to falter in their commitment to the RHP proposals at this crucial stage, it is likely that their credibility with other public agencies and the private sector as promoters and supporters of the tourism industry would be seriously questioned.[16]

The prospect of losing the confidence of the private sector was a real concern, since the Welsh Office had made it clear that its funding decisions would depend on increased efforts to obtain private sponsorship and investment. Local support by this time seemed to have melted away, both in Taff Ely and in the Rhondda.

(iii) 1988–1990: the Programme for the Valleys and the opening of the Rhondda Heritage Park

Taff Ely was eventually persuaded to stay on board, as, by the end of 1987, news was starting to circulate of a major new Welsh Office funding programme for urban renewal in the Valleys. The general election had brought new faces at the Welsh Office, and Peter Walker as the new Secretary of State was rumoured to be placing tourism at the heart of a new initiative: the Programme for the Valleys. Thatcherite free-market ideology was being vigorously promoted in the UK, but the Programme instituted a relatively interventionist economic development strategy for the Valleys. The Welsh Office retained a considerable hold, via various state quangos, over the economic management of the region and it was this context which spawned the distinctive interventionist style of Peter Walker (Rees and Morgan, 1991).

However, the *rhetoric* of the market – if not the reality – governed the Welsh Office's allocation of development funds in the Programme. The aim was to target funding at new tourism initiatives in the Valleys that would allow partnership between local agencies and the private sector (Prentice, 1993). Emphasis was to be placed on flagship local initiatives which the Welsh Office would 'enable', as part of a market-led strategy which claimed, at least, to eschew central planning. The rhetoric of 'enterprise culture' in Wales significantly depended, however, on the promotion of partnerships between local authorities, the quangos and – supposedly – the private sector. As we have seen, these partnerships were rendered extremely insecure by the competitive and divided relations between local authorities who differed from each other in key political, cultural and socio-economic respects.

Peter Walker's announcement sought to make it clear that the RHP was to inject new qualities into the Valleys' image, and that it was to play a role in 'rebranding' the area:

> I consider the provision of major tourism and arts centres to be a vital ingredient in my proposals to improve the valleys ... In the case of the RHP, I consider this to be an extremely exciting project which epitomises many of my aspirations for the valleys. Based on the industrial heritage of the valley communities it involves transforming a derelict site with its symbols of former glories into an attractive heritage park with much needed alternative employment. It will strengthen the local economy through the attraction of substantial numbers of visitors and help to *change many of the unwarranted perceptions that still exist about valley life.*[17] [italics added]

Here again is the now familiar call for the Rhondda to 'look to the future' and seek new sources of cultural identity. The Secretary of State positions himself as the provider of access to the Valleys' own 'former glories' at the same time as establishing the Welsh Office as the means of deliverance from 'unwarranted perceptions'.

Funding for the RHP was promised to the tune of £2.075 million. This, however, was to be matched by the local councils themselves, and further funding for future phases was to be dependent on new applications for Urban Programme grants. In addition, there were other strings attached. These focused especially on the demand that the RHP's management structure change from council control to private control, through the setting up of an independent company with a board of directors instead of the current steering group. This initiated a long period of close Welsh Office surveillance of the RHP's structure and organization, which tried to move it way from public control. Unfortunately for the Welsh Office, however, the private sector was hardly likely to take over a venture that was not only unprofitable but was actually generating huge financial losses. This meant that the Welsh Office instead became dedicated to seeing the project break even as soon as possible, in order that its cherished private-sector involvement could begin.

Welsh Office scrutiny added to the pressure on the RHP to hike up visitor numbers at all costs, by proceeding to the opening of a bounded attraction as soon as possible. This further contributed to the cracks that were already threatening to fracture the three-council consortium. Since capital development could now proceed, fast-track development at Lewis Merthyr was initiated. Architects were engaged to convert the colliery stores building into a visitor reception area and to refurbish the Trefor winding house. Heritage Projects, the company responsible for designing and building the Yorvik Viking ride in York, were commissioned to install a temporary multimedia exhibition in the visitor centre. Again, the rationale was to prepare the visitor centre and the Trefor winding house for opening as soon as possible, so that admissions income could start coming in. Still nothing was happening at the Taff Ely end.

Finally, in July 1989, the Rhondda Heritage Park opened to the public. It was, however, very different from the Gillespie vision of three years earlier. In the visitor centre visitors could see exhibitions of future plans for the park's extension in later phases. They could also visit the Heritage Projects exhibition which showed scenes from Rhondda social life. Outside, in the colliery yard, parts of the Trefor were open, and they could wander round the yard and buildings. Guides – some ex-colliers and some not – showed visitors around. However, the 40,000 visitor numbers projected for this initial attraction soon had to be scaled down. In the event, the first year of opening saw only around 11,000 visitors to the attraction. The Barry Sidings site was not yet integrated into the visitor experience, although by October 1990 a riverside walk, a small village park and some forest trails were all complete.

In the light of the much-reduced funding, Gillespie's then drew up revised plans for the rest of the Barry Sidings and Tŷ Mawr sites. These represented yet another change of emphasis, away from countryside interpretation this time and towards increased provision for business units, a commercial garden centre, car parking and a hotel. These would be developed privately. The only visitor facility, apart from the Hetty winding house, was to be an 'Environmental Resource Centre' to be housed in a bizarrely conceived 'Glass Mountain' and managed commercially. This change was a direct attempt to accommodate Welsh Office desires to see private-sector investment. Councillors in Taff Ely became convinced that their end of the site was being hived off for private development.

(iv) 1990–1994: consolidation and retrenchment

New funding was now needed urgently to progress development and fulfil the Gillespie plans. However, the Welsh Office, still unconvinced by the RHP's commercial performance thus far, requested yet more in-depth financial forecasts. Finally, in March 1991, the Under Secretary of State, Nicholas Bennett, communicated the Welsh Office funding criteria:

> I have heard your arguments about the need to develop the two sites in parallel, but I remain to be convinced that the market exists to make this a viable proposition. I do, however, appreciate the position of Taff Ely Borough Council. I have therefore decided that I will consider approving further Welsh Office funding only for the completion of the Lewis Merthyr site, including the Underground experience and the Village Street, the development of the pithead baths, the car park and the footbridge, and for the provision of infrastructure at the Barry Sidings site which would permit EITHER commercial/industrial development OR an extension of the Heritage Park. The decision as to which of these it should be will not be taken until the Lewis Merthyr site has been fully open for one financial year so that we have firm evidence of the financial position on which to base our judgement. I would expect the management of the Park to make every effort to cover running costs in that year.[18]

So nothing besides continued land reclamation was to happen at the Barry Sidings site for the time being, with future funding for heritage or leisure there available only once the full attraction at Lewis Merthyr was open. All effort was now focused on attracting more visitors to Lewis Merthyr. An Underground Experience was planned and, in May 1991, Heritage Projects' *Black Gold* opened (comprising three audio-visual shows in the winding houses and the fan-house: see chapter 5).

In effect, the Taff Ely side of the project was now seriously marginalized. The Barry Sidings and Tŷ Mawr sites had mutated from integral themed countryside and recreational areas to peripheral zones of possible commercial development that were to help pay for the 'real' visitor attraction at Lewis Merthyr. It was becoming increasingly difficult for Taff Ely Borough Council to justify continued expenditure at the RHP. Although certain Labour councillors were still supportive of the project, the local elections of 1991 delivered a Plaid Cymru majority on the council, which many felt had been achieved at least in part by campaigning on the promise of withdrawal from the RHP. Taff Ely Borough Council refused to commit any capital or revenue money for the 1991/2 financial year. The *Western Mail* carried the following report (5 May 1991):

> One of the three funding councils contributing to one of South Wales's largest tourist attractions may opt out of its £300,000 commitment. Taff-Ely Borough Council last night voted to rescind the minutes approving payment ... and though the plan to cut the money cannot be carried out until a full report has been submitted, it could spell a bleak period for the multi-million pound Heritage Park, which is preparing for the creation of an old-fashioned mining village and an 'underground experience' of mining to add to its attractions.
>
> The decision to rescind the minutes were pushed through by the new ruling coalition group on Taff Ely Borough Council, formed from a mixture of allegiances after the Labour group ... lost its majority at the elections in May.
>
> Labour councillor Henry Cox said ... Taff Ely should 'honour the commitments we have made' to the others.
>
> But Clayton Jones, whose Plaid Cymru colours dominate the coalition, said putting cash into the Heritage Park was pouring money 'down a financial drain'.

Once again, the RHP was in a critical financial situation, as the burden on the other two local authorities to match the funding pledged by the Welsh Office was unacceptably large. A decision was consequently taken not to spend most of the 1991/2 Urban Programme funding, and instead to await the results of the marketing and business plan requested by the Welsh Office, carried out by accountants Coopers & Lybrand Deloitte (January 1992). This was to be the study that finally laid to rest the ambitious Gillespie plan that had haunted the project since it began. The consultants concluded that not only should development proceed at Lewis Merthyr alone, but that the long-scheduled replacement of the footbridge and the conversion of the pithead baths were unnecessary.

Instead, a concentrated 'package of attractions' was to be provided at the colliery itself. *Black Gold* was already open and was to be enhanced by the provision of an 'underground experience' and a children's play area. The first would cater for those who wanted to go underground and provide a thrill ride that would enhance the 'fun' element of the attraction as a whole; the second would attract both families with young children and school parties. The mining village was again postponed. In effect, the proposals halted further expansion. The pithead baths site was to be sacrificed, and the baths were duly demolished. The RHP was now a one-site attraction. In March 1992, Taff Ely Borough Council formally confirmed that they were pulling out.

The implementation of the Coopers & Lybrand Deloitte proposals in effect constitute the form of the RHP as it is today. The children's play area, 'The Energy Zone', opened in time for the 1993 summer season, and the underground experience, *A Shift in Time*, followed the year after. Instead of the long-planned mining village, a small-scale recreated village 'street' was constructed inside the visitor centre. In 1996, the RHP was transferred under the provisions of local government reorganization to a new unitary authority, Rhondda Cynon Taff. Ironically, therefore, the RHP is once again controlled by a coalition of Taff Valley and Rhondda Valley councillors, and a council that owns *all* of the pockets of land originally sewn together in the Gillespie development plan. Currently, Rhondda Cynon Taff faces considerable financial deficits, and the future of the RHP – still a loss-making venture with low visitor numbers reflecting its scaled-down size – is uncertain. New development and upgrading of facilities are needed but extra funding currently seems unlikely.

3. The governance of heritage

The entrepreneurial direction forced upon the initial idea for commemorating the mining industry in the Rhondda eventually brought about its own defeat. The Welsh Office insistence on enhanced private-sector involvement and reduced public control had two implications. First, publicly funded countryside interpretation at the Taff Ely end was rejected in favour of small business and enterprise development to be set up on a commercial basis. Second, it meant that the generation of visitor revenue became an all-consuming preoccupation. Visitor numbers were to be increased at all costs, by concentrating resources on establishing and improving the visitor experience at Lewis Merthyr. Thus, the Welsh Office's increasing demands for greater marketization and greater independence from local authority control unwittingly pushed the park further in the Rhondda's direction by marginalizing Taff Ely.

The rhetoric of partnership envisaged rational local co-operation based on a happy coincidence of interests. Indeed, co-operation among different local and regional agencies of governance was absolutely central, especially in south Wales, which lacks the huge unitary metropolitan councils of England. In this vision, the local councils would be guided and supported by government agencies, allowing relations with the private sector to be cultivated and the fruits of private investment harvested. However, nothing could have been further from the reality of political culture on the ground. Under entrepreneurial governance, districts wanted to secure assets and funding at the expense of other districts, while counties were attempting to channel resources throughout the whole area under their control (Prentice, 1993). Competitiveness is built into the funding game. In addition, heritage is a cultural arena where long-established local political and social identifications are expressed and contested, and is crossed through with the competing interests of political groupings. The attempt to harness it purely as an economic asset is beset with problems where it ignores these cultural and social dimensions.

In this sense, the large-scale project failed because it forced the borough councils to deploy local heritage as a commodity, which – since it was unequally distributed between those who were paying for it – threw them into competition with each other. The co-operation needed disappeared because of the uneasy articulation between market ideals and the realities of the local political sphere. In particular, marketization forced the borough councils to compete over the ownership of heritage, defined very much as a resource for economic gain. What was Rhondda's gain seemed to be Taff Ely's loss. In this sense, the local social sphere 'bit back': the market, far from showing itself 'free' or 'rational', had to operate through relations of public governance, and thus succumbed to the sheer intractability of local political relations.

As for economic regeneration, the impact of the RHP has to be assessed as minimal. Only around 60,000 visitors come each year, and few jobs have been created. The vision of turning round the economic fortunes of the Rhondda by heritage and leisure alone, has turned out to be a mirage. Ironically, however, the failure of the grand heritage-leisure vision enabled the grassroots dimensions of local historical representation to come back into view, and it is these that we will be exploring in the next chapter. If marketization had succeeded, the RHP would have emerged as a large-scale development that had been thoroughly distanced from local social historical interest in the Rhondda. The translation of heritage into a multiplex heritage-leisure park might simply have presented itself to local people as an 'outside' initiative: a facility to use if money permitted, but not something they would expect to have much to do with their own lives and history. But with the failure of the large-scale multiplex model, heritage is left exposed to the critical gaze of the local sphere. This is the point at which local interests and identifications can reassert themselves, because planners are newly reliant on local markets and local acceptance. Chapter 7 takes up the story of local people and their relations with the RHP.

7

Heritage and local memory

Local residents are – potentially – both the subjects and objects of heritage. If invited to, they can be active assistants, consultants, even directors in the process of 'encoding' (that is, assembling the exhibitions of) heritage – through donating artefacts and memorabilia, helping in display design, volunteering their time and contributing local knowledge and memories. They are also its objects, in the sense that vernacular heritage claims to represent them and 'their' history. The new, vernacular heritage cannot simply ignore local people, since its experience-centred, personalized and ground-level tactics mean that it needs to draw on local oral histories. Whether these are gathered from books, professional researchers and social historians or whether they are sought amongst local people constitutes one of the key variables in strategies of heritage encoding.

Local heritage is about ordinary local lives. It claims to represent them with an authenticity, immediacy and realism that the traditional museum cannot provide. And, in the case of industrial heritage, these lives are likely to be sufficiently recently lived for there to be representatives and their families surviving locally, or at least family members with direct memories to contribute. This was the case with the People's Story Museum in Edinburgh, whose sponsors (the district council's recreation department) deliberately set out to 'tell the story of the life and work of Edinburgh people [and to] involve Edinburgh people in the presentation of their own history' (Marwick, 1995: 140). A local oral-history project, 'Memories and things', formed the prologue to an intensive period of collaborative encoding, with old people advising on the museum's displays, the layout of text, the writing of soundtracks and the preparation of artefacts. To some extent, there was a transfer of power from the curator to the public.

However, few heritage museums achieve or seek these levels of local collaboration, let alone anticipate the day of the 'autonomous, truly popular and professional-free museum' (Jenkinson, 1989: 147). While heritage has to feed off the 'colourful' and 'personal' local realm, its professional interpreters may also seek to manage it – to reorganize incoherent, multi-vocal and varied local testimonies into narratives and displays that are accessible to outside visitors as well as being entertaining. These two concerns may pull in opposite directions. Professional demands for spectacle and 'polish', orientated to a logic of exhibition, may work to exclude the messy inconsistencies of local oral history, orientated to memorialist values. Similarly, the reliance on professional, outside interpreters and consultants may alienate local feeling or pigeonhole local involvement into the niche of 'local colour'. Such risks and tensions are explored in the present chapter and the next.

In this chapter, I explore some of the local structures of feeling surrounding the Rhondda Heritage Park, and consider what kinds of roles it allotted local people in its development. I am particularly interested in how local enthusiasm for heritage is manifested: how residents give voice to, or, conversely, resist the opportunity to have memorials erected to a past which is – potentially – their own. Below, I discuss local enthusiasm for heritage in terms of a discourse of *memorialism*, and explore the ways in which this discourse is both articulated and contested. Local feelings about heritage are forged out of quite different spaces from those held by professional encoders, whose practice is orientated towards the capturing of a visitor market. In the next chapter, I turn to the professional practices of interpretation and examine how history gets turned into heritage through the transformation of local stories into public exhibitions.

1. Memorialism: getting the story right

In 1983, the Mardy colliery NUM branch secretary, Ivor England, was interviewed by Vincent Kane from the BBC for a television programme to mark the decline of mining in the Rhondda. As a way of finishing the programme, it was suggested that the recently closed Lewis Merthyr colliery at the bottom of the valley would provide a fitting closing shot. The idea of preserving Lewis Merthyr first began to take shape as a result of this programme being broadcast. Against a background shot of the recently closed colliery, Ivor made a plea for it to be saved:

> I said it should be kept as a memorial, if you like. Or perhaps that doesn't go far enough. It should tell the story of the Rhondda people. As a result of that programme, John Cornwell, who's a mining photographer and who liked the South Wales coalfield a lot . . . kept coming over on his own account by train, coming up to talk to me. We'd talk, he'd bring photographs over, we'd talk and talk and get things going. And then another two people came in . . . So it started as a small committee of people.

Ivor and John Cornwell called well-attended initial public meetings to generate local enthusiasm (one of which, in February 1985, attracted 120 people). In this sense, the project was conceived as a locally owned, locally managed museum intended to be a fitting memorial to the area's mining past.

Eventually, this 'small committee' assumed an official role in supporting the project's development, becoming known as the Friends of the Rhondda Heritage Park. As well as adopting conventional 'Friends' activities, such as volunteering their spare time to publicize the museum in the surrounding area and organising fundraising events, they also initially thought of themselves as quite central to the museum's historiographical direction. One of their major activities was to collect oral histories and artefacts from the local area, which were intended to provide some of the historical material for display. They were given office space in the pithead baths, and attended planning meetings.

However, once a formal museum management structure was put in place, based at the colliery buildings, the Friends began to feel increasingly cut off and marginalized.[1] They were encouraged to assume a more traditional 'Friends' role, in organizing promotional activities rather than being directly involved in planning or historical design. They also gradually assumed a more middle-class membership. The few ex-miners from the original committee were joined by newcomers, such as a BBC worker, a justice of the peace and a solicitor, and influential public figures were adopted as vice-presidents, such as Sir Donald Walters and a famous local sculptor. At the start, however, the Friends were an influential local voice concerned to have a serious input into the museum's creative development.

Memorialism meets Rhondda Borough Council

The original small committee initially made an approach to Rhondda Borough Council for funding, there being as yet no suggestion that the museum would encompass more than the Lewis Merthyr colliery and the pithead baths:

> We offered the Coal Board a pound for the pit, and that was the start. Then we went to Rhondda Borough, and asked them for a grant of £10,000 so that we could secure the site, because already every bit of copper pipe, and anything worthwhile had been taken from the pithead baths, the pithead baths had been stripped. So ... that was how Rhondda became interested, was when we went there and asked for the money. They said 'Whoa! We don't just give money out, we want to know why you want it.' And they sent a couple of representatives to the next few meetings, fishing for the Rhondda Borough. They reported back, and the next thing was we had the Environmental Manager come, and he said that he was very, very interested in our idea of keeping the building and telling a story, and that he would go back to the Council Chamber, and put it before the Council Chamber, which he did. They expressed an interest in what we were doing, and said that they thought there was some mileage in it as well, but they wouldn't be able to afford to do it on their own.
>
> (Interview with founding member of the Friends of the Rhondda Heritage Park)

When Rhondda Borough Council took on the idea, it, too, envisaged the suggested heritage project as a small-scale mining museum located in the colliery buildings alone. An early Rhondda Borough Council report drawing up details of the scheme triumphantly claimed the idea as its own, though it took pains to stress its local origins, the local availability of expertise and, significantly, local popular endorsement of the plans:

> Many local residents and men from both the Lewis Merthyr and Maerdy pits have expressed their delight that the Borough Council are capitalising on the unique opportunity which the Lewis Merthyr colliery presents to create a lasting tribute to Rhondda's 'coal age'. Miners from both Lewis Merthyr and Maerdy pits have offered whatever assistance they can give in this ... There is tremendous local interest and enthusiasm amongst voluntary groups and individuals who have expressed a willingness to assist in whatever way possible, and it is anticipated that much use will be made of bodies such as local miners' lodges, the

Rhondda Museum, the Manpower Services Commission, the Prince of Wales Committee. It is vital that the enthusiasm of such groups is sustained by ensuring that they have early involvement in the project.
(Rhondda Borough Council, 1983: paras. 4.1–5)

In this way, the council sought to position itself as the cipher for popular enthusiasm and the provider of a key local memorial. At this stage, local involvement was not merely understood as passive support, but as active 'assistance' – a very different proposition. A letter to Rhondda Borough Council from John Cornwell, the mining expert and photographer who, along with Ivor, was an originator of the initial museum project, indicates the level of expectation among grassroots enthusiasts at the time:

I feel that I must write to you, to draw your attention to the enormous amount of local interest and support for the proposed Lewis Merthyr Mining Museum; I have been interested in mining museums for many years but I have never ever seen so much enthusiasm in any community before. If and when the project gets off the ground, there are men from Lewis Merthyr Colliery and Maerdy Colliery who will offer their services to help you set up the museum; in fact, we will not only acquire material for the museum, we will arrange and display all artifacts and photographs to a very high standard.[2]

This letter makes it clear that in the minds of the local group at least, with whom Cornwell was closely involved, the visitor experience would follow the lines of a traditional artefact-based museum, the design of which was to be managed by the same miners and ex-miners who had worked the Rhondda collieries.

However, once Rhondda Borough Council applied to the Welsh Development Agency for land reclamation funds to purchase the colliery area, the heritage idea came to the attention of a wider layer of regional governance, concerned to find solutions to the intractable problem of 'what was to be done with the Valleys' (chapter 1). Ivor explains what happened next:

Then the official organisation took over and then it became slow and ponderous. They had people down here – site officers and things like that. Now me and all my ideas and John and all his ideas – we were finding it difficult to get through the bloody bureaucracy that always builds up around everything. As a matter of fact, [a man from the BBC] told me in a pub up the road, he said 'I'll tell you what will happen, Ivor. Your ideas of saving this colliery', he said, 'you'd better watch them bloody pinstripe wallahs don't come in with fancy accents or fancy bloody brief cases saying they're consultants, and then they'll be engaged by the local authorities at an enormous cost, and then they'll say yes this is the direction we should go'. And to some extent it was true.

(Personal interview with Ivor England, founding member of the local committee)

As a result of these tensions, John Cornwell ended his involvement with the museum. At one stage, Ivor decided to distance himself, too, as he felt it was being taken over by people who lacked 'affinity' with mining. Other local enthusiasts fell away due to the lack of activity or progress in the first few years. The problem that haunted the Park's relations with the local enthusiasts and the Friends association from early on was that a gap was allowed to open up between them and the professional developers and planners who moved in, just as Ivor's BBC contact had predicted. The Friends felt left out in the cold. As the founding Friends member commented, 'we still see the project as ours ... we see it as ours as much as the professionals who see it as theirs, because after all it was our idea.'

Memorialism, the locality and reminiscence

Understanding the dynamics of this tension requires gaining an insight into the dimensions of local memorialist feeling. The local mining enthusiasts and ex-miners who wanted to set up what was in 1984 still referred to as the 'Lewis Merthyr Museum' wanted it to be a means of telling a story. For Ivor, there were 'memorials to the Japanese who were killed in Hiroshima and Nagasaki up in the Rhondda, and quite rightly so'.[3] But the Rhondda mining industry, which had also cost thousands of lives, still lacked this public recognition. As Gaffney (1998) points out, a similar, belated recognition of local memorialist claims at nearby Senghenydd, where Britain's worst mine explosion occurred in 1913 causing 439 deaths underground, finally resulted in the erection of a memorial to the dead miners only in 1981, whereas the fewer local casualties of the First World War had received a timely memorial in 1921.

In this sense, claiming the right to heritage becomes a means of forcing bureaucratic public bodies to recognize the ordinary, lived histories of the locality. The small committee of original local enthusiasts was not concerned to exhibit the Rhondda as an imagined community, but rather to use the preserved colliery as a means of educating future generations about the history of the Valley coalmining industry and about the lives that were lived and lost around it. This was not a detached, purely preservationist urge simply to maintain the colliery as an epitaph to the past, but a social motivation to enlighten and educate. A founding member of the Friends explains:

> Some said [the colliery] should be kept as a landmark. Others said it should be kept virtually as an epitaph to all the people who had died in coal mining. But I and two others, we saw it rather differently. We said that we thought it should be kept as *a reminder*, both *of the past* and for *future reference*, for the children and grandchildren who would come, more or less to *tell the story of coal*. To tell the story of the cost of coal as well. It was all very well to read it from a book or see it on film, but to actually have a colliery, such as the Lewis Merthyr – which was the last of that type, and there had been sixty-three of those collieries in the Rhondda over time – we thought that *a story should be told*. We thought it was a story worth telling … Rather than just keeping it as a great big metal gravestone.
>
> (Personal interview with founding member of the Friends of the Rhondda Heritage Park; my emphasis)

In this extract, it is clear that the potential audience for the museum is envisaged as children and future generations, rather than outside tourists. The heritage project is understood as part of a project of popular education and the preservation of testimonies, based on a conviction that local heritage can provide an important forum for reminding local people about the area's past. Ron, a guide at the Park, commented:

> I think about it being a memorial. The importance of the place. It is a tribute, if you like, to the men that went down the pit, the men that suffered the pneumoconiosis, the men who died underground and the men who contributed in so many ways to this industry. This is a fitting memorial, I think. Always when I take a tour around, there is always the feeling that you are talking about something that has been the life and soul of the valley. This is the heritage of the Rhondda, and it is important that we should never lose sight of that … But you can't just think of it as a mausoleum. It's got to be living. It's got to be that people will come here and be entertained and informed.
>
> (From personal interview)

This is an instance of what I shall term 'memorialism': it is a mixture of the desire to create a 'tribute' and the desire to do more – to tell 'how things were'. Memorialist motivations for preservation potentially conflict with those of professional heritage practice, and this tension will be explored in the present chapter and the next. In what follows, I suggest some of the further distinguishing features of memorialism, as it was graspable from my research in the Rhondda.

The particular, the concrete and the familiar

Memorialism imagines the past as a record. It is the detailed, specialized and idiosyncratic memories that guarantee historical authenticity, the testimonies of those who were 'actually there'. It taps into those motivations for preserving the past which, as Johnstone notes, allow visitors to relive stories told by grandparents and to remember 'the personal and emotional resonance of the ordinary, the commonplace' (1998: 69). Local enthusiasts wanted to preserve the Lewis Merthyr colliery to enable the story to be told at first hand and *in situ*, rather than having just a 'big metal gravestone' or a history book. In this sense, memorials address themselves to onlookers as the inheritors of local historical identity. The memorial's function is not to supply new or arresting knowledge for outsiders, but to act as a repository for the everyday memories of the memorial-makers and provide a conduit for them to be passed on down generations of insiders. Professional, exhibitionary discourse, on the other hand, addresses a tourist-spectator for whom the knowledge is new and unfamiliar, encountered in the guise of spectacle.

The memorialist requirement for local testimony is well illustrated in the early struggle at the Rhondda Heritage Park between installing artefacts for the purposes of display and spectacle on the one hand, and for the purposes of rescue and safekeeping on the other. During the early development phase, key items of mining machinery and equipment were becoming redundant at nearby collieries as they closed down in quick succession all around. Ivor wanted to save them for preservation and display at the heritage site, and describes his frustration that the Park's management failed to respond:

Lewis Merthyr ... is a traditional pit, it's one of the old pits. It's one of the pits of *the familiar scene when I was a boy*. This headgear here was

the *same headgear*, virtually, as all the collieries in the Rhondda ...
I really believe they've done a good job of telling the story of mining,
you know, with the audio visuals, but *I wanted a lot more here* ...
I certainly would have liked to have all of this colliery with all the
paraphernalia *that we were used to* you know.

[The director] envisaged an arty farty bloody thing, with cobble
stones and gas lamps and things like that, instead of a colliery yard.
There was always a problem, right up to now – they wanted something
different than I wanted. But it's too bloody late now. It was a terrible
waste. There were engineers phoning me from Lady Windsor and saying
'Ivor, for Christ's sake are you going to come and pick this stuff up?
Because the scrap merchant's coming and they're going to have it, and I
don't want to see stuff going into skips but I can't hold it much longer.'
I got so bloody frustrated in the end I went over to Abercynon colliery
which was intact but closed, and we actually piled a load of stuff out of
the winding engine that we needed here into the boot of my car. And the
car was right down on its bloody axle almost ... Maerdy closed down in
1990 and the boys there had Communist gear, a lot of things, depth
gauges, mining shovels that we could have had. We could have even had
the bloody locomotives up because once the Board had finished with
them, if the winders were still working the boys had virtual control of
things and the management were sympathetic ...

(Personal interview with Ivor England; my emphasis)

It is the familiarity and recognizability of genuine artefacts, in this
account, that underpin the idea of a proper museum. The point was
to save the material signs of the past, because these were the
particular, concrete remainders of lived experience: 'the paraphernalia we were used to'. In the director's view, however, the aesthetic
dimensions of display and simulation needed to take precedence.

Memorialism also demands that the story to be told through
heritage reflects the complexities of remembered everyday life:

It's a *comprehensive story*. It's a story not only of miners going down the
shafts every morning, afternoon and night, but of the struggle of the
miners, a *unique struggle in the history of the British Trade Union and
Labour movement*. I said it would be wrong to the Rhondda if it all
vanished ... We kept it, we held on to it, but what it was going to be was
questionable. Of course I had my grave doubts when certain people were
coming in who had *no affinity* with the terrible struggles of the miners.
They wanted to keep it, but they were starting to say that if we're going to
keep it then it's got to be *a tourist attraction*, it's got to be *something
else*. Okay, perhaps I was naive. I thought, well, anything to save it. Not

anything, but there were some very convincing arguments saying 'there's nothing wrong with putting a bit of Victoriana around the place'.

(Personal interview with Ivor England; my emphasis)

There is here a palpable unease over how fully the story will be told, and a concern that those who have no 'affinity' with it, in the sense of having lived the same realm of experience, will be ready to turn it into 'something else'. The story is not about the uniqueness of the Rhondda as imagined community, but its position within a wider story concerning the Labour movement in Britain. It is both specific, yet simultaneously linked into this wider historical narrative.

Heritage thus creates the potential for linking local stories into wider, public narratives. Seeing the colliery simply as a 'memorial' thus 'doesn't go far enough'; it fails to tell the whole story. Instead, authenticity must be ensured through acknowledging both the wider connections *and* the specificity of the story, against the threat of generalized 'Victoriana'. The past is understood as an implicit critique of the present, in which 'the struggle of the miners' has been reduced and sidelined by official history. In this sense, heritage can be thought of as a local, political arena providing the material for a critique of the modern rather than being in any sense a decadent wallowing in nostalgia (see Crang, 1994). This sense of local ownership of the history and the industry was also expressed in terms of a hostility towards the professional outside consultants, and towards the Park's management (its first director came from a job in theatre management in Brighton).

Local residents interviewed by the author (see Appendix 2) underlined this concern over the ownership – and hence the authenticity – of local historical knowledge. Interviewees were ex-miners and their wives and relatives who were living locally in Trehafod and who were invited, in focus groups, to talk about the Heritage Park and the area's mining past. Five such groups were held, one of which comprised a mixture of men and women, one was all-male and three all-female. The mixed group (two ex-miners and two unrelated female schoolteachers who came from Trehafod mining families) were involved with the Friends of the Heritage Park, and therefore had a good deal of knowledge about the Park's development, as well as being likely to be enthusiastic supporters of it. This exchange, however, indicates a certain unease about the role of outside professionals:

M1: But, one thing that perhaps I would be critical of is that though they started off with very good intentions and they were working towards a goal, they then involved people from the leisure industry, people like the managers. I know you've got to have some, but they took over ... They involved too many people from the world of the leisure industries, and they didn't quite know what ...

W2: We said that, didn't we, we said that from the beginning.

W1: What we said was, it's a mining area, and ...

W2: It was too up-market.

W1: And couldn't we get a Welshman? That was what we said as well, wasn't it?

M1: Yeah.

W1: I mean, we wouldn't dream of going up the Yorkshire coal field and telling, like, Yorkshire people what to do, because you've got plenty up there who could actually do it, isn't it? That's why I sometimes find that they put people in key positions that haven't got a clue about mining, and mining in the valley, isn't it?

M1: You know, obviously they can offer something, because they can tell you how to, er ...

W1: Yeah, they can market things.

M1: To market the end product. But I think there has got to be something else ...

W2: You've got to be able to feel it.

(Extract from Focus Group 1)

This sense of being 'able to feel it' is held to derive from local knowledge, personal experience and belonging. The idea of a unique sense of place – here in Wales, not there in Yorkshire – is crucial, and articulated as an effect of personal, local structures of feeling and lived experience. This extract indicates the distance that was perceived to separate the Park's professional management from locally authentic experience.

Memorialism and identity

Memorialism, as the discussion so far reveals, is centrally concerned with identity (Urry, 1996). Ivor's reference to turning the colliery into 'something else' in the process of its conversion into a tourist attraction seems to hinge on a fear that the past may thereby be translated into a different language (which is precisely the aim of professional exhibitionary knowledge) – a translation that may render the stories no longer recognizable. This reflects an anxiety over the effacement of familiar narrative connections and links, an unease which centres on the collective and personal ownership of history. The narration of history is, thus, an identity-conferring practice, in that concern over historical authenticity is also a concern over identity – both personal and collective. Telling the story of the Rhondda potentially means, for certain local activists and participants in the heritage project, telling the story of the self and the community (cf. Ricoeur, 1988: 246). This potentially contrasts with exhibitionary discourse, which tells the story of the other.

In recalling the past, interview groups did make use of the conventional images of mining mythology,[4] but also made repeated references to particular, visually intense experiences and memories. What they remembered was the specific and the familiar together: the customary aspects of local everyday life which were also precise and idiosyncratic. Just one example, which all of the groups mentioned, was the coal drams being constantly pulled up and down the hillside to take mining waste to the top of the slag heaps, an unremitting activity that sometimes resulted in injury and death – to sheep if not to children playing upon them. This is a concrete feature of local life that is never mentioned in *Black Gold*, and which, particularly after the 1966 Aberfan landslide disaster, is a significant omission.

The identity aspect of memorialism is clear in some of the interviews with local mining-connected residents. One of the mixed interview group, a local schoolteacher at Trehafod primary school, who joined the Friends association early on in the RHP's development, said:

> I'm all for preserving the past in a way. Not making it just a museum – it's got to be sort of like a living museum ... I think you've got to have some sort of memorial to the past, because we are part of the past really, because that's why we're here at the moment. That's why I was born here, and not in some rural backwater in Somerset.
>
> (From Focus group 1)

Here, the connections between memorialism and identity are clear: the speaker makes the case for the RHP through framing it as something that can *explain* her own provenance. She was from a mining family that lived and worked locally for three generations. In this sense, telling 'the story' is not about access to knowledge of the 'other', as in exhibitionary discourse, but to knowledge of the self: the colliery becomes the material signifier of self-identity.

2. The contested spaces of local heritage

The desire to commemorate the Rhondda's mining industry has taken different forms over a long period of time. It had surfaced before the Lewis Merthyr closed in previous attempts to secure a colliery site for preservation (chapter 6), and has since resulted in various popular commemorative publications (Dai Smith's *Rhondda Lives*, for example, and Rhondda Borough Council's *A Tribute to the Black Diamond*, 1991) as well as television programmes. However, it was not uniformly shared amongst local people. The schoolteacher cited above continues:

> But there were people here who didn't want it to be remembered. They didn't want to remember the fact there was a colliery here. There were people who said, 'My father died in an accident in so-and-so and I don't want any memorial to it. You might as well raze it to the ground, because there's only bad memories.'

This position specifically resists memorialism in that the memories it stimulates are considered unwelcome or painful. Whether the mining past is judged as a positive or negative inheritance and whether it is seen as part of one's political, social or cultural identity are likely to be major factors in determining local feeling about heritage.

Memorialism thus needs to be seen as a site of contestation rather than being a feature of local social life. It should not be assumed as the 'voice of the Rhondda' and counterposed – in a facile local/outsider or grassroots/official opposition – to that of the professionals. Local people may have no 'affinity' with the mining industry or no sense of it as an identity relevant to them. Ex-miners themselves may consider the industry not as something to memorialize but as something to forget. As Peter, one of the guides at the Park explains:

> We used to be sort of termed as 'that white elephant' and 'why didn't they make it into a supermarket or swimming baths'. That was the first sort of reaction. But the more people that come here, the more people continually come back and bring visitors here, they are proud of the

place. Then there is another group of people who are local residents and residents in the Valleys in general who are anti this place, and always will be. They will never set foot in here. But if they did set foot here I'm sure they would be converted.

(From personal interview)

Local feeling cannot easily be identified, accessed or categorized. Answering the question of how widespread or limited memorialism is would require a large-scale survey of the locality, far beyond anything that was attempted in the present research. And yet such quantitative research would struggle to unravel the complexities of people's allegiances to the past. Local cultural space is divided along faultlines that are impossible fully to map, but which are made inevitable by the fact that no locality is a socially and culturally homogeneous unity (however heritage may like to picture it). There were, in fact, a number of voices raised against the heritage project from within local circles – not only impelled by its increasingly distant and controversial mode of development, but also voices which, from the start, had been resistant to the idea of preserving the Lewis Merthyr colliery.

A proud heritage?

In memorialism, past mining traditions are valued as inspiration for popular education and public display. However, local voices rejecting or devaluing these traditions favoured a 'new' Rhondda identity that would turn its back on values associated with the mining community. The two positions are well-illustrated in an exchange of letters in the *Llantrisant Observer*, the Taff Ely local paper, at the time of the first public rumours of plans to preserve Lewis Merthyr colliery as a museum. A letter from a Rhondda SDP (Social Democratic Party) representative, a Mr Nicholls-Jones, had appeared in the paper, attacking the museum plans. The following week, a reply was printed, written by a correspondent describing himself as a Labour voter:

Mr Nicholls-Jones is an opinionated, self-styled and self-appointed protector of our future. The council is working hard to create jobs in difficult times. Lewis Merthyr would be a tourist attraction that would show thousands of visitors what life was like in the Rhondda. With Mardy threatened, we soon will have nothing left of our past. Mr Nicholls-Jones would deny us that past and is typical of voices that would flatten everything in the name of progress. The valleys are dying, youth unemployed, the census has said that 10,000 people have left the valley. Our only hope for work is tourism. So let us use the beauty and exploit the tourist potential that would come to see our proud heritage.

(*Llantrisant Observer*, 13 July 1984)

A further reply to this letter came on 27 July:

I have worked down a pit for about 40 years, but I see nothing wrong with a man's opinion who wants to see removed, from the face of the Rhondda Valley, what must be the worse [*sic*] constructed pigsty you will find anywhere in Britain ... Let us exploit this 'beauty' to attract the tourist, says Mr. Williams. All I can say is, may God protect the children of the valleys from having such an aboriginal assessment of beauty forced on them ...

What, too, is this proud heritage he mentions? I, like thousands more, no doubt, had to work down a pit because that's all the work there was for us. Yes, I've got pride, but it has nothing to do with being forced down a pit! I and my wife are very proud of the fact that our boys went to universities. Now one has become, not a miner following his dad's unavoidable footsteps, but a director on the board of an international company. Another is a senior lecturer in an English University ...

Mr Williams can be sure there is plenty of pride in the valleys. Like a lot of valley people we are proud of what our children have done, and it has absolutely nothing to do with – pits! ... Too many of their mates have coughed their lungs away, to boast about mining, or to want to be reminded of it.

(*Llantrisant Observer*, 27 July 1984)

These extracts indicate opposing discourses over the memorialization of the mining industry in local circles. In the first account, mining is 'our proud heritage', which, it is feared, may vanish since 'we shall soon have nothing left of our past'. The memorialist desire to 'show what life was like in the Rhondda', is articulated to a pragmatic acceptance that 'our only hope for work is tourism'. It thus produces a version of the magical resolution between the area's industrial past and its post-industrial future that, I have argued, lay at the heart of heritage enterprise in the 1980s: if we cannot keep local industry alive, at least we can both commemorate it and turn it to our advantage.

In the second letter, however, the label 'proud heritage' is denied, and 'pride' repositioned as the opposite of local, industrial, working-class culture. Rather, pride resides in social and geographical mobility, 'progress' and leaving the mining industry behind. Mining equals death and disease – relics of old practices not found in the English universities and international company board rooms to which Rhondda's children can now aspire. It is difficult to locate this dissent in distinct political identifications, though the above extracts certainly suggest that the two wings of the Labour Party (which was at that time split into the Social Democrats and Labour) each claimed a different vision of Rhondda's past and thus of its future. In trying to present itself as the 'new' and modern alternative to the 'old' labourist traditions of the local Labour Party, the SDP was perhaps happy to disassociate itself from that strand of left opinion which celebrates historic labour struggles in the form of memorials and ceremonies. It was also, no doubt, anxious to contest the embedded localist claims of Labour, invested in a strong Valleys mining-identity. Whatever its provenance, there was, certainly, a divergence of local opinion over the canonization of the Valleys as the archetypal mining community.

Heritage as local resource

Another faultline of local contestation appears around the question of heritage as an accessible and usable local resource. The provision of an adequate memorial is not, in itself, sufficient to satisfy demands for local representation; it must also be seen to *belong* to the local sphere – not in terms of the story told, but in terms of the local benefit to be gained. There are, thus, two ways of understanding heritage 'representation': the representation of locally authentic stories, and the representation of people's claims over local economic and cultural resources (such as the built environment, public space, employment and the provision of leisure amenities). The Rhondda Heritage Park was often defined by local people I spoke to as a space they did not, in fact, own, and that had in some senses been taken away from them. One of the groups of ex-miners identified both a local ambivalence and a hostility towards the park:

M1: (ex Lewis Merthyr colliery official): I think most miners thought it was part of our heritage. I'm not saying they were deeply involved in it, because once they had left the industry ... But I would say the majority of them – though you never get 100% of people agreeing to anything – I think the majority of them think it's worthwhile.

M2 (an ex Tŷ Mawr miner): I think it probably started at the wrong time, when there was so much friction because they were shutting so many pits. There was a lot of bitterness about them shutting and putting so many little communities out of work. Then they want to build a Heritage Park costing so many thousands of pounds. It was causing friction in so many people, arguments as to whether it was a good thing.

M1: I have heard one or two people, ex-miners, comment that if they had put the money into the colliery that they have put into the Heritage Park, it would still be open today.

(Extract from Focus Group 2)

In this account, proper colliery jobs have been swapped, in an unequal exchange, for a heritage site. This clearly expresses the sense of dislocation produced in the transformation from an industrial to a post-industrial economy, suggesting that turning industry into heritage can be seen as obliterating identity rather than offering an expression for it. It captures the felt absurdity of a situation in which a colliery labelled uneconomic can nevertheless metamorphose into a loss-making yet sustainable and publicly subsidized tourist attraction.

This account turns on a critique of the Heritage Park's perceived appropriation of local economic resources. This was a major source of local hostility to the heritage project in the interviews I conducted with local people. It is also expressed in terms of cultural resources, for example, in a concern over public access to the colliery as both leisure space and centre for local culture. While the local area lacked its own children's amenity park, the RHP's smiling Energy Zone beckoned them in – at a price. This was reflected in claims that surfaced in all of the groups' accounts that local people had been excluded from the sights (or sites) of what they called 'The Heritage'. This was particularly expressed in terms of the lack of visible regeneration that the Park had brought with it, coupled with a feeling of exclusion from its public events:

W1: They held a *Songs of Praise* for [war evacuees] in The Heritage.
W2: Nobody knew it was going on. We saw it on the television.

W3: There were all the people who think they are somebody – they were there.

W2: But I looked through the crowd and I didn't see anyone I knew.

W1: You could see the buses coming down the valley, and from over the valleys and no one in Trehafod knew anything about it until the Thursday and it was happening on the Saturday ...

W3: They are ignoring the local people and we are the people who had to put up with all the mess and dirt, when all this [i.e. mining] was going on.

W1: I still think The Heritage has not done anything for Trehafod or Hopkinstown. The young people have still got nothing to do and nowhere to go. With all their big words, they were going to do this and that – I could put it more crudely but I won't – they were going to do such a lot, that everybody was thinking at least if they are closing the collieries there is something coming for the young people. Because in Pontypridd there is nothing at all for the young people, there is no community centre, there is no leisure centre ... Everybody was over the moon, but nothing has come from it.

(Extract from Focus Group 3)

In this account, heritage representation means keeping to promises made to provide amenities and jobs for the local area, and encouraging local public access to the park's resources. This suggests that the question of 'The Heritage' as authentic representation, then, is not necessarily concerned with historiography; it also means public access to material and cultural assets that are seen to belong to the locality itself. In this sense, local heritage that claims to be 'about' the people is also required to be 'of' and 'for' the people.

This critical perspective was most noticeable in the women's focus groups (Groups 3, 4 and 5), suggesting that, for women, mining heritage may not be the same identity-conferring practice as it can be for some (but by no means all) ex-miners. In the above extract, identity consists in feeling welcomed into the RHP's symbolic space as a local arena with cultural and material resources on offer. In Group 4, for example, which was made up of three women, all daughters and one the wife of ex-miners, the Park was unequivocally defined as an imposition, which took up a large amount of much-needed flat space in the valley bottom – swallowing up, in the process, land that could have been used for a children's playground or a sports centre. The demand for a sports centre, rather than a museum, was frequently heard at the time of the initial preservation plans at Lewis Merthyr, according to local people I spoke with.

On the other hand, the mixed focus group, made up of ex-miners and two female teachers and held at the local school, emphasized the positive environmental improvements the Park had brought:

> M1: The whole scheme, no one can deny – whether you're for or against it – the advantages to Trehafod.
> Bella: The whole scheme has?
> M1: Yes. The Heritage. Because it is situated in Trehafod and we have benefited. I don't think there has been any doubt about that.
> M2: Because it has fetched in the grant system as well, so houses have been having big grants – which has been causing some friction with some of the houses but ...
> M2: Because some have been having £40,000 and some have been having to pay.
> W1: Well, it depends on your circumstances, and it's not always quite as simple as circumstances is it, you know? So there is always going to be a bit of friction in that.
> M1: I was thinking, apart from the housing grants, I think other things have been done – like the station, which wouldn't have been renovated, I don't think, without the Heritage ...
> M1: We've got walks along the side of the river now, that we didn't have before. You know, now, if you wanted to have a walk along the side of the river when you were kids you ...
> W1: You were on the pipe weren't you?
> M1: Yeah, that's right!
> W1: A big huge drop into dirty water if you fell off it.
> M2: It was called scarlet fever water, wasn't it? It came from the old mine working ...
> W1: That's right. It was orange wasn't it? It's the iron-stone ...
>
> (Extract from Focus Group 1)

'Our' heritage?

At a more general level, there is a widespread sense that 'The Heritage' confers a positive identity simply through its physical presence in the valley. The group cited above, for instance, was in agreement that now the RHP was there it was a 'good thing' for Trehafod. Similarly, in Focus Group 2, an all-male group made up of ex-miners from the colliery itself, there was an appreciation that the colliery had been preserved:

> M1: The longer it's gone on ... I don't mean to say that somebody should have a blank cheque to run it, because that would be silly, nobody can get that today. But I believe the Rhondda – if it isn't, if it wasn't built on coal, it was built on nothing. The Rhondda *was* coal.
> M2: Coal. Full stop.
> M1: Right. Anybody that was outside the coal industry in the Rhondda, they had connections [to it] somewhere. And I think that we look at castles or people or things that happened you know 400 years ago and so on ...
> M3: *Why shouldn't we in the Rhondda have something?*
>
> (Extract from Focus Group 2; my emphasis)

Here, there is a certain satisfaction to be had in the fact that the RHP is in our village, representing our history, proclaiming the industrial foundations of our locality and inviting the tourist gaze, as a rebuff to the conventional tourist spectacles of 'other people's lives' in castles and ancient history. The very fact that the RHP exists affirms identity; the identity of the self confirmed via the identity of place and the past, through giving space to a set of peripheralized experiences (local mining) that have conventionally been denied entry to the realm of 'national heritage'. The mixed group were in agreement:

> M1: And I think it is also important to remember the importance of coal to this country.
> W1, W2: Yes, yes.
> M1: Because the economy was ...
> W2: ... based on it.
> W1: Coalfields kept the country going at one time ...
> M1: It's all part of history isn't it, and it's an important part of history. So yes. Whether it will ever be commercially viable, I don't know. I doubt it. But once it's gone, you can try then and build something else, but you can never ... this is authentic isn't it? You know, that the thing's still there ...
> W1: Oh, yes.
> M1: From the head gear there, that was what was there.

W1: Can you imagine walking up through Trehafod and not seeing the stack?

(Extract from Focus Group 1)

If the pit chimney stack were gone, this group felt that the locality would lose a local symbol and landmark. In this sense, the preservation of the colliery has at least allowed a significant material sign of the local industrial identity to be preserved.

We can see from the above extracts that memorialism was certainly contested. Furthermore, even where a memorialist stance is adopted, the museum's claims to meet its demands are often disputed. Local people's resistance was particularly directed at the RHP's appropriation of resources such as land, amenities, public culture and, of course, the colliery itself as local economic provider. However, in its purely historiographical function – to provide a space for local history where signs of the area's past can survive – it is seen as a repository for local memories and a display case for local history. In this sense, as Jacobs (1994) argues, economic appropriation does not subsume the social significance of heritage: even where the development process has distanced it from local people's involvement, it can still provide a memorial space for local memory.

What is interesting about the Rhondda project is that this local, memorialist feeling encounters – at a particular economic and cultural moment in the early 1980s – the entrepreneurial-governmental demand for heritage assets, as well as a more widespread and popular 'turn to community', both of which have been discussed in previous chapters. It also encounters the professional practices of heritage interpretation (which will be explored in the next chapter). Professional heritage relies on the production (through display, design and marketing) and consumption (through the tourist and commercial gaze) of community as spectacle. It is at this point that popular memorialist desire can be accommodated, since it can be brought into the service of economic regeneration and hitched to the opportunities opened up by new cultural values of consumption.

Yet the tension between memorialism and professional exhibitionary strategy constantly haunts the project, introducing particular conflicts and contradictions. The history of the encoding process at the RHP is to a large extent the history of this tension and its offspring: vernacular knowledge versus expert knowledge, history seen as authentic versus history judged inauthentic, local identifications versus non-local identifications, the educational versus the entertaining. These tensions are further explored in the next chapter, which turns to an examination of professional exhibitionary knowledge – the story of Ivor's 'pinstripe wallahs'.

8

The technologies of heritage encoding

This chapter explores how history is turned into heritage. This is a process that I have called, following Hall (1980), encoding. The study of encoding involves looking at the range of creative strategies used in displays and recovering the chronology of creative decision-making. In what follows, I examine how professional design practice worked in the process of putting the displays together. In section 1, I look at the social relations of encoding and the forms of knowledge deployed. Section 2 explores how local historical knowledge was harnessed within the technologies of exhibition design. Finally, I offer an illustrative picture of how a particular historical theme – the early industrial conflict in the coalfields – came to assume a narrative shape in the form of the three audio-visual shows of *Black Gold*. The objective is to illustrate how heritage works as a practice of historical re-presentation

The study of encoding involves situating exhibition design within the social contexts of the museum in its locality. In chapter 3, it was argued that encoding does not begin and end within the walls of the heritage museum. It is not only the result of creative decisions taken by exhibition designers and interpreters, but is also shaped by the wider social relations that characterize the heritage museum as institution, with its divisions of labour, frameworks of knowledge, and specific local, regional and national context. Thus, the encoding/decoding approach, which is based on a model of heritage as media, needs to be informed by a fully social model of communication (Dicks, 2000). Other chapters have discussed various dimensions of these wider contexts, and the last chapter focused on local structures of feeling amongst both supporters and critics of the Rhondda heritage project. The present chapter will bring the focus inwards – examining how the professional consultants who were engaged to 'interpret' the Rhondda's history went about their work.

The professional knowledge of interpreters does not alone produce a heritage experience. As interpreters go about the business of designing the displays, they are also seeking out and drawing on local knowledge in encounters with local informants and historical sources. In fact, three different kinds of expert knowledge are involved in the encoding of mining heritage. The local 'lay' knowledge of mine-workers and local residents is derived from their personal experience, work-based education and collective organization, and is orientated to the values of memorialism. The academic knowledge of local historians is concerned with the detailed historiographic content of texts, while the exhibitionary, professional knowledge of heritage interpreters is directed at the aesthetic and experiential design of visitor attractions.

Heritage texts, then, are the product of multiple forms of knowledge. These are organized into a hierarchy determined by the project's management ethos. In the case of the Rhondda project, local knowledge was sidelined through the project's metamorphosis into a multiplex, consortium-controlled product. Thus, it is professional knowledge which takes the helm. However, this professional knowledge remains dependent on local knowledge if, as new heritage seeks to do, it also claims to represent the authentic local voice of 'the people'. In heritage's increasingly vernacular aspirations, it is the recovery of experience rather than the deployment of material culture which is held up as the attraction (Jenkinson, 1989). What we find in the Rhondda case-study is that, in the process of trying to access and incorporate local authenticating stories, professional knowledge is itself transformed. In what follows, I explore how the separation of local historical knowledge and professional exhibitionary knowledge was enshrined in the project's divisions of labour and management structures, and how they were also, nevertheless, brought face to face in the process of encoding.

1. Professional, exhibitionary discourse

Who really 'authored' the texts at the Rhondda Heritage Park? There is no doubt that the research, design and creative encoding work was the preserve of the outside consultancy firms, who were engaged by management to produce the designs and oversee construction work. Whether consultants were landscape architects or audio-visual producers, they all offered the heritage project a particular realm of expert knowledge known as *interpretation*. Interpretation involves the creative aspects of the project, both the site hardware (design of buildings, interiors, landscaping, site layout and so on), and software (the displays, audio-visual shows, site dressing and theming, and so forth). It involves specialist skills such as landscaping, architectural design, interior design, video production, photography, scriptwriting, historical research, costume and model design. It also includes feasibility studies and market research, particularly in relation to tourism markets. By contrast, the knowledge brought to the project by its managers[1] was confined, on the whole, to local council/agency planning expertise and financial management.

The project's heavy reliance on commercial consultants, not one of whom was local to the Rhondda, the Valleys or – in most cases – Wales, is, from the perspective of an outside observer, one of its most striking features. We have already seen in the last chapter how locally placed mining and local-history experts and enthusiasts, including the vestiges of local NUM lodges, were progressively sidelined as the project developed. However, this still in theory left a layer of local knowledge and networks available, since some of the local government officers involved in the project's day-to-day management were intimately acquainted with the local area through both residence and occupation. Yet the business of doing local heritage is reserved for an army of outside consultants, who are specifically *not* tied to the local area. Indeed, the consultants were chosen because of their track records in *other* local heritage projects, such as the White Cliffs of Dover Experience, the Yorvik Viking Centre and the Wigan Pier Inheritance Centre. What was valued was the geographically varied knowledge of professional interpretation (see below), rather than the intimate and place-specific knowledge of local residents and workers. This feature of heritage representation (at least as it operated in the Rhondda) suggests an underlying principle to which we will return below: that interpretation first needs to construct local culture as an 'other' before it can transform it into an exhibition.

Divisions of labour

Heritage encoding, in this way, establishes a division between two separate domains of activity: the marketing and creative domain,

colonized by outside consultancy firms specializing in interpretation, and the practical, planning and financial domain, allotted to
the local management as 'client'. In engaging consultants, officers
were purchasing a realm of outside expertise that had to do with
knowing the market, targeting the audience and turning history
into heritage. Each stage of the encoding process was seen by
management as a discrete task which could be put out to tender as a
package. The early stages produced consultancy reports dedicated
to feasibility studies, market research, landscape design and architecture. Later on, once funding was secure and the project given the
green light, these packages comprised the more creative tasks of
producing the actual visitor experiences.

Management meetings, meanwhile, were, on the whole, confined
to the practical site-related and funding issues of the moment,
and left the content of the visitor experience to the expertise of
consultants:

> It was more the disposition of activities rather then the detailed concept
> of interpretation that tended to dominate discussion ... I mean at that
> time, you know, if it hinted at Yorvik, it must be good ... It was 'these
> are the people that have done it before, so you know, professionally, can
> we question them to any great extent in terms of the details of
> interpretation?' As I say the issues were more 'Well, is that the right
> place for that, or should it be there?'
>
> (Personal interview with planning officer from Mid Glamorgan
> County Council)

In this way a division of labour emerged, in which officers were
concerned with practical planning issues – what should go where –
and the job of interpretation was left to consultants. Officers saw
their business as those day-to-day practical aspects of site maintenance, labour and financing that constituted the progressing of
what they called 'the project'. Consultants in turn saw 'the client' as
merely the purchaser of their expertise, and unlikely to get deeply
involved in the creative decisions (as one of the *Black Gold*
consultants said, 'I can't remember a project I have done where a
client has discussed the research material itself').[2]

The technology of interpretation

Interpretation thereby came to be seen as a separate, specialist,
professionalized realm of knowledge distinct from the knowledge

that was available locally through mine-workers, their families or local historians. This was in direct contrast to the early Rhondda Borough Council proposal for a small, traditional collection museum, whereby artefacts and buildings were to be directly presented to the public by those who had first-hand knowledge of their use (the ex-miners). Heritage encoding instead deploys a mediating layer of knowledge which is inserted between the 'raw material' and the 'visitor experience'. Interpretation is thus not merely a field of specialist knowledge. It also entails the power to define the historical subject and translate this into exhibitionary forms.

It is useful to understand interpretation as a form of knowledge in the Foucauldian sense, whereby 'power and knowledge directly imply one another ... there is no power relation without the correlative constitution of a field of knowledge, nor any knowledge that does not presuppose and constitute at the same time power relations' (Foucault, 1977: 27). This alerts us to the fact that knowledge is not mobilized merely to establish abstract values such as 'truth' or 'authenticity', but for specific functions and uses in historical situations (see Alonso, 1988). Interpretation works as a 'technology of power', which is geared to defining how something is to be represented for a specific public (Foucault, 1981). The technology of interpretation identifies and names the subject to be represented (the Rhondda), and specifies the means of its representation (its exhibitionary forms).

What kind of power does interpretation bring into play? Another planning officer explains:

> [At the RHP we are] *interpreting a people*, or the history of a people – interpretation being the science or art of *telling the story of something* in a way in which people can *understand it*, and *be entertained,* if you like, by it. It's ... the telling of stories to people and the explanation of things to people ... We have to translate [the research] into *a workable product*. It would be easy enough to appoint an academic consultant who would come in and do a wonderful job of research and then write a brilliant treatise on the development of the Rhondda Valleys, and all we would be able to do is paste it on the wall like wall paper and nobody would read it ... What we have to do and what the group of consultants has to show that it can do is take that and turn it into a form that *people would actually enjoy.*
>
> (Interview with Mid Glamorgan County Council
> tourism officer; my emphasis)

Interpretation is not, then, academic (not a 'brilliant treatise'). It has to be 'workable'. The audience has to 'understand it and be entertained by it' and 'enjoy' it. It is therefore concerned with producing something for the purposes of public communication. It imagines an audience which is novice (needing the research to be interpreted for them to understand it), as well as one that demands enjoyment. Interpretation, then, entails a particular *mode of address*, envisaging the public as an uninformed audience requiring accessible and enjoyable products. Although it deploys knowledge in these particular ways and reproduces the real within its own terms, interpretation assumes the guise of merely mediating in a transparent way between subject and audience.[3]

Interpretation distances itself from traditional museum knowledge in the form of curation, which stands accused of failing to contextualize and enliven the objects it puts on display. Interpretation first developed in the early folk museums, discussed in chapter 4, and was later taken up by environmentalists working with public space in the countryside and city parks (see Uzzell, 1989). As competition for public funding became heightened during the 1980s, countryside planners had to ensure that green space was preserved in a way that made it accessible for users, so that public subsidy could be justified. Strategies of making the countryside accessible and desirable relied on interpreting it in ways that would help to attract the gaze (Urry, 1995). In Zukin's (1991) terms, green spaces have had to enter the economy of signs in order to survive. Interpretation is the means by which the site becomes a sight.

Interpretation thus defines the subject within the terms of its representation. It is the means by which 'the Rhondda' is imagined as a heritage community. The existence of the Rhondda Heritage Park, as a highly visual and concrete manifestation of the identity of the Rhondda does not only occupy local space or act as a memorial. It also marks out a heritage mining identity for the area which strengthens its deeply rooted associations with the ideal of community. Furthermore, it publicly affirms and promotes the area's unique sense of place, since interpretation, as has been noted, 'is about place and the concept of place, about putting people and things into their environmental context, restoring provenance to artefacts that have lost their roots so that their significance can once more be seen' (Aldridge, 1989). Interpretation thus contributes to the canonization of local place-myths and 'roots', which, potentially, can have far-reaching effects in terms of decisions over the deployment of local resources (see Shields, 1991).

If the knowledge mobilized in the development of the Rhondda project had been differently configured (if it had remained a community-driven initiative, for instance), the Rhondda would, undoubtedly, have been imagined differently at the site. As one of the planning officers described, the consultants' reports constitute the field of knowledge that produced the Rhondda as heritage representation: 'All those reports have gone through the sieve ... All those parts in the recipe have ended up with the meal that you actually get at the end.'[4] Interpretation, then, is the 'sieve' through which the ingredients of the recipe are sifted. The raw ingredients themselves, however, are taken as a given. They are thought of, simply, as the Rhondda and its history, which can then be worked upon to make a visitable attraction. This given, however, must already be represented as a temporally, spatially and socially defined subject with its own heritage identity before being interpreted. Thus, 'the Rhondda' is not a given 'thing' which is merely reflected through interpretation. Rather, it is always-already a representation, an imagined community, which constitutes a selection of ingredients for the recipe to work on.

Thematics: defining the Rhondda

The technology of interpretation needs to identify and imagine this subject which will form its raw ingredients. Following Silverstone (1989), we can call the study of this practice textual thematics.[5] Consultants imagine what the Rhondda *is* and *was*, before they decide how this 'it' will be displayed. As we shall see below, this initial act of imagination already imagines the Rhondda in terms of the archetypal mining community – even before formal interpretation takes place. This is because consultants have no access to 'the people of the Rhondda' other than by recourse to existing Rhondda place-myths, which – as we saw in chapter 4 – have long consecrated the area as the home of the archetypal mining community. I shall refer to this prior construction of the subject of interpretation as the 'really real' Rhondda (as opposed to the Rhondda which is finally represented in the exhibitions).

Positioning the 'really real' Rhondda as other is the primary principle upon which the encoding of the Rhondda-as-heritage depends. The 'really real Rhondda' is represented in encoders' discourse as a special, homogeneous, traditional and isolated place. This is both a topographical isolation (imposed by the steep valley sides) and a social one (epitomizing a special way of life). Consultants do not, however, set out to invent this special way of life, as theme-park designers or Disney imagineers might dream up a vision of the Wild West. Instead, they perceive their remit as carefully reflecting the reality of what they see as 'the community' laid before them. Their initial tasks involve gathering stories, images and information about the community, which they perceive as simply reflecting its identity. This material is later assembled into a 'workable product' and a 'visitable attraction', by being interpreted in scenes, props, themes and slide shows.

Pre-formed images of the archetypal mining community frame consultants' discourse about the Rhondda even from the earliest feasibility studies. However, it is interesting to note a shift in this imaginary, from one which posits a 'then and now' identity for the Rhondda, in which the area's great heritage is deemed to have been forgotten by its present-day residents, to one which affirms the ongoing 'spirit' of the Rhondda people today. In the early studies, consultants have limited contact with any local residents at all. Their reports are aimed at making the case for the project, and focus on presenting the Rhondda as, above all, needy. John Brown, for instance, asserts in the initial feasibility study of 1984:

> The context in which this suggestion is being made is that of a *seriously deprived* part of Wales – Rhondda and indeed the whole Valleys area – where it is realistic, indeed necessary, to consider major investment in a project which may begin to *reverse social and economic trends*, and to *renew the confidence* in the area of *both local people and the world outside* ... Such a project could substantially strengthen *Rhondda people's own awareness* of, and pride in, their home area and their heritage, and bring them *fresh hope for the future*; as well as *encouraging them* to look afresh at, and improve, their own environment, seeing beauty that *they may have neglected or taken for granted*. It would also be an important *educational* resource.
>   (Welsh Development Agency, 1984: 28–32; italics added)

Here, people in the Rhondda are imbued with a collective personality (lacking 'confidence', 'hope' and 'pride') which is in need of enlightenment by the 'project'. They are configured as indifferent towards their heritage, and isolated from 'the world outside'. The roots of this deprivation are located in vague 'social and economic trends'. This imagination enables the project to be positioned as the people's saviour, and effectively makes the case for substantial public funding. In such discourse, the really-real Rhondda *now* is characterized by a community imaginary which summons up a deprived underclass in need of rescue by outsiders.

If the Rhondda today is hopeless, its past only underlines how it has fallen from greatness. Composed of ideas with 'romantic power', the past evokes 'a stream of powerful images in the minds of people world-wide – coalmining, choral traditions, chapel, rugby, social struggle, human sacrifice, the industrial revolution' (William Gillespie & Partners, 1986: para. 2.2). This greatness is simply taken for granted as part of the received wisdom about how the Rhondda 'used to be'. However, the question of how this proud Rhondda was transformed into the new one that has lost this greatness is never clearly posed. There is never a cut-off point offered, as a means of dating when the old became the new. Where it is obliquely suggested that it is material and economic devastation that has wrought these changes, the implications of such a conclusion are contradicted through the proposition that it is attitudinal change on the people's part that can reverse the damage. The possibility that it may have been capitalist restructuring itself that caused the decline is simply forgotten.

Later on in the consultancy process, Rhondda people of today are configured somewhat differently. In the reports of those consultants engaged actually to carry out local research for *Black Gold*, the Rhondda's problems today are seen as offset by its people's resilience and 'grit'. Encoding *Black Gold* involved consultants in a more immediate encounter with local history (as the subject of the displays), and with ex-miners and local residents (as the voices of that history). The interim report for the visitor experience, in considering the approach to designing *Black Gold*, dwelt at length on the problematic relations between the Park and local people:

> It is said that Rhondda people are suspicious of the Heritage Park, despite the fact that most do want to have a worthy memorial to the Rhondda coal industry. The Heritage Park does not yet seem to have defined a clear role in the community; or the kind of contribution it can make, beyond the hoped-for boost to the local economy.

Some local people fear that heritage will not bring the liberation that is needed – a truthful and almost cathartic portrayal of their history and character ... A modern person looking back at Rhondda's past sees almost unbearable hardship and injustice, but this is to misunderstand the stoicism with which these were endured by people who themselves, and whose forbears throughout history, had known only ways of life that were little or no better. We must also show the pride, humour and enjoyment.

The people may have been defeated countless times in their upward struggle, but a hundred years of self reliance in the face of almost continuous social indifference to their plight has produced a community with a fierce pride and confidence in their ability to survive. If the test called for an emergence from starvation, bereavement and defeat with a positive, united outlook, Rhondda passed that test with honour.

(John Brown & Co. et al., 1988: 12–13)

This account brings into play elements of the 'good community' combined with aspects of the 'vanishing other', which I have argued underlies the trope of the archetypal mining community (chapter 5). It identifies a heroic yet suffering people – self-reliant, proud and confident – in contrast to the earlier claims about their apathy and despair. This change possibly results from consultants having been brought into contact with local people during the course of their research (see below). Because the project is locally situated, abstract and essentialized images of local people as apathetic are subjected to competing self-definitions from local people encountered. These are then re-presented in terms of positive images such as 'the good community'.

However, both types of discourse position local people as special and isolated: different from the outside world. In the 'suffering and defeated' version, the aim is to attract funding by spelling out the area's neediness so that the project can be presented as both essential and remedial. The later design consultancy, in contrast, is not charged with pleading the case for the project as a whole. There, a 'suffering but not defeated' discourse is mobilized. Local residents are pictured instead moving as one struggling yet homogeneous mass through the years. Nevertheless, the common thread in both versions is that the Rhondda is a special, homogeneous and 'other' place, a time capsule either holding on to or losing its greatness through the vicissitudes of history. In this way, the boundaries around it are clearly marked out and it appears as a recognizable identity still surviving in its essence. Above all, it is worlds away (and times away) from consultants' own professional cultures in the urban cityscapes of Manchester, Leeds and York.

This gap is perceived as simultaneously a spatial, temporal and social one. In the view of project managers, however, it merely reflects a pragmatic need for outside, expert knowledge:

> Although its seed started very much a little weakly seedling from within the community, all the manure and all of the water has come from outside. And it may be too that a lot of the fruit has been plucked from outside because all of the consultancy teams [are people from England]. But it had to be. If you are going to develop a proper project, you've got to have the best. It just so happens that the best doesn't grow, in that particular industry, in South Wales. You've got to import it.
>
> (Personal interview with Tourism Officer, Mid Glamorgan County Council)

The officer here suggests that what was imported was merely the neutral expertise of interpretation. But it was also the importation of a perspective – one that is essential to the encoding of place for the tourist gaze. Creating a 'unique sense of place' is a strategy that is central to the demands of image-driven contemporary tourist consumption, in which the widespread choice of leisure destinations and activities means that each site has to offer a particular appeal – yet one that is not difficult to decode (see Urry, 1995: 147–50). The requirement is for attractions and sites that will both offer something different from the norm, yet appeal to as wide a number of visitors as possible. In the process, the tricky business of attracting visitors to an ex-colliery in a peripheral area of the UK will depend on carefully translating the specifics of the history into the familiar tropes of community which will be recognized by outside tourists. There is, thereby, a tension within heritage encoding between the generalized demands of the tourist gaze and the parallel need for authenticity, a unique sense of place and the credibility of the spectacle as vernacular history.

2. Local forms of knowledge

Professional interpretation on its own does not produce heritage. The new heritage's claim to represent 'ordinary lives' means that encoding has to incorporate local, vernacular, personal voices that can provide the authenticating effects that constitute its appeal. This was fully recognized by the management at the Rhondda Heritage Park. It was not, however, only the cynical aim of creating authentication that impelled the search for local voices. As other chapters have shown, there had long been, and continued to be, an entrenched problem with the park's local public relations, in that it had attracted considerable controversy and hostile press comment (with suggestions in the local press that it was a 'white elephant'[6]). Since a committee of local councillors from each of the three consortium councils was ultimately holding the project's purse strings, it was necessary to respond to local feeling and to be seen to involve local people in the representation of a heritage which was, after all, their own.

The consultancy team that handled the historical research for the *Black Gold* exhibitions, consequently, was charged by the Officers' Directing Group to produce what it called 'an interpretation of the valleys' heritage which will not only meet visitors' needs, but provide an essential link for local people with their past'.[7] This instruction reveals the contradictory remit of the project: on the one hand, the exhibitionary aim of 'meeting visitor needs'; on the other, the memorialist aim of 'providing a link for local people'. The brief goes on:

> Emphasis should be placed on the personal – *what it was like* to work in that environment. Wherever possible, the re-creation should be influenced by the many *personal memories* and *memorabilia* associated with the mine. The designers should work closely with the Friends and the Mid Glamorgan County Council Community programme Research Team.
>
> (1988: 21; my italics)

This encoding strategy implies a happy coincidence of objectives: local people's 'links with the past' need to be catered for and visitors require 'personal memories', so the solution is to ask consultants to base their research on the 'memories and memorabilia' of local people. The Friends of the Rhondda Heritage Park (see chapter 7) and the Manpower Services Commission team of local oral history-gatherers (see below) were to be co-opted in the process.

The consultants who worked on *Black Gold* were thus instructed to ensure that any artefacts used in the theming of the colliery head gear, and in the photographic slides for the audio-visual shows, would be recognizable and thus 'authentic' for local people. The consultants were thereby directed towards significant local individuals (such as Ivor and other ex-miners), with whom they were to consult on the appropriateness of both artefacts and historical detail. This meant that consultants were involved in tracking down locals in search of concrete and particular 'native' knowledge. Such activity, however, only contributed to the them/us divide that had haunted the Rhondda project from the beginning. Local knowledge was provided free by local people, but became a commodity for consultants in their efforts to track down authenticating effects. Ivor explained:

> You'd get people asking you, 'Oh, Ivor, what was it like in a typical street in the '30s, the '40s, the '50s? ... Could you tell us what it was like when you were a boy? What did you and your sisters play in the street?' I did co-operate, but I co-operated grudgingly because I thought 'No, why should you have my bloody knowledge? At the end of it all, you'll present it in a great big glossy kind of consultancy study and then you'll get paid handsomely and then you'll go away.'
> (Personal interview with Ivor England)

Local knowledge is thus commodified by the consultants' need, as outsiders, to obtain it *from* insiders. The lead *Black Gold* consultant commented that he 'had never known a project where the dividing line was so severe, where [locals] have been either an open book or a closed book, people would either talk to you about it or they didn't have the time of day for you' (personal interview with member of production team, *Black Gold*). This suggests that, during their field research, consultants met various local people who were resistant, even hostile, to the project.

In addition, consultants found themselves surveyed by the memorialist gaze, facing the scrutiny of local enthusiasts over, for example, the degree of cleanliness required of an apron on a model, or the thickness of a woman's eyebrows in a close-up shot. Such concern for detail clashes with the demands of exhibitionary knowledge:

> Because of the nature of the project and the people involved, we had to be really, really particular about it, and search out individuals who could give us a definitive yes or no: yes, that lamp was in use at the time,

or no, they wouldn't have used those tools, they'd have used others ...
But you might miss certain details – out of choice not out of ignorance.
... Because a lot of things that people present you with, although they
may be intimately interested in it and think it's of value, ultimately to a
school party visiting from Bristol or from Edinburgh, it doesn't have
much relevance really.

(Personal interview with member of *Black Gold* design team)

In exhibitionary discourse, then, insistence on local authenticity
may be seen as a burden because the signs of the past have to hold
the attention of the visitor as other; they do not, as in memorialist
discourse, have to be recognizable as self.

Part of the gap that appears to divide professional exhibitionary
discourse from local memorialist knowledge can be explained by
recognizing the different functionality of each. As the last chapter
showed, local historical feeling is impelled by the desire to record
the specific details and idiosyncrasies of the area's previous way of
life, which can only be represented by reassembling the fragmented,
often contradictory mosaic of individuals' particular memories.
By contrast, exhibitionary knowledge is geared not to a recording
function but to a logic of display, in which the historical material
is mined for its communicative and spectacular potential – its
capacity to attract and hold the tourist gaze. Two of the encounters
between consultants in the Rhondda project and local informants,
explored in what follows, illustrate this gap particularly clearly.

In search of local memories

In the first encounter, the professional researcher for *Black Gold*,
hired to assemble a portfolio of themes and stories that would form
the basis of the three audio-visual shows, set off to interview a
group of local people in order to collect their personal memories.
This group, which included the remnants of the original committee of local enthusiasts who had agitated for a 'Lewis Merthyr
Museum', had been employed by the Park's management through
the then Manpower Services Commission community scheme to
undertake some oral history work in the locality. They had been
instructed to collect anecdotes from older local residents on tape,
but so far none of this material had been utilized by the designers.[8]
The group had been given the use of a Portakabin, which was situated in the pityard, which, according to the researcher, tended to

reinforce the impression that they had been 'banished' to a marginal position in the Park's development.

The researcher described the group as profoundly dissatisfied with the seeming absence of any material end-use for their oral history work:

> For them the story was the reason they were there, the reason the project was in existence, the reason the money was being invested. That was where they came from and so they couldn't understand why people didn't realise how this was, and why people hadn't taken any notice of what they were doing, and why it had never been used ... I found myself in sympathy with them, and I felt they had been mishandled ... There was very much a sense of ownership there, I think that was the problem. They felt they owned it, and yet they had no rights of ownership. They were not offered any rights of ownership, or any real part in the decision-making.
>
> (Interview with researcher for *Black Gold*)

In this account, the researcher notes a conflict of interests between the MSC group and the project's management. The consultant, sympathetic to their situation, wants to be their cipher, a medium through which their concerns and their 'story' could be accommodated in the displays. The consultant wanted to tell 'their story': 'I was always very, very concerned that this should be a recognisably authentic story for local people, that local people would walk in and know that it was true.' All thus seemed set for a happy transfer of the story from the local to the professional sphere.

However, this strategy began to lose its way when problems emerged over the content of the story. 'Their story' could not, it seemed, meet the demands of the professional, exhibitionary story. Interpretation, as we have seen, requires a story which is easily readable and digestible by the tourist gaze. This requirement eventually forestalled the strategy of using local people's memories as the content of that story:

> I wanted to get at what they felt was important, and I would ask them questions like '*what do you want to have said about you?*', 'what do you want to have said about mining in the Rhondda, about the community you lived in, about the families who were involved?' Nobody had ever asked them that question before, I was absolutely convinced that no one had ever asked that, and there were some silences ... It was hard, very

hard for them to step outside and think 'well, what would we like to
have said about ourselves?'. They felt sure no one would say it right, but
when asked to grasp it they couldn't easily find the words ... What I
had were *a mêlée of impressions and feeling*, from people in the
community that I talked to, but there was *no one who could interpret
that*, there was *no channel through which to pass it*, no one person.
    (Interview with research consultant for *Black Gold*; my emphasis)

This account reveals the convoluted subjectivity of the heritage
text. The awkward phraseology of the question 'What do you
want to have said about you?' betrays the confused authorship
relations of professional encoding. It asks people to present their
own lives as polished statements for a public audience. In its use
of the passive voice ('have said' instead of 'say' or 'us to say') the
question both avoids the naming of an author, as though 'what
people want' can be directly reflected in the text without mediation, and also positions the group as both subject and object ('what
do you want'/'about you'). The effect is to position the consultant
as the mere conveyor of messages *from* people *about* themselves, a
bridge between local voices and their public representation.
    The last sentence of the quotation suggests that the bridge is,
however, uncrossable. Exhibitionary discourse cannot utilize these
local voices because they lack coherence (being a 'mêlée') and are
impressionistic. This shows that interpretation, despite its claims,
does not act directly upon unmediated reality, but requires the
ephemera of the social world to be *already encoded* into text and
thus already organized into accessible images, before it can be made
into an exhibition. The absence of an organized, single-authored
account (through a 'channel' or a 'person') threatens to unravel this
intertextual structure. To regain it, an 'expert' form of local historiography was enlisted, that of local professional historians.
    Professor Dai Smith, an eminent local historian of the Valley
coalfields, was 'a wonderful find' in that he could provide that singly
authored account which would still be 'recognizably authentic ...
because he still has his connections in the Rhondda community'.[9]
The *Black Gold* consultancy team engaged his services to write the
scripts for the three audio-visual shows. Born in Tonypandy into a
working-class mining family, Dai Smith is the author of several
well-respected and prominent local histories and co-authored the
acclaimed *The Fed* (Francis and Smith, 1980), a history of the south
Wales mining union. He could offer a local historiography which

was both coherent and, crucially, sufficiently locally esteemed and rooted to be capable of substituting for local 'lay' voices. Thus, we can see that the texts have not been authored by the consultants, nor, in spite of what is claimed, by the people themselves. Instead, they are a complex interweaving of existing texts which are already structured for the purposes of public communication (as opposed to the messy mêlée of first-hand accounts), and yet which can still claim to be 'of the people'.

In search of the personal voice

Although Dai Smith's stature as a local historian was considerable, the fact that he was a professional historian still ran the risk of losing the grassroots, authenticating quality of the narratives. Thus, consultants continued to search for a 'real' local person, who could serve as the narrative voice for the 'people of the Rhondda'.

> N: 'What we wanted to do was to find a character who had family members who had worked at the colliery from the time it opened to the time it closed. And we found this one character, Bryn Rees. I think it was his grandfather who started work at the colliery when it opened and then his father, and then him and I think his son followed him into it.
> Bella: What was your thinking behind that?
> N: To *personalize* it really. To get somebody who could remember and who we felt, *knew the pit*. Knew the pit because they had worked in it, who could *have those memories* ... To be able to have that through the grandfather and father and then him and then his son. I think it gave it a *credibility*. It's coming from the words of *the people who have done it*, ... someone who's *lived it*.
> (Personal interview with lead designer on *Black Gold*; my emphasis)

This account values experience, 'direct' knowledge and roots, as a means of guaranteeing the 'authenticity' of the representation. Thus, finally, access to the lived, the situated and the personal is secured. Yet it is access which is structured and disciplined: the consultants interviewed Bryn[10] once or twice, and then the script-writer worked his reminiscences into the script. It is a strategy that avoids unruly encounters with local people, and substitutes the voice of the single individual who can nevertheless offer vicarious access to others: the grandfather, the father and the son. Thus, 'Rhondda miners' can be personalized into three subjective, vernacular voices, and temporal change can be reified into three 'times': the time of each generation of this one family tree.

At the same time, as with Dai Smith, using Bryn's story offered another means of linking in with local memorialism. As the other *Black Gold* consultants described, the officers were concerned about what 'the locals would make of the story':

> As soon as you get a local family, like the Rees family involved, that was a big plus point. They loved that idea. Oh yes, because it carried all the local people – that one of their people was actually in there and was being made a hero. So that was quite important for them.
>
> (Personal interview with member of *Black Gold* design team)

Thus, we have another example of the 'magical solutions' that this heritage project claims to provide: by simultaneously abiding by the rules of exhibitionary discourse (to tell an engaging story of real, lived experience) and the rules of memorialism (to accommodate local memories), a magical resolution is proposed which will supposedly satisfy both the tourist and the local gaze. Again, we can see how the relations of production outlined in chapter 6 (which work to exclude local people as active participants) then produce counter strategies in encoding practice, designed to retrieve the lost 'voice of the people'. However, the notion of access to the people is here translated into the search for the personal, as though one, manageable voice can be the cipher for the many voices of the social.

In search of popular participation

A similar, and ultimately equally compromised, attempt to harness local voices in the encoding process occurred during the design and construction of the miner's cottage and street in the visitor reception centre. Unusually, the team working on this did not come from the professional heritage industry, but from the field of theatre design, and was committed to a model of community participation in 'devised shows' – a technique whereby local residents are co-opted into play-writing and rehearsals in community theatre initiatives. Accordingly, the theatre team asked the RHP management for local contacts in the area, people connected with the mining industry who would come and participate in workshops. These were intended to generate a vision of 'how things used to be', based on people's actual memories of their houses and streets. However, the one and only workshop held was a 'disaster':

> We were in this tiny little classroom thing, with a large group of people. We started off by sitting round. We'd got a structure to work on, but we never got beyond the first section, because I think that these people had been briefed to come and just tell their story, as it were, in one way or another. They were all desperate to unload something ... like this woman had written a poem that she wanted us all to hear, which took her about half an hour to read ... By the time we'd gone round the whole group, and been very fair with people and let them have their say, they'd say, 'Well, I've written this down because ...' And they'd launch into a story about their great Aunty Lilly, which was why they'd wanted to come in the first place. So it was kind of fatal, really.
>
> (Personal interview with theatre design team)

This account suggests an opposition between memorialist discourse, in the form of reminiscences composed of the personal, the detailed and the idiosyncratic, and a spectacle-orientated theatre model where fragments and impressions are sought for the mixing pot of images. In the theatre workshop, the virtuoso performance from the single individual is exactly *not* what is required. Again, it seems, accessing local voices resulted in unmanageable and unusable kinds of material.

It was as a result of this failure that the team finally resorted to cutting out extracts from local period newspapers, local historical accounts and local novels, and literally pasting these onto the walls of the cottage:

> I wanted to prioritize people who were living and working and writing in the area at different times. A lot of that was very witty and very pithy, and had, if there is one, *the voice of the Rhondda.* I don't know if you can identify that as an outsider. I mean, I was born in Ely [in Cardiff] but I don't think of myself as Welsh, even. So I saw myself as *standing outside the community* and *trying to identify what this voice was,* and how *we could express* that voice and feeling. Okay, we've failed miserably with talking to local people ... But we can at least use the voices of people who lived in the area as opposed to perpetuating my standpoint as an outsider by using so and so working at the University of Wales.
>
> (Personal interview with theatre designer; my emphasis)

In a similar fashion to the *Black Gold* consultants, the designer is searching for that elusive self-expression of the vernacular, 'the voice of the Rhondda'. Once more, the search is frustrated, and once more it is the written word that substitutes for the first-hand account of ordinary residents. The team's desires to be inclusive and people-centred were defeated by the complete lack of established and meaningful channels of communication between the museum and local people.

3. The encoding chain – an illustration

I have been arguing that encoding involved the incorporation of local vernacular voices into more manageable, coherent accounts, and that this amalgam ultimately meant relying on professional written, rather than oral, accounts. This process is well illustrated by piecing together the different interpretative texts which made up *Black Gold*. The first of these was the two-volume *Report of Research* (Sally Wright Associates, 1990a, b). This report comprises dense, detailed summaries of the major developments in the area's industrial, political and social history over the past century and a half. On the basis of these, the audio-visual production team, Centre Screen Productions of Manchester, then prepared a creative treatment (Centre Screen, n.d.), a document describing how the history would be transformed into three shows in Bertie, Trefor and the fan-house. Finally, the producers appointed Professor Dai Smith actually to write the final three ten-minute audio scripts, based on this creative treatment. The audio-visual company then had the task of assembling a sequence of photographic slides to illustrate the script, and producing special sound effects to accompany the spoken narration. This resulted in the production of a 'story board', the final recipe which recorded the chronological ordering of narration and accompanying stills. The last task was to engage the professional actors (for example, Glynn Houston) and personalities (for example, Neil Kinnock[11]) who would record the spoken narratives onto tape.

The most striking element in the *Black Gold* encoding chain is the series of historiographical transformations that take place during the operation of this division of labour. In particular, the initial lengthy *Report of Research* is transformed into the dramatically reduced creative treatment, before being expanded out again into the final three scripts destined for the audio-visual shows in the

Bertie and Trefor winding houses and the fan-house. This chain underlines the thoroughgoing intertextuality of *Black Gold*: the researcher begins with academic history books from the library plus interview material from the authors of written histories; the production team then condenses these into three stories in the creative treatment, and finally the scriptwriter produces the three ten-minute scripts. So history is written and rewritten down the chain until the final scripts emerge, laden with the remnants of the prior texts that constitute them.

To give an example of the transformations involved in this process, let us consider one aspect of the historiography that finds its way into the final audio script of the Bertie show. This is the account of industrial conflict from the middle of the nineteenth century until the Depression of the 1930s. This story goes through three stages of encoding:

(i) Research report

In the research report there is a detailed description of the mid-nineteenth century sliding scale for wages,[12] miners' increasing resistance to it and the eventual setting up of the South Wales Miners' Federation (popularly known as 'the Fed') in 1898. According to the report, this increased resistance was caused by the spread of large colliery combines, the continuing frequency of mining disasters, the spread of 'education and socialist ideas' amongst miners, and the downward pressure on wages. The report devotes six pages to a description of the Cambrian Colliery strike of 1910–11, including a detailed account of the Tonypandy Riots. It describes how the strike was conducted by a workers' committee, and how, after the miners' defeat (enforced by the presence of British troops), a growing number of miners rejected liberalism and turned to radical politics. As a result, *The Miners' Next Step* appeared, a revolutionary pamphlet calling for workers' control of a 'new industrial democracy' to replace capitalism, instead of the Labour Party's official policy of nationalization. However, the report documents how the Depression then hit the coalfields, caused by oil-demand replacing coal-demand, and how many pits closed in the 1920s and 1930s. This was in spite of the efforts of A. J. Cook, as leader of the Fed during the national strike of 1926. The strike, caused by the owners' simultaneous reduction of wages and increase of the working day by one hour, saw miners organizing around Cook's slogan 'Not a penny off the pay, not a minute on the day'.

(ii) The creative treatment

The creative treatment covers the same historical period, but concentrates on detailing *how* the story is to be got across. It gives W. T. Lewis – the owner of Lewis Merthyr colliery – a large chunk of the narration, detailing the scale of mining exports in the south Wales coalfield. He is 'a figure described as one of the greatest benefactors of the South Wales Coalfields', it is noted. A later note reads: 'W. T. Lewis was for many years the standing arbitrator between employer and employed making him highly qualified to talk about the class differences from an objective point of view.' The document continues:

> Lewis describes the Sliding Scale for wages, which he was instrumental in introducing in 1875 ... helping to give South Wales immunity from labour troubles for many years.
> With the rush to the Valleys, never before had there been so much work around or so much money to be made, and spent ... on things other than mere subsistence ... But underneath this facade it was really still a poor society, far removed from the grand life of the great landowners.
>
> (p.6)

Next, 'suddenly there is an enormous explosion and flashes of light, and from speakers behind the audience the noise of the whole ground rumbling builds dramatically. Everything goes black ... Images on the screen depict the horror of an explosion under-ground.' The narration switches to John Rees, a local Lewis Merthyr collier (and the father of Bryn Rees, who started off the narration at the beginning of the show):

> The bosses just wanted to get the best coal out as fast as they could, often at the expense of safety. That led to a lot of conflict, says John. He talks about the Cambrian strike of 1910 and the Tonypandy riots are conveyed with dramatic force through the First World War to the 1926 National Coal Strike.

A cameo shows 'the spot-lit figure of a union leader [and] we hear the voice of the Union leader shouting out, calling for solidarity.

On the window screens we see banners ... "Hungry as L", "S.O.S. – Struggle or Starve". It is 1926, the year of the general strike, when the miners were joined by all trade unions'. John Rees retires due to ill health 'glad to see the back of [mining].' There is no mention of the cause or outcome of the strike; instead, 'the main a/v screen takes the story through the years to the 50s ... enormous unemployment, emigration from the area, local people taking part in the hunger marches, Nationalisation in 1947'.

(iii) The final Bertie script

The creative treatment was then given over to Dai Smith, who was to produce the final scripts. What visitors finally hear is the following account of this same historical period, with Lewis Merthyr miner Bryn Rees as principal narrator:

> Skill and muscle power win the coal but its price, how much it fetched, was what decided how much a collier would get for every ton he cut. The Sliding Scale they called it. William Thomas Lewis thought that one up. Smart man, W. T. Lewis. By 1880, as well as his own collieries, he was looking after the mineral rights of the 3rd Marquis of Bute, the heir of the greatest land-owning family in South Wales.

Here, there is a cameo of Lewis at Cardiff Docks, with Lewis's voice describing the Rhondda's role at the heart of Britain's coal production. After another cameo, showing the marquis of Bute preparing plans for Castell Coch, Bryn continues:

> You lived with danger in the pit all the time. You 'ad to. But there had to be a better reward than a tidy funeral. In Tonypandy, in mid-Rhondda, in the winter of 1910, the men had had enough. When wage demands were turned down, they struck. 12,000 men came out. And stayed out for a year. Blacklegs were imported, to man the pits ... and police to protect them. There were fierce clashes. The middle of Tonypandy was wrecked. That's when they sent the troops in. And they stayed till the strike was smashed. New leaders were needed for these new times. The South Wales Mining Federation, the Fed as we called it, was demanding a minimum wage and public ownership of the pits. Some wanted workers control even. South Wales became a cockpit of strife, joining in with the rest of Britain's miners in the great strike of 1921 ... 3 months that lasted ... and 1926, was the general strike and lock-out, this

time for 9 months. The leader of the British miners then was our own A. J. Cook, who'd come from Somerset to work in the Rhondda and had first gone underground in the Trefor pit ...

[*Cameo of Cook*:] Not a penny off the pay, not a minute off the day! That must be our watchword, comrades! And not just because this fight is for decent wages and a decent home life for the miner and his family but because it is a cry from humanity to humanity for one thing – and that thing, my friends, is justice! Justice! Justice!

A. J. Cook, worn out by that struggle for justice died in 1931, aged just 47. And the miners fell back, away from unity, into their own areas. Defeated yes, but not beaten. The coal boom was over as the navies of the world switched to oil and foreign coalfields expanded. The great strikes seemed in vain. Nothing we did could stop the pits closing, men out of work for years on end and people fleeing the valleys.

Heritage chains

These three transformations illustrate the differing demands of interpretation at each link in the encoding chain. In the *Report of Research*, the coal-owners are described as 'remote entrepreneurs' concerned merely to increase profits by reducing wages. In the creative treatment, however, W. T. Lewis is transformed, bizarrely, into an 'objective', 'standing arbitrator' and 'one of the greatest benefactors of the South Wales coalfield'. He is also assigned a large chunk of the narration. In telling the particular story of *this* pit in *this* valley, rather than the story of 'coal owners' in general as in the *Report of Research*, the creative treatment confines the story to the major 'personalities' on the Rhondda and Lewis Merthyr stage. W.T. Lewis appears to be seen as a neutral voice, something which betrays a profound ignorance of the power relations of the early coalfields. He seems to be allotted a mediating position between the 'great landowners' and the miners, as though social conflict could be explained through a simple landowner–worker cultural divide. In short, the creative treatment simply writes out the complex historical events documented in the research report and reduces the variety of causes behind industrial strife to the single issue of inadequate pit safety.

However, in the final script, which is the outcome of a negotiated process and thus a compromise between the audio-visual producers and the scriptwriter (Professor Dai Smith), it is Bryn Rees rather than W. T. Lewis who has undisputed narrative authority. Bryn's framing of W. T. Lewis is ironic, characterizing him as a pompous and calculating figure – a 'smart man' who 'loved to talk'. The final script is, of necessity, greatly simplified and shortened compared with the research report. It is also focused on the local sphere of action at the expense of wider contextualization, and relates history in terms of local, colourful 'personalities' which allows the show to include visual cameos, dramatic exchanges and different voices. Yet the story that is finally presented does manage to achieve a surprisingly high level of historical detail, considering that it represents only ten minutes' worth of script. The creative treatment's exclusive preoccupation with dramatic staging and holding the gaze is supplemented in the final text by an attention to explanatory frameworks. Above all, it spells out a labourist understanding of history told from the miners' own perspective. What finally emerges is a hybrid, compromised narrative, trying to meet both the demands of exhibition for the tourist gaze, as well as the demands of political and cultural credibility in the local sphere.

IV. VISITING THE PAST

9

The rhetoric of heritage: placing the visitor

Heritage addresses a public audience. It offers visitors a theatre in which to imagine the past (as well as being a resource for local economic and political interests and a field of interpretative technologies, as discussed in other chapters). It is a public *text*, which – in the act of being 'read' by visitors – defines and elaborates a historical place-identity (Dicks, 1997b). But what does this identity look like to visitors? What place do they imagine they have visited as they pass back out through the turnstiles? Or, to put it another way, where have visitors actually *been* during their visit? This is an area of enquiry which has frequently been subsumed into discussions of texts themselves: scholars have often been content to present their own analyses of exhibition narratives as their 'meaning'. Against this, we need to recognize that the heritage text is designed for public communication. Since 'the public' is not a pregiven, homogeneous entity but rather an endless activity of visitor encounters with exhibitions, neglecting to explore visitors' readings of heritage rather reduces the public exhibition to a solipsistic and private encounter between critic and text. Studying the *rhetoric* of heritage means both identifying the ways in which the text itself addresses an audience *and* analysing how the visitor makes sense of the text.

This chapter and the next take our discussion into the realm of decoding (Hall, 1980). There is now a growing and multidisciplinary body of work on museum visiting, and there are several useful overviews of studies both in Britain and elsewhere (for example, Bicknell and Farmelo, 1994; Graf, 1994; Hooper-Greenhill, 1994, 1995; Uzzell, 1989). However, much of this work has been dominated by questionnaire surveys that severely limit our understanding of heritage communication. Market-research-style surveys have been much in evidence, categorizing text–visitor interaction through closed questions that itemize the 'information' that visitors absorb or the 'enjoyment' they obtain from the exhibition. Such individualistic approaches have been subjected to growing criticism as museums studies have moved away from administrative and market-dominated research into different areas of academic specialism. In particular, there has been a call for the use of interpretative, qualitative methods that can unpick the complex ways in which visitors interact with displays (for example, Hooper-Greenhill, 1994). More than this, however, it is necessary to consider how heritage exhibitions play a role in constructing public discourses of place and in shaping wider social and cultural relations, such as, for example, class.

1. Museums, class and cultural capital

The influence of social class on people's propensity to visit museums has long been a major preoccupation of the literature. Museums have become associated with high cultural values and high social class, stemming from their Victorian and Edwardian usage as reforming instruments to instil hegemonic scientific knowledge and 'civilizing' cultural values into the middle and lower classes (Bennett, 1995). As Bennett further points out, however, in practice museums' appropriation by social élites tended to undermine their supposedly educational purposes, as museum visiting became established as a means of communicating social-class distinctions. Indeed, the decontextualized and minimally informative modes of exhibition traditionally employed in collection museums suggest they intended to display the opacity of élite knowledge rather than to educate the 'masses' (see Lewis, 1980).

The connection between class and museum visiting received empirical confirmation and theoretical elaboration in Bourdieu and Darbel's well-known studies of art museum visiting in the 1960s (Bourdieu and Darbel, 1991 [1969]). They concluded that the art museum requires of its visitors considerable skills of artistic appreciation – knowledge in turn predicated on high levels of formal and informal education. In Bourdieu's approach, class exerts its influence not only through the material advantages offered by high levels of economic capital, but also through the translation of this capital into cultural knowledge, acquired through the cultivation of 'habitus' (Bourdieu, 1984). Museums, in his argument, are a key domain for the communication and display of 'cultural capital'.

Since Bourdieu's empirical surveys of the 1960s, social research has remained attuned to the class basis of museum visiting. Although there is no national statistical profile of visitors to UK museums, several surveys show that ABC1s are more likely than other social classes to visit museums. The Henley Centre's 1995 survey showed that 34 per cent of ABs and 23 per cent of C1s visited museums in 1993–4, as opposed to only 14 per cent of C2s and 10 per cent of DEs (Selwood et al., 1995). In addition, museum visitors tend already to be members of heritage organizations, to be in the 34–64 age bracket, and to be in full-time employment or retired on company pensions (East Midlands Museums Service, 1996). The East Midlands survey did, however, indicate that the proportion of C1, C2 and DE groups visiting museums might be higher than the Henley Centre data suggest.

There is, in fact, some debate over the accuracy of the assumption that museum visiting is predominantly a middle-class activity. There appear, first, to be regional differences in patterns of museum attendance. Myerscough (1988) surveyed museum visitors in different areas of the UK, and found that in Merseyside museum visitors were roughly equally divided between the ABC1 category and the C2DE group, with 53 per cent of visitors from the first half and 47 per cent from the second, while in Glasgow, only 30 per cent of visitors were C2DE and 70 per cent were ABC1. Hooper-Greenhill (1994) concludes from research like Myerscough's, which takes regional differences into account, that the standard categorization of museum visitors as predominantly middle class is not necessarily accurate. This is particularly the case where museum visitor statistics are disaggregated from art-gallery attendance, which does tend to attract a more consistently middle-class visitor body (Heady, 1984; Merriman, 1989).

Secondly, it is important to consider the different appeals of different kinds of heritage site. A survey of a sample of three categories of Welsh heritage attraction found that, whilst the managerial and professional classes were over-represented at all three categories of attraction, there was a higher percentage of visitors from the skilled, manual classes at industrial sites (the Welsh Slate Museum, Dolaucothi Gold Mine and Cefn Coed Colliery Museum) than there was at ecclesiastical sites or castles

(Light and Prentice, 1994). Similarly, Divall (1998) suggests that visitors to the National Railway Museum are closer to the socio-economic average of the general population than is commonly the case in other museums.

A major difficulty of museum surveys is that the term 'museum' embraces a wide range of diverse attractions, covering both art galleries at one end of the spectrum and heritage theme parks at the other. Recent trends such as the incorporation of themed and interactive elements into museums and the explosion in heritage centres offering simulated experiences rather than displayed collections (see chapter 2) make the question of classification increasingly difficult. As traditional museums, impelled by squeezes on public funding, reach out more insistently to a broader range of visitors, studies of their class profile become increasingly difficult to interpret. More research is needed here. It seems likely that the class profile of visitors to heritage sites such as the Rhondda Heritage Park, Wigan Pier, Yorvik Viking Centre and so on, will be more diverse than that for the unreconstructed national collection or art museum. Aggregating visitors to the Tate Gallery with those to Snibston Discovery Park is not likely to provide particularly illuminating insights into the links between social class and heritage consumption.

Motivations for visiting

Various motivations to visit museums and heritage centres have been suggested – including gazing on the exotic other (Urry, 1990), reminiscence, 'roots' and intergenerational family life-histories (Urry, 1996; Johnstone, 1998), leisurely wandering (Mellor, 1991), informal education (Light, 1995), entertainment (Walsh, 1992) and the communication and affirmation of social distinctions (Bourdieu, 1984; Merriman, 1991). Most current research concludes that cultural factors (such as interest in history and perception of museums in terms of cultural value), rather than structural ones (such as access to money and transport), provide the most convincing explanations for why people do or do not visit heritage attractions (Merriman, 1989). Several surveys show that heritage visitors have a high level of motivation to find out about the past, and that many have a developed interest in the particular historic period represented at the site they visit (Light and Prentice, 1994; Merriman, 1989).

Light's (1991) study of four ancient monuments in Wales, for example, set out to understand what visitors learnt from their encounter with the interpretative displays offered at the sites. Visitors were asked to select from certain statements after their visit – of which only one was the 'correct' one. The problem with such an approach is that it assumes that heritage communicates relatively unambiguous items of information that can be straightforwardly identified by testing visitors' pre- and post-visit understanding. This failing is replicated in much of the market research and museum administrative studies, which limit the investigation of visitor interpretation to the question of how the heritage 'product' is 'consumed' – as though heritage could be reduced to a clearly defined and measurable set of data. This neglects the ways in which information is situated both within wider ideological narratives of the past which structure individuals' historical understanding, and also within the particular biographical contexts of people's emotional and social lives. The complex intersection of culture and biography is difficult to map, but is a necessary challenge which a quantitative, informational model entirely neglects.

The ways in which visiting constructs particular 'visions of the past' cannot easily be identified and interpreted. For a start, it is important to distinguish between different kinds of visitor experience. Visitors to Llancaiach Fawr, the seventeenth-century restored manor house in south Wales, are likely to be interested in learning about domestic living arrangements of the time; the visitor to the Rhondda Heritage Park, on the other hand, may be primarily concerned with recovering personal memories or visiting the places connected with childhood stories told by grandparents. Whether heritage is about accruing specialist knowledge, simple entertainment or about recovering roots and memories will depend on the temporal, spatial, social *and* emotional proximity of visitors' lives to the heritage itself. This suggests that visitor studies need to ask quite probing questions about the visitor's own understanding of history, the past and their relation to the self.

2. Historical knowledge and consciousness

People's historical consciousness is not just a collection of historical information. However, little is known about how visitors actually make sense of heritage displays. The ways in which visitors position and define the past – as 'vanishing other', or as aids to understanding the present, for example – are important in framing heritage as a source of knowledge and information about the past. The quantification of who visits museums and what they learn is, consequently, less illuminating for the present purposes than the question of visitors' interpretative frameworks. The broad-brush approach of Bourdieu and Darbel (1991), for example, does not enable us to understand the different messages and impressions of the past that museum visitors take away with them as they pass back out through the turnstiles. A more qualitative approach, focused on a particular heritage museum, can allow us to understand how the encoding strategies employed in professional interpretative strategies (see last chapter) are given meaning through the active decoding practices in which visitors engage. This allows us to compare the rhetorical construction of meaning by designers with the rhetorical construction of meaning by visitors (see Silverstone, 1989). Such a task is initiated in the present chapter, while the next chapter explores visitors' interpretative frameworks more closely.

Various methodological approaches have been utilized in an attempt to understand how visitors respond to museum displays. In a study of a cross-cultural anthropology exhibition in the Birmingham Museum and Art Gallery, for example, Jane Peirson Jones (1995) devised nine different methods of visitor research. They included an exit questionnaire, covert observation of visitors' paths through the exhibition, a post-visit follow-up study of visitors' memories and an analysis of visitors' written comments. On the basis of these enquiries, the researchers concluded that 'quality learning' was taking place at the exhibition, something which occurs when 'old and existing beliefs are permanently discarded in favour of new propositions which are found to be relevant and intelligible' (Peirson Jones, 1995: 268). This was evidenced in visitors' affirmations that particular exhibits raised new questions in their minds and dislodged existing assumptions about other cultures. The exhibition did, it seem, enable new forms of knowledge to take shape in visitors' minds.

This study, though offering a valuable contribution and employing quite sophisticated and innovative methods of enquiry, nevertheless relies on an abstracted model of communication. It sought to identify learning moments and messages in visitors' interactions with different exhibits. Through comparing an exhibit's thematic content with visitors' responses to it, the extent to which effective communication has occurred was measured. Museum communication is thus seen as a 'loop' connecting exhibitions and their visitors, so that visitors' perceptions are seen as responses to stimuli issuing from the content of exhibitions (see also Hooper-Greenhill, 1995). The problem with this approach is that it tends to isolate historical understanding from its embedding in wider ideological and cultural discourses, by conceiving of that knowledge as the outcome of the museum's self-contained dynamic of message and response. It thereby neglects to situate visitors' knowledge within the contexts of their lives as social subjects and within the cultural frameworks that organise knowledge into public discourses of time and space.

A more sociological approach would want to examine how visitors' social positioning and cultural identifications (including class, ethnic and generational understandings) along with their personal biographies and family histories, shape their understanding of displayed times and places. This could be achieved through adopting an ethnographic approach which would investigate a range of different domains for the mediation of history in people's lives. There has been a tendency, particularly in museum market research and in many of the quantitative surveys, to delineate visitor characteristics or to categorize visitor knowledge rather than to investigate the social contexts of people's various engagements with the past and with place. This involves attending to the visit as part of people's more general political and cultural understanding, producing an ethnographic account of how historical knowledge is configured in real social contexts.

Fyfe and Ross's (1996) study of heritage sensibilities in Stoke goes beyond an inquiry into visitor markets or the attributes of individuals and is based instead on an extended piece of locality-based ethnography. In this study, inquiry was not confined to the post-visit interview, but reached instead into households in a heritage area (Stoke-on-Trent). Instead of a closed-question survey approach, participants were 'invited to reflect at length on their lives, their uses of non-work time, their social backgrounds, consumption, living in Stoke, and their senses of place and time' (1996:131). The authors wanted to examine how class could be understood as a cultural matrix of experiences rather than reducing it to a variable such as male occupation. Different class experiences shape different orientations to the past: for example, museum visiting may be refracted through the lens of a nostalgia for community based on an attachment to 'natural' values in the past, or it may be shaped by a more cosmopolitan appreciation of specialist, high-cultural and aesthetic knowledge which has little to do with personal attachments to place. Such an approach allows us to see how wider cultural codes intersect with individuals' own biographical occupational and familial experiences.

Biography/culture

Heritage displays offer a space for the intertwining of public, exhibitionary space and private, biographical space. Crang (1994) appropriates the term 'journeys' to refer to the multiple ways in which heritage provides an intersection between public narratives and people's own biographies and experiences. Rather than concentrating on the abstracted analyses and descriptions of the heritage debate, where writers are preoccupied with producing 'maps' which unify heritage into a single field, we should be examining the different journeys that visitors construct as they appropriate the space–time narratives of the displays into their own life stories. Viewed in this way, heritage is a constantly shifting performance, in which 'to each exhibit, people bring a host of metonymic others – personal resonances that are set off, memories and connections triggered by the display' (Crang, 1994: 345). In this perspective, heritage is not so much sight-seeing (the public display of the other) as cultural biography (the public recognition of the self and its stories). And these stories are not merely internal monologues inside visitors' minds, but are re-enacted and multiplied through the conversations and social interactions of visitors in their groups – visiting together as families, couples, friends, societies, schools and so on (see McManus, 1989).

Such journeys are not only the pathways that visitors plot as they move through and interpret exhibitions, but are also the metaphorical or literal journeys which constitute the social life stories of individuals. Geographical journeys from place to place, for example, provide one source of heritage-laden biography. The study by Fyfe and Ross mentioned above points to the importance of locality – in terms of geographical fixity or displacement – in different kinds of class habitus. The geographical location of early memories – a changed but enduring 'here', for example, or a half-forgotten but enticing 'there' – provides a narrative for understanding the past as a journey. Historical exhibitions, particularly of the vernacular, new-heritage kind, activate these different narratives of the self. As Johnstone (1998) suggests, heritage museums can function in this way as 'substitute heirlooms'. They preserve the material culture of past generations that has gradually disappeared from families' own homes, thereby offering visitors the pleasure of seeing 'their own' personal realm displayed and verified in the public collection – 'my granny had one of those!'.

This is particularly the case where family members have become cut off from previous generations, through geographical displacement in various experiences of diaspora. These relocations do not only reflect voluntary middle-class mobility; they are also the result of forced industrial and colonial migrations, producing generations of families who have had to leave areas to find work. This in turn creates a potential swathe of descendants wanting to return much later on as part of a recovery of 'roots' and the elaboration of a family history. These autobiographies are not, it should be reiterated, the products of purely internal, personal reflection conducted in the private realm of the individual mind. Instead, these journeys of the self and its past are shaped into narratives and *made sense of* through the public, collective stories that circulate both within and outside the heritage museum itself. Heritage culture thus grants the private self a public narrative: in place of the solitary perusal of a personal snapshot collection, heritage offers the visitor collective recognition by organizing these snapshots into epic narratives and cultural figures and putting them on public display.

Self/other

The biography/culture intersection occupied by heritage suggests a particular category of tourist gaze – one which seeks the means of encountering or fantasizing the self *as other*. The quality of otherness is necessarily part of the heritage gaze, if only through its temporality – we are gazing on the past rather than the present. However, there are multiple gradations of otherness involved here, from a gaze which mirrors the self (as in local mining families

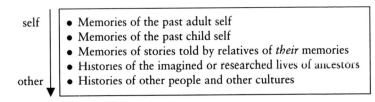

self
- Memories of the past adult self
- Memories of the past child self
- Memories of stories told by relatives of *their* memories
- Histories of the imagined or researched lives of ancestors

other
- Histories of other people and other cultures

FIGURE 9.1 Self/other relations potentially set up by heritage

visiting a local mining museum) to one which reflects the other (as in Westerners visiting an ethnographic museum of African culture).

In Figure 9.1, tracing the arrow down, there is an increasing distance between the heritage on display and its relation to the visitor-self. This movement also, arguably, entails a weakening of the visitor's demand for experiential detail in the display – that is, for the idiosyncratic and everyday particularities of lived memory. A childhood experience of profound change – occasioned by geographical migration, perhaps, or the sudden loss of an industry that had previously defined the home town and one's family life – may produce in adults a strong desire to gaze again on those remembered childhood vistas. Here, the historical detail provided by the display will be considered sufficiently authentic only if it stimulates personal recognition and accords with childhood memories. Conversely, if there is no self-identification with the heritage on display, as in the case of the outside, disinterested visitor looking to accrue anthropological knowledge, perhaps, or simply to journey into the past, the demand for historical detail is motivated quite differently. The authenticity of the exhibition will be judged more in terms of its accordance with received ideas about the subject on display than by memories or personal experience.

This self/other distinction is a dimension of the heritage gaze which is often neglected in discussions which tend to take for granted its 'othering' functions. Urry's (1990) distinction between the collective versus romantic tourist gazes captures something of this relation, in that the first involves gazing on the familiar while the second involves gazing on the awe-inspiring and the auratic. Yet Urry's argument is focused on the gregarious versus solitary aspects of the distinction, which is not perhaps its most significant element. Rather, it is the social and cultural distance between audience and text which seems to be important. The self-recognition effect of vernacular heritage that I am describing depends on the degree of cultural and biographical proximity between the exhibited world of the heritage subjects and the lived world of the visitor. In this sense, academic disputes about the objectivity and historical accuracy of heritage texts may be an effect of a particular text–reader relation where the reader occupies the position of the informed outsider judging the historical authenticity of exhibitions on the basis of formal, acquired knowledge. Other, 'closer' and more subjective text–reader relations may judge authenticity on a different basis, that is, through the degree of recognizability and familiarity the exhibition sets up between the historical world and the visitor's stock of family memories.

Authenticity, then, is produced in the interaction *between* exhibition and visitor, text and reader, rather than being a property of the text itself. This suggests that investigating the cultural proximity between visitors' lives and the lives 'in the texts' is a necessary dimension of understanding heritage communication. Moreover, it also has implications for understanding the relation between encoding and decoding, since one would need to consider whether the texts themselves succeed in inviting these potential moments of self-recognition on the visitor's part – particularly if they are oriented to an audience conceived of as the tourist from afar. To this end, one would need to examine how the visitor is 'imagined' or addressed by the displays, a question which concerns the *rhetoric* of exhibition (see Silverstone, 1989). This rhetoric in turn depends on strategies of encoding. For instance, the discussion of encoding in the Rhondda case-study suggests that the area's heritage was conceived by its designers as a product to be consumed largely by non-locals. If the rhetoric of the exhibitions positions the visitor as 'other', then the historiography may be judged bland or lacking by those visitors seeking self-identifications with their own past on display. This is a faultline that is explored further in the next chapter.

3. *Placing the Rhondda visitor*

One way of exploring these self/other relations is to examine the relations between visitors and the way of life represented in heritage texts. In the case of local vernacular heritage, the question of visitors' relations to the locality is of particular importance. Below, I discuss the question of social class and place in relation to a small-scale visitor study (see Appendix 2) carried out at the Rhondda Heritage Park, a full account of which is provided in the next chapter. As a way of mapping the objective social and spatial connections between visitors and the place-identity of the exhibitions, I shall examine the provenance and social profile of these visitors to the Rhondda. (The limits of such an exercise should be borne in mind, however, in that it is vital to consider the ways in which these formal links are actually experienced as subjective identifications. That is a task requiring in-depth interpretative analysis, and one which I shall leave until the next chapter.) In the final section below, I turn once more to a discussion of encoding at the Rhondda Heritage Park – but this time to explore how the visitor is imagined or *placed* by the interpretative practices of display design.

The Rhondda visitor and social class

The visitor study discussed here was conducted at the Rhondda Heritage Park during a three-day period in August 1995. The sample of visitors was recruited at random by requesting post-visit interviews with naturally occurring groups who were waiting to join the guided tour in the museum's reception area. In all, twenty groups were interviewed, comprising forty-five adults and a number of children.[1] Many of these visitor-groups were families, both two-generational and three-generational, although there were also friendship groups amongst the sample. Whilst the average age of the adults, at forty-six years, accords with other research (for example, Eckstein and Feist, 1991), it would appear that the class profile of the interview sample was somewhat at odds with other visitor surveys. In particular, a survey by Prentice et al. (1993) studied 207 visitors to *Black Gold* during August 1993. They found that no fewer than 63 per cent of summer visitors to the RHP were from social classes A or B, and that more than a third (37 per cent) of visitors had a university degree, with only 11 per cent holding no formal qualifications. Prentice et al. conclude that 'the predominantly working-class heritage presented at the Park is being interpreted to essentially middle-class contemporary visitors' (1993: 142). This suggests that there is a potential social and cultural as well as temporal distance between the visitors and the heritage subjects on display.

The class profile of the visitor sample interviewed by the author contrasts strongly with the 1993 study. Here, only 9 per cent of visitors interviewed were from social grades A and B. The largest group in the sample (53 per cent) was the C1s and C2s, although no fewer than 38 per cent were from grades D and E[2] (see Figure 9.2). In terms of the manual/non-manual worker divide, Prentice et al. (1993) found that 70 per cent of RHP visitors came from non-manual households (the ABC1 category), and 30 per cent from manual households. As Figure 9.3 shows, my sample was much more evenly distributed, with roughly half (49 per cent) from the non-manual and half (51 per cent) from the manual grades (see Figure 9.2).

Furthermore, the class identity of the present interview sample is confirmed in terms of educational attainment, with only 13 per cent holding a degree or higher qualification and those with no formal qualifications comprising 40 per cent. One way of accounting for the differences might be that Prentice et al. classified visitors according to head of household, rather than on an individual basis as in the present study (though this is not made clear in the 1993 report). However, reclassifying my interview sample in this way actually increases the discrepancy between the two pieces of research.[3] Whilst Prentice et al. found a 70/30 non-manual/manual divide in their visitors to *Black Gold*, my interview sample was divided either 49/51 (based on individuals' occupations) or 40/60 (based on male head of household).

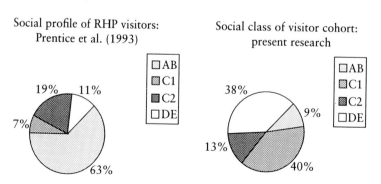

Social profile of RHP visitors: Prentice et al. (1993)

□ AB
▨ C1
▩ C2
□ DE

19%   11%
7%
63%

Social class of visitor cohort: present research

□ AB
▨ C1
▩ C2
□ DE

38%
9%
13%
40%

FIGURE 9.2 Social profile of RHP visitors

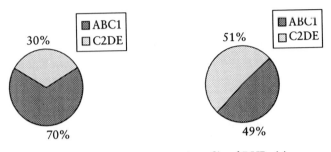

FIGURE 9.3 Manual/non-manual profile of RHP visitors

It should of course be recognized that my sample (forty-five individuals) is too small to be compared with the 1993 research (207 individuals), and that my intention was not, in any case, to conduct a representative survey of RHP visitors that could be generalized to the wider population. The differences are, however, puzzling. Most likely is the possibility that the earlier study included a larger number of younger visitors, which would help explain the lower incidence of manual workers, as well as the higher incidence of formal qualifications. There is also the possibility of a merely fortuitous higher incidence of C2DE visitors on the three days in which I carried out my interviews. My sample does, however, accord with some of the research reported in section 1 above, that is, that class profiles of visitors to the more local and 'popular' heritage attractions are closer to those of the general population than those to traditional collection museums.

The Rhondda visitor and locality

There is one important point of similarity between the two visitor studies, however. Prentice et al. (1993) found that no fewer than 69 per cent of visitors to the RHP claimed links with the south Wales Valleys, and 65 per cent named an interest in local history and in the local area as a 'very important' motivation for visiting the RHP (1993: 144). They found, moreover, that most visitors to the park are not tourists as such but are local in provenance, making a day trip out from home. Similarly, in the present study, it was striking how many visitors had connections with either the Rhondda or the mining industry and, in a significant number of cases, both. In fact, nearly all of the visitors interviewed claimed that they had some kind of connection with the heritage on display at the Park. This was largely due to the high proportion of visitors who could be termed *returnees*: people whose families had at some time moved away from the Valleys and who were now on return trips to the region, usually bringing friends or family members to whom they were showing their history. As Busty, one of the guides currently working at the Park told me:

> You can typecast some visitors. They're descendants of people who left the Rhondda or left the Valleys of south Wales years ago, settled in other places and now come back here, you know. A lot of these people were born in places like this, here and around. And they hear stories from their grandparents, and this is the Rhondda and it tells a story, you know. They might not be from the Rhondda, they might be from the Rhymney Valley, but it would be the same way of life. So, in an hour and a quarter here, the stories they've heard from the grandparents, they can put into pictures.

In the visitor sample, no fewer than fifteen of the twenty groups (75 per cent) had specific family connections to the Rhondda *and* to the local coalmining industry (Table 9.1). Of the five groups without these dual links, four had other connections either to the Valleys or to mining. In fact, only one group – group 11 – conformed to the tourist-from-afar category, in that they had no local or mining links at all and were simply holidaying in the area. The pattern of visitors' linkages with the Rhondda coal industry is shown in Table 9.1.

This table shows well how thoroughly this group of visitors is infused with family links to both the local area and its major industry. Indeed, it would not be improbable, were one to trace some of the links in more detail, for a number of historical common acquaintances and ancestral family networks to emerge among this collection of complete strangers. Many of them are bringing to the museum a spouse, friend or relative who has no link to the local area, and to whom they are introducing the setting of their childhoods or of their handed-down memories. A couple of them are on specific trips of rediscovery, from the Rhondda diaspora in Canada and New Zealand (groups 1 and 10). If a large number of visitors to the Rhondda have these local links, this suggests that they

TABLE 9.1 The nature of visitors' links with the Rhondda and its
coal industry

Group	Nature of links with Rhondda and local coalmining
1: Mr A	Mr A's grandparents were from Tonypandy mining families, though they emigrated to Canada before his mother was born.
2: Mr/Mrs B	Both Mr and Mrs B had uncles who worked in Rhondda collieries.
3: Mr/Mrs C	Mrs C's grandfather lived in Trehafod, next to the Lewis Merthyr colliery, though worked as a builder rather than as a miner.
4: Mr/Mrs D	Mrs D's mother's family worked in Rhondda mines and lived in Treherbert.
5: Mr/Mrs E; Mrs/Ms W	Mrs W was born in Porth and her father was a Rhondda haulier at Cymmer colliery. Mr E's father was a miner in Tredegar (Gwent valleys).
6: Mr/Mrs G	Mr G currently worked as a Yorkshire mining surveyor.
7: Mr/Mrs G1	Mrs G's family came from Treorchy in the Rhondda, and both her grandfather and uncle worked in Cymmer colliery.
8: Mr/Mrs H	Born and bred in Cardiff, though they had several friends who worked in the mines.
9: Mr/Mrs J; Ms. E	Mr J was born and bred in Ystrad, Rhondda, where his uncles and brothers were coalminers. Ms E was also born and bred in the Rhondda, and is the daughter of a Rhondda miner.
10: Ms L + Mr E1	Mr E's father was a miner in Maerdy colliery, in the Rhondda, until he emigrated to New Zealand in 1970. His aunt still lives in Maerdy, where the couple – who had travelled from New Zealand – were guests at the time of interview.
11: Mr/Mrs M	This group comes from Northern Ireland, and its members have no links with the Rhondda or mining.
12: Ms J	Born and bred in the Rhondda, Ms J's father and uncles were colliers in Maerdy and Tylorstown, in the Rhondda. Her father-in-law worked in Lewis Merthyr. She moved to north Wales six years ago.
13: Mr/Mrs P	Mr P was born and bred in Barry, South Glamorgan, but went to a Welsh school in Pontypridd, at the mouth of the Rhondda Valley. His family were originally miners in Wrexham, north Wales.
14: Mr/Mrs P1; Mr/Mrs P2	The two couples are cousins. Mrs P1 was born and bred in the Rhondda, where her father and grandfather were miners.

(continued)

Group	Nature of links with Rhondda and local coalmining
15: Mr/Mrs R	Mrs R was born in Tonypandy, Rhondda, where her father was briefly a coalminer, and all her uncles worked in the mines.
16: Mr R1; Ms P2	Mr R1 was born and bred in Trealaw in the Rhondda, where his father, cousins, grandfathers and father were all miners.
17: Mr/Mrs W1; Mrs L1	Mrs W was born in Porth, in the Rhondda, the daughter of a Lewis Merthyr miner, before moving to London. Mrs L1 was born and bred in Tonteg, Rhondda, and all her husband's family were miners.
18: Mr/Mrs W2	Mr W2 was born and bred in Bedwas, though his family are from the Rhondda, where his grandfather was a miner.
19: Mr/Mrs W3 Jr; Mrs W3 Sr	Mrs W3 Jr was born and bred in Tonyrefail near the Rhondda. All of Mrs W3 Sr's family worked in the collieries of Abertillery and Six Bells.
20: Mr/Mrs W4	Mrs W4's grandfather was a Yorkshire miner. Her mother worked in Windsor colliery as a nurse when the family moved down to south Wales.

may be looking for a reflection of their own historical connections to place rather than seeking the 'vanishing other' as objects of an anthropological tourist gaze.[4]

This is not to argue, however, that just because visitors are from south Wales they necessarily possess a meaningful sense of personal connection to the history presented in the museum. On the contrary, the considerable cultural-spatial differences within south Wales mean that the constructs of The Valleys and of 'the archetypal mining community' may be entirely 'other' to the visitor from, say, Newport or the Vale of Glamorgan. Indeed, it is very difficult to draw any reliable conclusions about visitors' identifications with heritage representations from questions that simply ask about their provenance or social class. Nevertheless, the large number of family connections to the mining industry do suggest both a geographical and a class proximity, even if this is in the fairly distant past. It also suggests that the designers of the Rhondda Heritage Park were making some rather misguided assumptions when they envisaged their major consumer base as the outside tourist-from-afar. If visitors are predominantly on 'voyages of rediscovery', retracing their family roots, this suggests a different text–audience relationship than that set up by the encoding process. As we shall now see, the encoders' imagined visitor was a passive spectator of an alien world, rather than an interested journeyer through a family past.

4. The rhetoric of display: the visitor as cultural novice

Given these characteristics of RHP visitors, how is the public addressed in its exhibitionary rhetoric? For all the marketing pronouncements insisting on its differentiation from traditional museums, currently fashionable principles of interactivity find little expression here. Instead, the public is principally addressed as spectator, not participant. In contrast to the interactive technologies developed recently in science museums, which allot an experimentalist, proactive role to visitors (see Barry, 1998), the RHP has almost no exhibits that could be termed properly interactive. It is rather the visitor's gaze which is constantly solicited. While the Museum of Welsh Life and other open-air heritage museums, such as Beamish, Ironbridge Gorge or the Black Country Museum invite visitors to construct their own itineraries through an open-air site, the Rhondda Heritage Park guided tour largely restricts the visiting experience to a spectatorial role. This is not to say that the visitor is allotted only a passive form of interaction, for – as in televisual viewing – the consumption of texts is an active practice of reading and decoding rather than a matter of passive absorption.

The visitor tour at the Rhondda consists of communicative encounters between visitors, human guides and audio-visual technology. The visitor's communicative role takes two forms: that of the *film spectator* in the case of *Black Gold*, the three-part audio-visual element, and *the cultural novice* in *A Shift in Time*, the underground experience. In the former, the visitors sit in darkened auditoria, listening and watching as the slide shows and narrative weave their stories. In the latter, the visitors are physically led on a journey through an alien environment – the colliery buildings and underground roadways – tutored by their mentor, the guide. The latter is the more interactive domain, in that visitors are encouraged – in the manner of cultural initiates – to ask questions and to engage in conversation with their guide. The tour as a whole invites the visitor to embark on a cumulative journey of revelation. While free-flow galleries in traditional museums tend to disaggregate historical knowledge into localized segments displayed by each exhibit in a pick-and-mix layout, the tour-guide model rather encourages the opposite – a gradual inculcation into a total, represented world revealing an unfolding story to a spellbound audience. In constructing the visitor experience, professional interpreters set themselves the task of ensuring that visitors would be enthralled and interested – above all not bored or indifferent. Visitors are imagined as uninitiated yet demanding media consumers, looking for emotional engagement rather than detailed knowledge, as we shall see below.

The audience as spectator

The idea of using multimedia or audio-visual shows at the Rhondda to narrate the 'story of coal' had been inherited from the very first feasibility study of 1984. By the time of the major design for the visitor experience in 1989, this strategy had become the key foundation of the attraction. Its final achievement was in *Black Gold*, where visitors' attention is divided between the slide screen suspended high in the roof space of the winding houses, illuminated dioramas or *tableaux vivants* in different parts of the buildings and soundscapes issuing from the darkness all around. The *Black Gold* lead designer explained how he approached the design of the dioramas:

> You're not pulling the wool over their eyes. You're not saying, 'This *is* Castell Coch'. You're just using it as a backdrop to telling a story. But the fact that it's *this* big ... Well, we could have just put a couple of monitors there, we could have put some nice seats in, and we could have told the same story. But I don't think it would have had the same impact. It's the scale, you know, it's a big subject, big equipment, it needs that kind of scale of interpretation ... But you're not kidding anyone, are you? Nobody thinks that is Castell Coch, or that is the dock side. They're only to set the story off, just like a little stage set.
>
> (Personal interview with lead designer)

Thus, the project of telling a story is bound up with the parallel aim of constructing a highly visual and auditory environment that will hold the visitor's attention and have 'impact'. A sense of reality is not created through naturalistic reconstruction but through a sensory environment that evokes the 'feel' of the past. The most common metaphor used for the design work was that of the 'black box':

> It's a black box to me, you know. Like an artist starts off with a white canvas, we start off with a black room. It's brilliant. We start off with a black room and we sit people in a black room and it's magical ... What you illuminate is what people see. So you can use the place as you want to use it ... portraying the bits that fit into the story ... Just using the bits you need to use. The place becomes a theatre.
>
> (Personal interview with member of design team)

Creating authenticity does not, therefore, consist in verbal detail or iconic accuracy but in the dynamics of a show, whereby visitors are subject to a range of technologies that manipulate the senses.

There are similarities here with the televisual mode of representation, though the big screen and sound effects make a comparison with the cinema more apt. In the cinema, the audience is particularly 'under the spell' of the projected images, due to the totally controlled environment in which the spectacle unfolds (Ellis, 1982). However, the experience is even more compelling in *Black Gold* due to the technique of supplementing the screen images with three-dimensional dioramas and light sequences. The designer describes how he was aiming to make the visitor more 'receptive' by using multimedia techniques:

> The mixed media thing is when you're talking about smell and scale, not only the different media but the different scale of things. Being able to do something life-size, being able to create an environment where you can make it cold, make it hot if you want, you can make it smell if you want ... That's interpretation. It's stimulating the senses ... You become much more receptive then to the information that's being given.
>
> (Personal interview with member of *Black Gold* design team)

The aim is to enthral the audience, so that they become more pliable, more under the spell of the interpreted environment.

This focus on sensory experience has consequences for the type of story that is sought out by the professional interpreters. The story must produce the variation in audience feeling and mood at which the designer is aiming as part of the strategy of holding the gaze:

Obviously you need an opening that really engages people, that's what you're looking for, something that just draws them in to the story quite quickly ... You're looking for those sudden, you know, like the explosions, you're looking for sudden moments like that, you're looking for moments when people suddenly stop and think, 'God!', you know, 'was it really as bad as that?' And then you go for more dramatic moments like, you know, the fighting, where you get the conflict between the miners and the police ... a bit of action, you know, and that way, everything sort of comes alive again. Then you get more philosophical sort of passages. It's just story-telling in the traditional sense ... Just like any film maker.

(Personal interview with member of production team, *Black Gold*)

This emphasis on directing and controlling visitors' responses means that the story itself is understood as a piece of entertainment, capable of provoking specifiable responses at particular moments.

The spectator as outsider

The imagined audience is one that craves constant stimulation. Encoding frames the communication as an attention-holding novelty – and not a reflection of prior knowledge, as in memorialism. The professional skills required are all understood as the routine business of 'telling stories' and 'making films', in which members of the audience are positioned as the recipients of an attention-grabbing story. This involves addressing the audience as spectators of an imagined world, composed of signs and images quite distinct from and alien to their own lives. The audio-visual team described how they put the creative treatment together and assembled three stories from the mass of available historical detail:

D: It's what's significant to you – there's always subjects you'll come across that are new to you and it's what *strikes* you ...
T: What *hits* you as individuals ...
D: And what you think would strike your kids, or your wife. You know, that's what I suppose you're going for in the storyline, in the way that it's produced, isn't it? ... If it's new to *you* ... so whatever comes across as *amazing* or *remarkable* or *interesting* ... you're fairly sure that the visitor's going to find the same.
T: If you are *new to something* ... that's why it would probably be more difficult if it was a producer in south Wales, to give such an

objective ... well, assuming it was objective in people's eyes, but in
order to have an objective view of a situation, you have to be quite
removed from it ... and pick out a few features of a story that, that
make *an impact*. And *make people remember it*, and enjoy what they
see. I think that's important.
 (Personal interview with members of production team; my emphasis)

The assumption here is that visitors will be like the interpreters
themselves – novices and outsiders to the Rhondda's history. The
communicated story has to be that which will 'strike' the audience
through its novelty and difference from their own lives. This can
only be achieved by an outsider looking in – the 'view from the
hills'.

In this way, much of the encoding and planning processes in the
Rhondda project were dominated by an exhibitionary discourse
emphasizing the cultural strangeness of the Rhondda as imagined
community (chapter 8). This clashed with memorialist concerns to
preserve the authentically detailed and the familiar (chapter 7). The
presupposition of the planners at the RHP that the attraction was to
pull in hundreds of thousands of visitors from afar, together with
the emphasis on interpretation as an outside, non-local prerogative,
combined to envisage the visitor and the displays as culturally and
socially separated. This means that the displays' principal address
may be at odds with the expectations or knowledge-base of its
major visitor constituency.

The visitor as returnee

This 'othering' approach contrasts with the approach of the guides
at the Rhondda Heritage Park, who recognize that the visitor is
likely to have a biographical connection with the Rhondda and its
history:

I think what we give is the reality of it. The realism. They come here and
they look at this place and they say, 'Well, I know where my father
worked now, I know where my grandfather worked', or – these days –
'I know where my great-grandfather worked'. And then anything else
really is, as far as I'm concerned, peripheral to that. The main point is
the personal experience from their point of view. The facts and figures
don't really matter so much; they're just something to say as you take
them around. But it's the feeling, the putting into sort of bricks and

mortar or timber, and whatever. What they've learnt in an academic situation they can then relate to their own past and their own family, and have some understanding of what it was all about.

(Personal interview with Ron, one of the guides at the museum)

In the underground part of the tour, *A Shift in Time*, visitors have the opportunity to explore these family connections further. Being able to see 'what it was really like' for grandparents and relatives involves a different decoding relationship to the displays than being engrossed in a spectacle of 'other worlds'. There is, thus, in the guided parts of the tour (*A Shift in Time* – the colliery lamproom, headgear and underground roadways) the possibility of human interaction between experts (guides) and novices (visitors) in which visitors can also talk about their own knowledge and memories. A space is created for this interaction since guides themselves are telling their own personal stories and anecdotes as they take the group around. However, the social, non-work aspects of this local knowledge – those that centre on the memories of place rather than industry – are not the focus in this part of the tour. It is rather the details of colliery work itself (experiences confined to men working as miners) that are under the spotlight. Thus, the opportunities for more interactive and communicative engagement with history are confined to encounters with the colliery as place of work, whilst the 'social life of place' is presented to visitors as a filmic spectacle requiring a hushed audience. The opportunity, therefore, for visitors to explore and discuss the lives of, for example, female ancestors cannot be taken up so easily.

The extent to which visitors do interact with guides during *A Shift in Time* varies considerably, as repeated participant observation of many such tours reveals. From the guides' perspectives, they are having to manage groups in which there may be a wide spectrum of expertise and experience in relation to the coalmining industry. One major source of concern for guides, who themselves are ex-miners, is the credibility of the underground space in the eyes of other visiting ex-miners. This particular category of returnee has the most critical gaze in relation to the material authenticity of the recreated roadways. If the underground reconstruction does not ring true for other ex-miners, the guides themselves feel exposed to ridicule. Similarly, the ex-miner visitor is a knowing insider who can easily 'catch out' the guide who stumbles on small details or misrepresents

the idiosyncratic experiences of different miners. As Gary, one of
the guides, describes:

> Some of the boys I worked with at the pit have come over here. And I've
> taken some around. And I hate it because you have that little smile –
> because you do exaggerate. You have that little wiry smile at the back:
> 'You bull-shitting bastard!' But at the end of the tour they love it. They
> talk about their own experiences.

Such a visitor contrasts strongly with the wide-eyed schoolchild, the
visiting tourist and the returnee who left the area long ago and has
never seen the inside of a coalmine. All of these different kinds
of self/other relation are set into motion by local, vernacular
heritage – and it is a tall order for exhibitions to enable them all to
be adequately represented, and thus for authenticity to be achieved
in all its different guises. In the next and final chapter I take these
questions further by examining in detail how visitors' relations to
the subjects of heritage shape their interaction with the exhibitions,
and how the imagined community of the 'people of the Rhondda'
assumes a form and identity in visitors' discourse.

10
Visiting the Rhondda

Heritage is a communicative encounter between visitors, museum personnel and exhibitions. Visitors are not on the receiving end of messages emanating from within the exhibition; rather, these messages are constructed in their interaction with the texts. Decoding is an active practice of untangling the multilayered narratives, impressions, ideas and images of heritage, which visitors assimilate into their existing repertoires of historical knowledge. The self/other and biography/culture relations explored in the last chapter are played out in terms of visitors' own memories, knowledge and expectations during their encounter with history. Thus, we cannot talk about the 'meaning' of particular heritage exhibitions in isolation from the sense-making interpretative activities in which visitors are engaged.

This chapter presents further analysis from the RHP visitor study. The research consists of semi-structured, in-depth interviews carried out with twenty visitor groups (comprising forty-five individuals in total) over a period of three days in summer 1995. Visitors were asked to say briefly what they already knew about the Rhondda before they started their visit, and then they were interviewed again at length immediately after they had finished it.[1] In the post-visit interview, they recounted what they had seen and heard, and described how they would now characterize the Rhondda, the people who lived there and the history of the area. Visitor decoding was analysed along three principal axes: how visitors imagined the past (the history of the Rhondda), place (the Rhondda as community) and the social (mining as a way of life).

In all three of these axes, it is not only a question of what forms each imaginary takes, but how the self is positioned in relation to that imaginary. So, for example, if visitors imagine the Rhondda as a traditional close-knit mining community, is this as object of a distanced, anthropological gaze which views it as a 'vanishing other'? Or is this place imagined as part of the self's own subjective history, and thus peopled with remembered characters, events and situations that are familiar and concrete? These relations of self are important dimensions of heritage communication and serve to underline the argument that heritage decoding is not only about the communication of identifiable messages or information, but also about visitors' cultural and biographical relations with the past.

1. Visiting the past

How do visitors characterize the 'thing' which is represented in heritage exhibitions? Is it, for example, a coherent story, a mêlée of impressions, an evocation of the 'old days'? Textual rhetoric may address the visitor as 'other', but we cannot assume that visitors position themselves in relation to the text in the same way. For instance, what might to the critic seem a powerful and coherent ideological narrative may be to the visitor simply a springboard for their own memories. Visitors may not pay much attention to 'the story' itself, whilst still engaging quite profoundly with certain aspects of the history presented. The text's authority to define the past as a distinctive place in visitors' minds will depend on how elaborated a sense of that past the visitor already has. Those that have close biographical relations with the history presented are likely to judge its authenticity on a different basis from those for whom that history is a distant and vague apprehension of the 'old days'.

The Rhondda interview data analysed by the author suggest visitors adopt three different decoding *orientations* to the history on display, each of which accords the texts of *Black Gold* a different degree of authority. They correspond to different self/other relations, or different relations of proximity, with the Rhondda and its past. Moreover, they deploy different kinds of knowledge – about history as a subject, about family 'roots' and about home and self-identity.[2]

(i) Distant places

In the *distant* orientation to the past, visitors are caught up in the story. They have little direct knowledge of the Rhondda way of life and few detailed personal memories of place. Instead, they are immersed in the revelatory content of narratives. This means that they focus most attention on the points at which the texts reveal knowledge which is new or surprising, yet which resonates with the memories they do have, or with their existing frameworks of knowledge about 'life in the past' or 'the Valleys'. In general, both the *Black Gold* texts and the guides' discourse occupy an authoritative role in the distant orientation. What visitors have been told during the tour largely determines the agenda of the interview: visitors accept the authenticity of the accounts presented. This is not to say that visitors are a blank slate written on by an all-powerful text, for they continually bring their own experiences, insights and knowledge into play. However, these are largely provoked by specific elements recalled from the texts themselves, rather than arising from visitors' own memories.

In the distant orientation, there is often mention of a historical detail which has made a particular impression. In fact, it is the cultural strangeness of the past – its ability to shock – which is the focus in accounts of the visit. Visitors express amazement at 'how bad things were then' or 'how different things were then'. Mr A, for example, was on a trip to Wales from Canada. His mother (who did not take part in the interview) had also been born in Canada, but her own family had originally lived in Tonypandy, Rhondda, and worked in the mines. Mr A's own links with mining, then, were two generations distant. Nevertheless, as a politics professor, he was very interested in learning about local history:

Mr A: I hadn't understood quite why it was so dangerous, what was there about the methane gas that led to so many accidents, and what you could do about it. [The guide] also talked quite poignantly about the 'black lung', and that, however many people had died in explosions, how many more had died quietly but very painfully through the kind of disease they had to ingest through their working lives. Maybe I understand now why my great grandfather emigrated and got the hell out of it.
Bella: What about before the tour?
Mr A: Before the tour? That was a movie audio-visual about the owner of the mine here. What was his name, Lewis? And how long it had been a mining area. There were new things there again. I hadn't realized that – mining is so much part of my mental image of Wales, because of my family talking about it a lot – I didn't realize that in fact it was

relatively new. It came here in the 1850s in a major way in these valleys. I thought it had always been a mining area since the Romans. Well, I guess it had, in a small way. So, the fact that this was a boom industry with all the urban issues of massive overcrowding, I didn't realize that before.

In this account, Mr A positions himself as a novice, having become initiated into a realm of knowledge that he had only inadequately understood before. In this sense, the history presented is accorded an authority and authenticity that fills in gaps in his own knowledge. Heritage, in this orientation, plays an educational role.

This orientation does not, however, imply a visitor with no local knowledge base at all. Mr and Mrs C, for example, also had only distant links to the Rhondda. Mrs C's grandmother's family had lived in Trehafod, although they had been builders rather than miners. Mr C's father used to repair coal wagons at Barry Docks, though there were no connections to the Valleys. They brought knowledge of their *own* local area into play, however, throughout the interview. Mr C would pick up on specific details of the Bertie show which struck him as particularly noteworthy, and relate these back to his own knowledge of Barry (South Glamorgan), where the family currently lived:

Mrs C: There was that fear all the time. The mine-owners...
Mr C: Well, that's it. They wanted the money and that was it. Same when they built Barry Docks. They'd blow the rocks out and you'd get twenty tons falling on half a dozen blokes. They'd say 'I'm sorry to lose you boys', and carry on working.
Bella: What can you remember from the film before the tour?
Mr C: What stuck in my mind was the marquis of Bute and William Burges saying, 'Great. We've got plenty of coal, now we'll build a castle. You bring the coal up. We'll spend the money.' I know when they started shipping coal through Cardiff, the marquis of Bute charged so much that David Davies from the Vale of Glamorgan, he actually turned round and built Barry Docks. It was cheaper to run from their own area, than it was to run from Cardiff. And Barry has still got the world record for shipping coal – it was thirty million tons in a year.

Dominating the conversation throughout, Mr C was a lot more talkative than his wife. He was eager to focus on those parts of the history that allowed him to deploy his own frameworks of knowledge. These were not memories so much as items of historical information picked up about his own home town, where his father used to work in the docks. Particular details of the Bertie show had stuck in his mind and these were ones which connected in some way with his existing repertoires of knowledge. *Black Gold* allowed him to reflect on and imagine life in the past of his own home town.

(ii) Childhood places

In the *childhood* orientation, the exhibitions are a reminder of personal memories. There is usually only one generation dividing the visitor from the 'Rhondda mining community'. The texts do not reveal new knowledge, except to confirm or enhance personal memories, and are conceded little authority. Instead, they are a bridge to access and retrieve visitors' own childhood experiences and reminiscences. Visitors relate to the texts as voices from their own pasts, inviting them to resurrect old memories. A large proportion of interview discourse here consists of visitors talking about themselves – their families' lives, their own memories and handed-down stories – rather than what they have gleaned from the displays. The stories told by *Black Gold* and by the guides fade into the background, for they are less significant in themselves than in the spaces they open up for visitors to recall their own pasts.

Indeed, the *Black Gold* narrators and the guides take on the character of conversational partners, themselves engaged in reminiscence about the *same* past. There is clearly a high degree of pleasure obtained through visitors' matching their own life stories to the ones narrated, so that a common and satisfying description of 'how it used to be' emerges. Although visitors add to, expand on and often adjust the *Black Gold* account of the past, they do so not through finding the *Black Gold* version lacking, but by interacting with the text in the role of bearers of a more detailed and personal level of knowledge. The most noticeable aspect of this orientation is that gaps in the texts' accounts of life in the past are simply filled in, rather than not being noticed (as in the *distant* orientation), or being identified and critiqued (as in the *self* orientation – see below).

These visitors are the most typical of the 'returnee' category, that is, those returning to the Rhondda to show their families the scenes of their childhoods. This is an extract from group 17: a London couple in their sixties, Mr and Mrs W. They were visiting an older cousin, Mrs L1, who lived in the Taff Valley, south of the Rhondda. Mrs W had moved to London in 1936, but was born in Porth in the Rhondda, the daughter and granddaughter of Lewis Merthyr miners. She wanted to show her husband, who came from Middlesex, what the local way of life had been like. Mrs L1 was born and bred in Tonteg, near Rhondda, and all her husband's family were miners:

> Mrs L1: Well I enjoyed the first film.
> Bella: Did you? What did you particularly enjoy about that?
> Mrs L1: Well it was quite realistic from all that I have heard of the Rhondda and from my uncles working there. I remember my mother talking about the first strike. I suppose it was when her brothers were up here and they were starving and she was working at that moment on the farm as a young girl in Pembrokeshire, and one night, well apparently miners used to walk down to Pembrokeshire to try to get something to eat and there'd be a little job for them on the farm. And I remember it quite well, her talking about how one night some of the other boys on the farm said that they'd been down to the village and two miners were desperately poorly there for lack of food, and she had this pre-monition that it might be one of her brothers, and it was. I remember that quite well.
> Mrs W: And I was interested in the talk about accidents, falls and things, because I had an uncle who was in an accident. I'm not sure which one it was, but he was terribly burnt. I felt terribly emotional going around ...
> Mrs L1: Especially when you're near someone who worked in those conditions, you see.
> Mrs W: That's right, and I could've very easily sat and wept whilst we were going around because I found it very, very emotional. It's brilliant. It's the best place I've been to. Fantastic. Really realistic, you know, you don't feel like it's an exhibition, it's like you are experiencing it. It's wonderful.

Here, my interview question as to why the film was particularly enjoyable is answered not by reference to the film itself, but by its fit with Mrs L1's own memories. Thus, the topic of poverty presented in *Black Gold* is elaborated on in the answer by the recounting of a personal story that illustrates this poverty, just as the topics of 'accidents and disease' and 'children working' provoke similar offerings of evidence drawn from personal experience. The films are judged realistic because this linkage has been activated, particularly in the case of Mrs W, whose father and grandfather actually worked in Lewis Merthyr.

A similar orientation, highly dependent on reminiscence, was visible in the interview with Group 9. Mr and Mrs J were a couple in their forties, currently living in Ystrad, Rhondda, where Mr J was born and bred, and where his grandfathers, uncles and brothers had all been coalminers. Ms E, in her late fifties, was also born and bred in the Rhondda, and was the daughter of a Rhondda miner. These connections to the local area and to mining were very close.

Ms E: I've been here a few times ... And I never fail to feel very proud that I'm a miner's daughter, very much so. Especially the first time – because of course, when you've been a few times, you get to know what to expect – but the first time it took my breath away. The impact. Oh, I am a miner's daughter and I'm proud to say it.

Mr J: And it was nice to bring up what I remember from my father – the twist, the stick of ... tobacco which they could take underground and chew on, because obviously they couldn't take cigarettes. And I can remember going to the shop and getting a shilling of twist. That's £2.35 now. There were various flavours ...

Mrs J: And apart from that, it's also been very interesting looking at the houses and the shops, and some of the things I remember. The washing board and the old boiler. I mean, I've seen those when I was a little girl. And the mangle, it had the same name: Mermaid ...

Bella [to Ms E]: You just said that when you first came here it really took your breath away, and you really felt this sense of being proud. Can you remember what it was that made you feel like that?

Ms E: I think the aromas of actually going down the pit shaft to the bottom, and the men working in appalling conditions ... I think it was the smell that came back to me because, as a little girl, we used to go, my father and I, to collect his pay, and the smell of the colliery, it's a certain kind of smell. I think it's too deep for me really to tell you, but I think that I felt that these sort of caring men were also very resilient people. There's something that I can't really put my finger on. I'll have to think about it. It's too deep.

Mr J: What I could understand as well is when they were saying that they had to walk two and a half, three miles, and I can remember my father and my brothers saying, they worked in Gelli colliery and they'd have to walk to Clydach, which is about two and a half, three miles away, underground, before they'd get to the coal face. So I could relate to what he was saying, because I was told that 30, 35, 40 years ago ...

So I knew what he was saying today was true, because my father had done it, and my brothers. They were six foot six.

Part of the pleasure in the visitor experience here lies in the fact that it not only reflects the personal realm of individual biographies, but also authenticates and legitimates them. It reminds visitors of their own personal memories yet also allots them a public significance. The constant back-and-forwards dialogue between public text and private reminiscence sets up relations of equivalence between the history presented and visitors' own lives. The history seems authentic to visitors because it accords with their memories, and in turn, those memories themselves receive public authentication. Visitors thus experience a sense of self-recognition that can be intensely emotional.

(iii) Placing the self

In the *self* orientation, the exhibitions are judged as a public display of self-identity. There is both a close biographical relationship between the visitor and the history presented, and a deep concern over the authenticity of that history. This is the most critical orientation, in that it questions the historiographical adequacy of the displays and claims ownership of the history. Instead of being caught up in the narratives or seeing them as a springboard, the text *as text* is brought into view and critically examined. This involves bringing into the interview a whole range of knowledge which is not contained within the texts themselves nor within guides' discourse. Instead, visitors are comparing the adequacy of the Park's version of local history with their own knowledge or expectations, based on a thorough familiarity with the history of the local area. Ms J1's critical review of the Bertie show provides a good example of this orientation (emphasis added):

Bella: What impression do you think the Park gives of the role of women in the Rhondda Valleys?
Ms J1: It *doesn't give* any real impression of the role of the female. It's all centred around the role of the male. They talk about the children going underground, well, children were boys *and* girls, but they certainly only mentioned boys. Then again, girls didn't work under-ground after a while . . . I tell you what they *didn't do* is depict how dirty

and dusty everything was, because the winding gear is all painted and polished, you know, and it was filthy where my grandmother lived. She'd scrub her front and she'd clean her windows, anything up to two or three times a day, because of the dust from the colliery. And they *didn't show* little snippets, like, I can remember my father used to have two or three loads [of free coal] per year, and ... they delivered the coal to the front door where my parents lived, and I used to dread days when the coal was being delivered, because my mother would have lifted the carpet in the passage and it wasn't fitted in those days, it was just laid down. Newspapers laid down, newspapers down in the sitting room, out into the kitchen, and us kids would have to come from school and if my mother hadn't carried it all through, we would have to end up carrying the coal through the house, down the steps and into the coal shed ... *None of that was shown* or some of the general little bits and pieces.

B: Would you like that sort of thing to be shown?

Ms J1: Well I think that would give an idea. You know, how would a woman today react to having a ton of coal dropped outside her front door? It just doesn't happen, does it? I mean you can imagine her reaction, can't you?

Born and bred in the Rhondda, Ms J1's father and uncles were colliers in Maerdy and Tylorstown, in the Rhondda, and her father-in-law worked in Lewis Merthyr. She moved to north Wales only six years ago. She found the historiography presented at the Park inadequate. This judgement was not founded on a rejection of *Black Gold's* general interpretative framework, but on a conviction that the films had not done justice to the 'real' nature of life in the Rhondda. Thus, Ms J1 presented herself as having a much wider, more detailed and more accurate body of local knowledge than that which is on offer at the Park – hence her focus on the gaps: what *Black Gold* failed to do. This echoes the requirement of local, memorialist discourse that the represented past be recognizable as a reflection of self-identity through being specific, familiar and detailed (chapter 7). *Black Gold* is judged deficient in failing to represent the specifics of lived experience and thus of local/self-identity.

This is mirrored in the accounts of the local residents interviewed who had visited the museum. In four of the focus groups, there was concern over the ways in which local people's lives were represented within the museum's exhibitions. Here is one example:

W1: I think what they've attempted to do is excellent. I hate those models, though.
W2: Oh, yeah, yeah.
W1: Have you ever seen anybody so ugly in your life? And the fella's got anaemia, but that's a small point. (*laughter*)
W1: And I think that they've attempted to address the village as it was in those days, but it's over-sanitized. There's no mention of men coughing their lungs up into bowls.
W2: No there's not. Like Ann said, I think they glossed over it a lot, because I've seen [my grandfather] suffer. He had dust, and he had bottles there and he had oxygen, he had little cups to spit into and ugh ... I mean, I've seen the other side of it as well ... I liked it, yes I did. But I think they glossed over it a lot.

(Extract from Focus Group 4)

Here, the 'authentic' representation would hinge on a portrayal of locally recognizable experiences, which relate directly to the specific knowledge of place. It hinges on an anxiety over the representation of self, as opposed to the representation of the other. In both of these extracts, this anxiety is centred on the claim that hardship has been 'glossed over'. In contrast to the childhood orientation, which is content to see an evocation of the personal world, the self orientation is concerned about the public image conveyed by this world as represented in the museum. In this sense, there is an anxiety about the kinds of messages the museum is communicating to others *about* the self. This suggests a much stronger self-identification by visitors with the historical lives represented, as though it were their own lives that were on display. It is not only a reflection of personal memories and feeling which is required, but a public narrative which can be trusted to 'get the story right'.

Place, past and cultural proximity

In these three orientations, there are quite different degrees of personal investment in and identification with the history presented. They involve different relations between the self and the past. The first orientation is the least personally engaged in the history, though this does not mean that the Rhondda is turned into a romanticized 'other'. Indeed, visitors still draw on frameworks of knowledge which enable them to place the Rhondda within their own frameworks of knowledge, as in Mr C's excursus on Barry Docks. Thus, there can still be, here, a sense of cultural, if not biographical, proximity between the self and the history. However, this is not the emotional proximity of the second orientation, which uses the text as a route into personal reminiscence.

The second orientation, in many ways, produces the most visitor pleasure. The relationship set up between text and visitor is, it seems to the visitor, almost the mutual one of conversing with a fellow time-traveller from one's past. It is also the most emotionally engaged. It is not, however, particularly demanding as regards the level of historical detail expected. The third orientation, on the other hand, whilst involving the closest relations of self-identification with the history presented, is also the most detached and critical, since the history is reconfigured as a set of public messages about the adult self. It is both a question of recognizing the self within the stories told, as well as endorsing the public version of the story to be told. Authenticity is conferred by the visitor him/herself, not by the texts themselves. Thus, the self orientation is more demanding than the childhood one, in that the latter wants only to relive memories of life 'there', now left behind, whilst the former demands to see reflected the memories of life still identified as the history of 'here'.

2. Visiting community

We have begun to see the significance of the relations of social proximity set up in heritage encounters. In what follows, I explore the more substantive historical meanings reproduced by visitors in interview accounts: meanings about, for instance, the imaginary of the Rhondda as community. This represented a key line of enquiry during the visitor interviews. In the pre-visit interview, when visitors were asked what their impressions were of Rhondda people, twelve of the twenty groups offered the unprompted comment that 'community' or 'friendliness' summed up their idea of the Rhondda, with six groups actually using the term 'close/close-knit community', and nine groups producing statements equivalent to 'the people are very friendly'. This suggests that the trope of community as a Rhondda-specific commonplace is already embedded in the majority of visitors' cultural repertoires before the visit commences.[3]

After their visit, however, all twenty groups used the term 'community' in describing the 'people of the Rhondda', suggesting that its continual use throughout the audio-visual shows and also by the guides provides visitors with an instant and automatic label for the Rhondda. Rather than simply bandying the term community around, however, visitors drew on a particular discourse of community that could be termed the 'it was hard, but' discourse. In this, the ready acknowledgement of the past's difficulty and harshness is linked to an insistence on the compensatory or palliative effects of community, that is, of Rhondda people's friendliness, helpfulness and mutual support. This discourse could be summed up as 'They had a hard life, but they were a close-knit community', and is clearly related to the imaginary of the 'good community' (the utopian community ideal of mutual aid, collective action and common interests). It was articulated in six closely related ways: three principal ones (1–3), and three less-prevalent versions (4–6). Many groups produced one or more in combination:

1. 'They had a hard life, but they were a close-knit community': eleven groups explained the 'history of the Rhondda' in this way.
2. 'They had a hard life, but they didn't take it lying down': nine groups produced this interpretation of the history.
3. 'They had a hard life, but they helped each other': nine groups made this observation.
4. 'They had a hard life, but they made the best of it': four groups.
5. 'They had a hard life, but they had self-respect': three groups.
6. 'They had a hard life, but they still had fun': two groups.

There are clear links here to the imagined community of *Black Gold* discussed in chapter 5. That imaginary – of the Rhondda as energetic, resilient, close-knit and disciplined – is fully echoed in this discourse of community.

We can see an indication of the 'it was hard but' discourse of community in Group 18:

Mr W2: A lot of people came into the Rhondda in a very short space of time, so there was pressure on housing, pressure on beds, even. People would share beds, because they couldn't build any quick enough. And then amongst all this mixture, a community developed, you know, with brass bands, choirs, sports, schools, and different activities ...

Mrs W2: It was obviously an up-front community. People would count on each other, as they do in close communities. I suppose it would be quite a stifling community. Everybody would know your business. But with the poverty in those days, you needed to stick together and help each other.

This is a good example of versions 1 and 3. Version 2, on the other hand, is well-illustrated by Mr A (Group 1):

Mr A: You had the bosses, Mr Lewis, and the boom in Cardiff and so on, interspersed with the coal; it's called 'black gold' ... Some people made a hell of a lot of money off it, but the fruits of that labour were not well distributed and these people, these miners, didn't take it lying down. That's what also comes across, that people here weren't lackadaisical or supine. They didn't win, I don't think, but they fought back time and time and time again. It's a demonstration of the human spirit if it's not a demonstration of justice.

Group 6, Mr and Mrs G, provide an example of a combination of versions 1, 3 and 6:

Mrs G: They worked very hard, any sort of leisure time they had they really appreciated. They did have a hard life, but they were a close-knit community.
Mr G: They did everything together. They worked together, they lived close in the streets, they lived together, they went on holiday together. Even the Bank Holiday, they all went to Barry Island or whatever. They seemed to move en-bloc, moving to different parts of the area ... They worked hard and no doubt they played hard at the end of it.

A combination of version 4 and 5 can be found in Ms L and Mr E1's account (Group 10):

Mr E1: Oh, the people from then, like now I guess, but especially then, it was such a busy area, people with a lot of pride and self-respect, even though they were doing a pretty dirty, grotty job, you know. They'd still respect themselves. With the organized protest marches, they'd all be in their Sunday best. It was good.

We can see that these readings position the characteristics of the 'good community' as factors that rescue people from the harshness of past life. Thus, community is seen as a characteristic of the past, a compensation for the harshness of past life.

However, most visitors also suggested, as we have seen from the
pre-visit interviews, that the Rhondda was *still* a 'community' even
though times had certainly changed. In this sense, the underlying
opposition seems to be less a 'then' versus 'now' one, in which
community is understood to have disappeared, and more a 'here'
versus 'there' one, in which it is held to survive here in the Rhondda,
but not there outside. The people of the Rhondda seem to have a
special community spirit which they carry with them, which marks
the place out as distinct and different from other places. We can
see in operation here the discourse of both the 'good community'
(as a place of struggle and mutual aid) but also echoes of the
community as the 'vanishing other' (it being out of synch with
modern life elsewhere). Community is thus seen as a special attribute of *those* people *then* and *there*, a quality that exists in the
particular historical identity of a unique and special place. In this
very general sense, most visitors read the Rhondda as 'other' – that
is, as an identity removed both temporally and culturally from
visitors' own lives.

3. *Visiting politics*

However, if all visitors felt that community marked Rhondda
people out as special, there is still the more significant question of
how visitors defined and judged the community spirit itself,
particularly in relation to collective action and politics. As we
saw in previous chapters, *Black Gold* does flag up the union –
'the Fed' – as the authentic voice of the miners, and does frame the
strikes and struggles of the miners as a legitimate cause. This
certainly seems to be the way that *Black Gold* is decoded, too.
Without exception, visitors read the historical efforts of the people
to improve their working conditions as the story of a 'struggle for
justice': that is, a legitimate cause. At first sight, this reading seems
consistent with a discourse of the 'good community', in that it
appears to celebrate and legitimate working-class activism. However, it is the question of how visitors locate this story in relation to
the present that is really at stake here. Indeed, this narrative might
also be framed as the community of the 'vanishing other', where
people's struggles figure merely as narrative events in the special
way of life that was led back in the 'foreign country' of the past.

Historical understanding is not only a question of messages about the past, but of how the past is *framed* in relation to the present.

In fact, visitors were divided as to the present-day relevance of the people's 'struggle for justice'. The most widely expressed framing is that 'things are different now' (nine out of the twenty groups), suggesting that Rhondda people's concerns are no longer relevant to the present day. A significant minority (six groups), on the other hand, framed the story in terms of explicit parallels between 'then' and 'now'. Five groups were more ambivalent, in varying ways – one of which was that they questioned the wider validity of the stories presented. We thus have three differing articulations of past–present relations: an alien framing, a parallel and an ambivalent one.

(i) Alien framing

Mrs R's account[4] offers a good example of the first. Interviewed with her husband, she describes the Rhondda's history as follows:

> What I picked up was that the gentry were making money out of the poor old working class of the mines. That came across to me when I watched it. The big wigs, and Lord Bute, or whatever his name was. Built all these houses off the backs of the workers. I know it's an awful thing to say, but that came across to me. Whereas the miners were living in squalor, the upper class were living in luxury, where they could afford to build Castell Coch and all these places.

Several terms here suggest that the framework of knowledge drawn upon envisages an *old* social order based on an exploitative upper class/working class division: the 'poor old' working class are oppressed by the 'gentry' and the 'big wigs' – both labels with old-fashioned connotations. The comment, 'I know it's an awful thing to say', suggests that to identify class inequality is a rather extreme, and not usually justifiable, act. Whilst this account appears to conform to the predominant reading, that is, of the people's 'struggle for justice', later on in the same interview, the following exchange takes place:

> Mr R: Well let's put it this way, I suppose in the days that they did go through, they deserved more. They just outdid themselves in the end, didn't they? I don't know whether they got too greedy or whether they

just thought they could get coal cheaper from abroad, I don't really know that. But, years ago, the strikes were necessary, weren't they? Like you say about working a twelve hour day for nothing. But towards the end I thought they did get beyond...

Bella: What did the Park tell you about that type of issue?

Mrs R: ... I think, to me it seemed that the early struggles of the miners were more, more legitimate...

Mr R: More desperate...

Mrs R: More desperate than the later miners. Obviously they did stick together, and you still get that very friendly approach up this way, but I don't think the struggle up to the 50s and 60s... I think modern-day mining is not the same. To me it's not the same as your going back fifty years ago and, you know, beyond that. Modern-day mining isn't in the same class is it?

Bella: Did the Park tell you much about modern-day mining and...

Mrs R: No, no, not really...

Mr R: Not as much as I thought, it was mostly the older...

Mrs R: I think it was the olde worlde type.

Mr R: He explained that they did do it with machinery...

Mrs R: Obviously, people aren't interested in that. I mean people want to know the heritage part of it and what happened 50, 100 years ago down the mines. I don't think I'd be interested really in the modern.

Here, we can see that the narrative of the *struggle for justice* is reconfigured through a distinction between 'deserving' and 'undeserving' causes. 'Modern-day mining' is sharply distinguished from mining in the past, and this is offered as an explanation as to why modern miners' struggles are less 'legitimate'. In addition, there is a clear preference stated for stories about mining in the past – 'the heritage part of it'. The message is that heritage is rightfully preoccupied with the past, which has little to tell us about the present. Just audible beneath the exchange is an implicit condemnation of the 1984/5 miners' strike, when the miners became too 'greedy'.

(ii) Parallel framing

The second 'parallel' framing does not position the past as an 'other' which is finished and complete. Instead, specific points of comparison and contrast are drawn between the past and the present, so that 'the people then' are brought into visitors' explanatory framework for understanding their own lives. Here is an exchange between Mr and Mrs H:

Mr H: It portrayed it as a boom town and it was great, but when you saw how they lived, it wasn't that good, like. The conditions underground. They valued the animals more than the humans. It made me more sympathetic to the miners, miners' causes and all that. Not so much the money, but the closing down of it, and the better conditions.
Bella: Really? What were your views on that before then?
Mrs H: I don't know really, because it didn't interest you really, it was just what you saw on the news.
Mr H: Yes, [the TV] brought you the violence of it, you just saw the picket lines ... All you ever heard is they're just striking for more money, more money, like. You don't get to hear about better conditions. [... *Here, Mr H mentions some friends who have recently joined him in the factory where he works, and who used to be miners.*] Although it was all really dirty and everything, they said there's a better camaraderie, I suppose, between each worker, whereas in our place if there'd be any action there'd be no union between the workers. It's a modern factory. It's just different, like ... That's what Stuart was saying – if another job comes up, he'll go [back to mining]. He's working in a Japanese factory where they don't think about the workers. You know it all looks glossy on the telly, but it's rubbish really ... There's better unity in the mines, than our, than this type of factory I'm working in. Because, if somebody got sacked tomorrow, for whatever reason, people would just say, 'oh, too bad', like. But, in the mines, I hear it's more like if you got the sack, then they'd all get together. You know striking's not always the answer, but they get things sorted don't they? It's a very selfish type of attitude in our factory. Everybody's out for their own. They don't care about other people. It's clean, our place. It's warm and everything, but it's just a dead-end type of job.

In this account, life in the Rhondda is not consigned to the past. The discussion turns on a comparison between Mr H's factory work and the work of his friends, who left mining to join him in the factory. The Rhondda is held to be a place of camaraderie and unity; these values are located in present-day mining too, which is explicitly compared with the speaker's own experience of work. In fact, mining and factory work are discussed in terms of two axes of comparison: the unity/non-unity axis and the dirty/clean axis. This means that there is no simple assertion that 'things are better now', as there is a more multi-faceted identification of both differences and similarities between past and present.

It is clear that it is Mr H's immersion in a work culture where ex-miners talk about mining in relation to the factory that helps to open up this type of engagement with the heritage under discussion, whereas his wife stays largely silent during this part of the interview. This suggests that both class and gender may have a bearing on the ways in which visitors negotiate with the narratives presented. It is striking that in four out of the six accounts that articulate this second reading, it is spelled out in most detail by working-class males, suggesting that a shared male working-class experience of insecure work provides a ready bridge between the present and the past.[5]

(iii) Ambivalent framing

An example of the more ambivalent framing is offered by Mr and Mrs G:

> Mr G: I thought the feel of the whole thing was very sort of that the community had been exploited, sort of downtrodden working class. They had a terribly tough time working out all this valuable coal, and not being rewarded properly for it ... Yes, a story of exploitation and mass action, community feeling.
> Bella: Mass action? Can you explain a bit more what...
> Mr G: Well, about the strikes. They went on for a year and that sort of thing, but the strongest theme was the fact that they all did it together. So it was a community, when they all went marching, and then very soon after the Arthur Scargill strikes, they all closed down...
> Bella: How do you think that story came across really?
> Mrs G: I don't think it's particularly biased, really. You'll [to husband] probably disagree violently. I mean I think obviously they were trying to sort of show that the workers were exploited, but I didn't think that it was over done. You know I'm amazed at how they put up with it for so long.
> Bella: [to Mr G] What would be your view on that?
> Mr G: I think that's the way that the community here would view it. We had a look through the newspaper, and it had a list of the local councils, and it had nineteen Labour and four Plaid Cymru I think, and so it sort of reflects the whole feeling. So this would be an authentic view, and they wouldn't want anyone else's view of it. That's the way they see it, and it's not wrong. I wouldn't argue with their interpretation, but I can see that other people would have put the history of coal in a different way. Yes, people from different viewpoints...
> Mrs G: If the mine-owners had written the script. [laughter]

Here, there is a very interesting negotiation of the *struggle for justice* narrative. First, the coal-owners versus miners division is decoded as the story of the 'downtrodden working class'. This is an appellation which constructs the working class as an other, and as victims rather than activists. Historical change is seen simplistically as the substitution of one type of mass experience ('they all went marching') with another ('they all closed down'). Secondly, this 'mass experience' is explicitly attributed to local Rhondda Labour Party hegemony, so that its wider relevance is thrown into question and is only considered authentic for 'them' – that is, the Rhondda people. There is a clear political disagreement visible in this exchange, with Mrs G appearing to be more convinced of the legitimacy of the Rhondda's people's cause than her husband. All in all, there is a rather sophisticated argument about how local 'bias' might or might not be at work in the encoding of the narratives.

Othering the Rhondda

We can see that the alien framing defines Rhondda people as different from self, whereas the parallel framing establishes connections with the self. The alien framing suggests that there is little to connect the Rhondda way of life – past *or* present – with visitors' own lives. Interestingly, there is a synergy between this and the 'it was hard, but' discourse, which is much more prevalent in the 'alien' framing, than in the 'parallel' one.[6] This suggests that viewing the people as other is connected to viewing community as a compensatory aspect of 'life then'. Thus, Rhondda is framed as the site of outmoded ways of life which endure only as relics or residues of an older social order. Just as community is seen as a thing of the past, so too is the Rhondda – as the epitome of community – a past-orientated place.

Black Gold's insistence on the dynamism and endurance of community in the Rhondda thus does nothing to prevent its framing by many visitors as a relic – interesting, but outmoded. This is because the texts also insist at the same time that the Rhondda is 'special' and 'unique' (chapter 5). In those interview accounts, on the other hand, where no strict past/present split is articulated, the trope of 'olde worlde' community is not mobilized so clearly, because neither the past nor the Rhondda are categorized as special/ other. We can say, therefore, that although the interpretative thrust of exhibitionary discourse encodes the Rhondda as other for the tourist gaze, this effect *can* be transformed in decoding into an articulation of self, where visitors manage to find personal and political resonances with the particular heritage world on display.

4. *Encoding and decoding*

This book has been exploring the relations between encoding and decoding, and I have tried to demonstrate the interconnectivity and interdependence of these practices throughout. Following Hall (1980), we can say that there is a specifiable circuit of determination – or, better, articulation – between the three linked domains of encoding, text and decoding. In other words, what visitors carry away with them as an imaginary of the Rhondda at the end of their visit is in some way related to the conditions under which the Rhondda Heritage Park came into being. In chapter 5, we saw that two discourses of community – the 'good community' and the 'vanishing other' – are both implicated in defining and imagining the Rhondda at the heritage museum. This prevarication between a pat, anthropological evocation of community and the appropriation of a humanist voice of collective action reflects the divided and uneasy conditions of production within which encoding took place. This leaves the texts open to equally divided decodings.[7]

   Although, at one level, there was general agreement on visitors' part – that the people's collective action constituted a 'struggle for justice' – the visitor interviews also suggest that the framing of this very general reading varies considerably. The twenty visitor groups related in quite different ways to the stories presented. Whilst a large proportion viewed the Rhondda as a place and people both socially and temporally 'other', a significant grouping drew on frameworks of knowledge that brought 'the people then' into relations of equivalence and comparability with 'people now'. This suggests an active and questioning engagement with history. Even those whose readings 'othered' the Rhondda at least left the Park with a clear impression of the hardship of early mining, which rather undermines the claim that heritage romanticizes the past. However, it does reflect a tendency to pick up on the tropes and figures of community as a people belonging to a place in time (the vanishing other), rather than to hear the message about the ongoing march of history and local activism (the good community).

As we saw, visitors arrived at the Park with varying kinds of preconstituted image of 'the Rhondda', which were organized around prevalent tropes of the mining community ideal: friendliness, togetherness, closeness, etc. These tropes organize the meanings of heritage both within and 'outside' the texts in question, but they do not foreclose on the possibility of a critical reflection on past/present relations. It is how the boundaries of community are envisaged that is important: whether these are seen as temporally and anthropologically closed, or whether they are conceived as more open and porous. As we saw in chapter 8, encoding organized the texts around both: professional exhibitionary discourse deploying its nostalgic tropes of community, while professional historical discourse preferred to emphasize a different kind of trope, in the 'ongoing march of history'.

Thus, the three framings identified are indicative of different forms of self–other identification: in the alien framing, visitors hear only the discourse that turns community into an 'other'; in the parallel framing, they heed the utopian call to enter community and view it as 'self'; and in the ambivalent one they remain 'on the fence' so to speak – neither inside nor out. Such identifications seem to confirm those views of encoding/decoding which suggest that all readings are negotiations (for example, Morley, 1992). They are less the outcome of decisive decodings, than of relations of relevance/ irrelevance – between readers' own social positionings and interpretative frameworks, on the one hand, and the text's negotiations of the differently accented relations of encoding on the other.

I would argue that it is at the level of childhood reminiscence that there is the greatest fit between the encoding and decoding of *Black Gold*. For returnees, in particular, the desire, it seems, is not so much for the museum to inform in a challenging way, or to present an unfamiliar or extensive body of knowledge. Instead, it is for a reflection of visitors' own rather distant memories or handed-down stories. It does not need to do more than to stimulate reminiscence through alighting on the appropriate topics at an appropriate level of detail. These reminiscences are largely of scenes and scenarios, of places and people, of stories and anecdotes. It is this imagination of the past that the RHP succeeds in matching, since it offers the vignettes, the scenes, the old photographs, the snatches of dialogue, the highly visualized and vivid events and situations, which satisfy the gaze of the self returning to the memories of childhood. It is not, perhaps, a coincidence that this imagination is also situated midway between professional interpreters' vision of the Rhondda as other and the local historians' identification with it as self.

Conclusion: Heritage, place and community in the Rhondda

The new, vernacular heritage represents local community simultaneously for the tourist gaze and for the commemoration of place-identity. It thus deploys community both as a commodity to market the special appeal of vernacular place-myths, but also as a cultural arena in which meaningful connections can be ignited between past and present lives, between 'here' and 'there', 'us' and 'them'. I have suggested that two competing definitions of community underlie this duality: community as nostalgic appeal to a timeless, other place (the community of the 'vanishing other'), and as utopian collectivity which promises to grant the 'voice of the people' a belated public recognition (the 'good community'). In the history told by the Rhondda Heritage Park, discourses of the vanishing other and the good community are knitted together, thereby proclaiming community as both an anthropological unity (as in the images of traditional Rhondda) and a political unity (in the people's collective struggle for justice).

Encoding community

This dual imagination of community is the product of contested and locally situated practices of heritage encoding. In this process, the exhibitionary discourse of professional heritage designers encounters a particular indigenous Rhondda place-myth (that is, the Rhondda as the heart of the labourist, industrial Valleys traditions) which it transforms into the story of 'a special people'. Heritage smoothes these contradictions into a 'view from the hill' (Dicks, 1999), in which the essential, unitary identity of place is always-already assumed. Heritage interpretation 'discovers' this unity and re-presents it as watchable pictures and dramatic stories for an audience conceived of as outsiders and tourists. Thus, exhibitionary discourse works to draw boundaries around its subject-matter, in order to encode it as a special attraction for the tourist gaze. The local labourist voice, insisting on the continuing vibrancy of the Rhondda's collective spirit, is still, however, audible in *Black Gold*. The encoding of the mythologies of left-leaning, working-class 'good community' discourse into the tropes of the 'vanishing other' does not obliterate the former, but transforms it into an index of the archetypal mining community, in which the special character of the people is mapped on to place and period rather than class (thus consigning the working class to history?).

Decoding community

This contradictoriness is also confirmed by practices of consumption. On the one hand, the visitor research conducted suggests that the 'view from the hill' is also adopted in decoding, producing an understanding of historical change that simplistically envisages community and place as the people's salvation. This enables the visitor to recognize and endorse the message that the miners' was a 'just struggle', yet at the same time to avoid framing it in political terms relevant to the here and now. On the other hand, I have argued that visitors are not blank slates upon which heritage imprints its message. The visitor may not adopt an anthropological or spectatorial gaze from the hills, but may instead descend the hill and interpret the predicament faced by Rhondda people as linked to ongoing, wider political and social struggles in the present day. This confirms the argument that different types of tourist gaze exist (Urry, 1990), but also suggests that different gazes can be mobilized by the same 'view'.

I have also suggested – though only tentatively, given the small scale of the research conducted – that the view from the hill offered by *Black Gold* invites a particular self/other relationship between the visitor and the Rhondda, which translates it into an object of childhood reminiscence. This means that it is the rather distant yet emotionally evocative scenes and anecdotes of personal memory which constitute the principal 'pleasure' offered by the visitor experience. This indicates that the nature of the interaction between visitors and heritage is not only about the hermeneutic decoding of messages but also about self-recognition and identity. Thus, the gaze from the hill can be a gaze on the childhood self rather than on the other. In relation to places like the Rhondda which have released sizeable diasporas into geographically and socially distant places, the ex-local returnee may seek – and find – only self-confirming commonplaces on his/her 'return' via the heritage museum. For the returnee, the pleasure of the heritage experience lies in the reflection of memory (what the Rhondda was like then) rather than in confronting new interpretations that interrogate those memories and bring them up to date with the Rhondda now.

An entrenched perspective on the Rhondda that looks *back* on itself as an archetype of past experience is already a familiar element in public images of the Rhondda as community. *Black Gold* seems to mirror such an imagination, thereby suggesting once again that the Rhondda's true identity lies in its past. In claiming that 'the Rhondda spirit' lives on, but doing so by framing this spirit as 'heritage', *Black Gold* risks producing the Rhondda's true identity as reminiscence rather than actuality. Exhibitionary discourse works to produce this 'olde worlde' community as object of the tourist gaze, while memorialist discourse counters this by insisting on the continuing relevance of collective memory. As an amalgam of both, *Black Gold* and the heritage site as a whole ends up trying to have it both ways. It tries to proclaim the Rhondda's continued vibrancy, but inevitably reproduces the Rhondda as anachronistic. In this way, the museum hitches the Rhondda to connotations of 'olde worlde' tradition, thus merely underpinning those 1970s fears described in the first chapter in which the Rhondda was felt to be on the brink of extinction. Certainly, 'dying communities' do not usually attract large amounts of new funds, or have large amounts of public resources directed at them.

The olde-worlde appeals made in *Black Gold*, however, are offset in important ways, by the live, face-to-face commentaries of the guides during the underground part of the visitor tour. Here, at least, history is made present – present-ed through the immediate accounts of ex-miners, both young and old. It is this part of the tour that really comes alive. It is, however, a history that is mainly focused on mining as a job, rather than on the Rhondda as place. Perhaps if women were to be employed too as guides – and the

remit extended to include community life – more could be made of
such 'live' encounters with local people.

Local contexts

The tensions of *Black Gold* are produced through the particular
divisions and dissonances that characterize encoding. However, the
museum's exhibitionary logic also needs to be placed within the
particular historical and spatial conditions of its local social contexts. The Rhondda Heritage Park sought to tap into new forms of
cultural consumption through the display of the vernacular realm
rather than specialist knowledge or élite lifestyles. It thus needs to be
theorized as part of a wider cultural turn to community, in which
representations that celebrate the lived, situated, ordinary and
familiar realms of human sociality are proliferating in both urban
design and exhibitionary practice. There is, however, something
slightly bogus about the claims of vernacular heritage to grant access
to the fullness of community. When these images of community
become encoded into heritage centres such as the Rhondda Heritage
Park, they are translated into spectacles which are clearly inviting the gaze of audiences and not the participation of community
members as such. Vernacular heritage offers the past as a peculiar
blend of community as presence (the materiality and authenticity of
old buildings; the local credibility and personal testimony of ex-
workers) and absence (the reliance on spectacle and technological
mediation). Thus, to suggest that heritage can grant access to the
vernacular hides the fact that the visitor is not experiencing community, but gazing upon it. Moreover, local residents metamorphose from the subjects of the history into objects of that gaze.

However, heritage cannot be completely subsumed into object for
the tourist gaze. Exhibitions and restorations take place within
particular local 'structures of feeling' (Williams, 1961) and historical conditions. If a museum promises to *represent* community,
local people may well interpret this as a promise to promote
and accommodate their interests. Thus the community as spectacle
is always subject to other more concrete usages of the term
'representation' in the locality. We noted, for example, how the
discourse of local memorialism made itself heard at every stage of
encoding practice, helping to ensure that local heritage was not

entirely separated from its definition as local representation. Indeed, it was these *other* meanings of community, which claim material resources for the locality in terms of jobs, space for local services and amenities, as well as a respectful and dignified space for the commemoration of local history, which intruded into the museum both as text and as material structure.

Textually, these other meanings underpinned the (albeit belated and compromised) attempts to enlist local people's involvement in encoding, and helped to ensure that the scriptwriter chosen was local, sympathetic to and indeed expert on local history. He was the cipher through which the narrative of Rhondda as utopian-radical working-class community became inserted into the intertextual tapestry of *Black Gold*. In terms of its materiality, the contested meanings of community representation ensured that local struggles over the political control of the project, and over the negotiation of 'inside' versus 'outside' input to it, were sufficiently potent to prevent the museum from fulfilling its early exaggerated mission – that of turning the entire area into a mixed heritage, leisure and business development. Had the three-council alliance discussed in chapter 6 held, there is no doubt that the three-site development would have proceeded (though whether it would have been commercially successful is another matter). Taff Ely's fear that the community benefit argument put forward by the planners to attract funding was merely an empty promise finally prompted them to depart from the consortium. Thus, we can see that the appeal to community has to be very carefully negotiated within the local spaces of heritage projects. The Rhondda case-study shows how the meaning of community – appropriated by different parties in different ways – becomes a site of social contestation. In order to exhibit community for tourists and to exploit the fame of the Rhondda, the heritage museum is also asked to provide benefits to the local area. These, I have suggested, are not always clear when the major preoccupation becomes that of attracting visitors and tourists, rather than providing the infrastructure and physical improvements demanded by local residents.

Political contests

And yet it is the essentially contradictory roles played by heritage in the locality which is the clearest point to emerge from the analysis presented in this book: its simultaneous economic usage as advertisement for the area's future *and* as tourist attraction based on the area's past; its cultural usage as memorial to labourism (by Rhondda Borough Council) *and* as sign of labourism's demise (by the Welsh Office); its social usage as reminder of local self-identity *and* as confirmation that this identity is past. Local heritage initiatives, then, can be thought of as magical resolutions to the crisis of local identity (economic, cultural and social) at the juncture of deindustrialization. They promise to market the past for visitors at the same time as preserving it 'in the interests of local people'. Unfortunately, as the Rhondda case-study has shown, magical resolutions can evaporate when put into practice in actual social contexts. The knots that tie them together unravel, as the various allegiances to the site in its various contexts part company with each other.

The major reasons for the unravelling of the Rhondda magical resolution can be traced to the fundamental incompatibility of local popular representation (whether as memorials for place-identity or spaces for local amenities) and entrepreneurial regeneration (the exhibition of community for the tourist gaze). The unravelling that occurred in the consortium, with the departure of Taff Ely Borough Council, and thus the contraction of the whole scheme into a single-attraction heritage site, cannot be understood in isolation from the contested place-mythology within which the different boroughs staked their claim to political autonomy. Rhondda was always happier with the identity of 'archetypal mining community' than Taff Ely. Nor can this contestation over place-myths be under-stood outside of the economic entrepreneurialism that has forced localities into competition with each other for scarce economic resources. Place-competition cannot, it seems, be set aside for the sake of project unity, when the economic and cultural rewards for doing so do not appear to be equally shared.

Local identity is thus co-opted into heritage in quite complex ways. Simply to conclude that heritage anachronizes local identity by exhibiting it *as* heritage neglects the more locally specific appeals that heritage also makes, which arise from its cultural, political and economic usage in the locality. Heritage may also instigate a realignment of local political power relations. The Rhondda Heri-tage Park was part of a wider entrepreneurial – though publicly funded – package sponsored by the Welsh Office as a means of fostering regeneration through leisure and tourism as substitutes for the labourist identity of the Valleys. It involved Rhondda Borough Council ceding control to a consortium led by the county and by the Welsh Development Agency. This loss of local political control occurs, paradoxically, in relation to a heritage project which publicly *asserts* local cultural distinctiveness and autonomy. The heritage site offers a platform for this local (labourist) identity by giving it a symbolic afterlife at the Heritage Park. In this sense, the cultural tries to stand in for the economic.

Nevertheless, local political control is not lost forever where much-vaunted commercial success fails to materialize. In that situation, the public purse continues to pay the bill. Financial control over the Rhondda heritage museum has remained in public hands because the project failed in commercial terms. Furthermore, it recently returned to a Valleys-dominated local authority (Rhondda Cynon Taff), created by local government reorganization in 1996. The Welsh Office, the Welsh Development Agency and the now-defunct county council can no longer take the helm because the project is no longer developing, and no longer chasing development funds. This means that the museum is bereft of new funding which it desperately needs if it is to develop and expand. Nevertheless, it provides a neat example of the Welsh Office's ultimate failure to wrest the heritage project from 'parochial' hands where the brave new world of enterprise leisure has simply failed to materialize.

Indeed, any surviving councillors or officers of the old borough council who can still remember the early days can perhaps barely contain the odd smile of satisfaction. Rhondda Borough Council would have had to enjoy its local autonomous control over the small community museum that it first planned in 1983 within a very tight budget. It is doubtful whether much more than basic buildings and machinery restoration could have been attempted. As it was, the project was able to attract millions of pounds of funding, thus allowing a high-tech, sophisticated attraction to emerge. Now that the Rhondda (in coalition with neighbouring ex-boroughs) has reasserted local control, it finds itself with a highly capitalized asset – even though it is one that continues to underperform in visitor numbers and to require continual public subsidy. It has by no means succeeded, however, in regenerating the Valleys. For the future, the considerable problems of unemployment, ill health and an ageing population that continue to afflict the area suggest that locally derived or locally focused political-economic solutions will be difficult to find. As the decline of local *economic* distinctiveness continues, there is a question mark over the survival of local labourist traditions (Adamson, 1991). The heritage park attests to their continuing *cultural* vigour, but, increasingly, this strong local identity – which, in any case, has long been a contested one – may become merely a commodity rather than a narrative which is embedded in the realities of local social life.

Indeed, we can conclude that what the heritage museum puts on display is neither the 'spirit of place' nor the 'voice of the people'. As we have seen, the claim to represent and mirror the vernacular fails, in that exhibitionary discourse cannot be reconciled to memorialism. Consultants begin and end with a Rhondda that is, inevitably, an *imagined* community. Local voices have been sought out in order to retrieve the personalized and authentic 'voice of the Rhondda', but this is not the mirror image of the contestation, multivocality and inconsistencies that characterize real social space. There is, in the end, no unmediated access to community, for it is only – as Bauman (1992: 138) suggests – a retrospective unity. Community emerges through the 'communal cloud' of heritage, which settles over various views from the hill.

Appendix 1
Black Gold *audio-visual shows*

To give an idea of the narrative composition of the three audio-visual shows in *Black Gold*, the following table shows how each show can be broken down for ease of analysis into sub-stories, each with its own theme (lexia[1]). Some of the material is directly quoted from the soundtrack; the rest is indicated through a summary (main elements of story). Throughout the three shows, and especially in the Bertie winding house show, different voices belonging to different historical figures take over the narration, and so the table also indicates how this narrative organization is constructed (emplotment). The final column offers an interpretation of each lexia in terms of its contribution to the imaginary of community which *Black Gold* constructs (significance).

TABLE A1: The Bertie show

Lexia	Main elements of story	Emplotment	Significance
The coal rush 'The old Rhondda is changing out of all recognition. So many new streets, homes and shops are springing up. Like mushrooms overnight, that a man can't find his way 'ome in the dark – especially if he's 'ad a good drink on a Saturday night'. 'Not so long ago these valleys had no coal worked in them at all ... the big change came when they did prove the steam coal was there up at Cwmsaerbren farm, top end, where they do call it Treherbert now ... just before Christmas 1855 the first train of Rhondda steam coal, 38 clanking wagons of it, went bumping down the valley to the new docks at Cardiff. Since then it's been nothing but coal going out and people coming in to dig it.'	• first trains of coal leave the Rhondda • sudden expansion of Rhondda pits • sudden influx of people from the rest of UK • new houses and shops are built	As visitors enter, three life-size figures, a collier and his wife and small son are lit up in a cameo *tableau*, speaking Welsh. Then, a disembodied voice booms out from overhead, introducing himself as Bryn Rees. He explains that the man, Thomas Rees, is his grandfather, and the boy his father, John. He locates their time period as 1880 (in the past tense), and hands the narration over to Thomas. Thomas narrates through voice-over and projected photographs, in the present tense.	The sociological story of modernization, technological innovation and urbanization sets up a view of the Rhondda as new, modern and emergent. Community is seen as originating with the discovery of coal, suggesting that it springs up naturally as the Rhondda's material resources are laid bare, creating a symbiosis between people and environment.

Lexia	Main elements of story	Emplotment	Significance
The life of the miner 'I been working in the pit since I was 10. Like most lads I started as a doorboy, opening and shutting the heavy wooden air doors, sitting there for hours in the pitch black .... You get used to the rats running around, but I did take fright at first, all on my own. After that I helped the collier to shovel his coal, and when I was only sixteen, I came a collier, with a boy of my own to 'elp.'	• constant threat of accidents • growing up meant conquering fear • wages only reflected the price of coal • the Tynewydd pit disaster and rescue: five survivors entombed for nine days	Thomas continues the story, through voice-over and photographic montage. Bryn Rees takes over momentarily to give more information on the miners' lives and the famous rescue at Tynewydd colliery. Then, as a funeral bell tolls, the screen shows statistics written large of the death figures caused by mining.	The emphasis on the difficulty and danger of mining represents it as a vocation with its own rites of passage, into which the young novice is initiated via the overcoming of youthful fear and the passing of time.
The fame of Rhondda coal 'The Welsh nation owes to coal the prosperity that has provided us with a university, with fine civic buildings and mighty ports. Coal has made Cardiff into a veritable Welsh Chicago. The coal bunkers of the Empire, from the Cape to Aden, from Bombay to Port Said are stocked with coal from south Wales,	• Cardiff Docks rapidly developed and expanded • Cardiff gained a university and 'fine civic buildings' • the world demanded coal at ever-increasing rates	Bryn Rees explains the expansion of W. T. Lewis's mining empire, and describes the wealth of the Bute family. A *tableau* is lit up of W. T. Lewis and a shipping agent, against a background of Cardiff Docks. They converse about the expansion of Cardiff and the world-wide demand for coal.	The story of the global role of the coal industry and the vast wealth made from it imputes a historical agency to coal, and to Rhondda coal in particular. Thus the 'special status' of the Rhondda-as-place is confirmed.

Lexia	Main elements of story	Emplotment	Significance
The fame of Rhondda coal (cont.) with coal from the Rhondda … with coal that has come up, in endless streams, from this very colliery.' 'Make no mistake, we have made the name Rhondda and of Lewis Merthyr ring out around a world that needs coal as it needs oxygen itself.'	• the marquess of Bute built Castell Coch, with 'exquisite designs' • W. T. Lewis 'sank shafts' • a 'real jamboree on high days and holidays' before 1914	Bryn Rees, resuming the narration momentarily, then invites us to listen to W. T. Lewis. W. T. Lewis's voice takes over the narration (voice-over with stills). He pays tribute to the Bute family. A *tableau* is lit up of the marquess and his architect, against the background of a Castell Coch interior.	
The miners' collective struggle 'In Tonypandy, in mid-Rhondda, in the winter of 1910 the men had had enough. When wage demands were turned down, they struck … New leaders were needed for these new times. The South Wales Miners' Federation, the Fed as we called it, was demanding a minimum wage and public ownership of the pits … The leader of all the British miners then was our own A. J. Cook.'	• 12,000 men struck for a year • blacklegs were imported • troops sent in, the strike was 'smashed' • the Fed wanted a minimum wage, and public ownership • south Wales became 'a cockpit of strife'	Bryn Rees narrates (voice-over with stills), in the past tense. Then he introduces A. J. Cook, and the third *tableau* is lit up. It shows Cook on a platform in the middle of a speech. The speech is heard above the shout of crowds supporting his call for 'justice'.	Here, the image of the miner as archetypal proletariat is activated, through the description of united, collective action and the image of a strong, popular leader. In contrast to the received-pronunciation and pompous tone of the voice of the coal-owner, W. T. Lewis, Cook's

Lexia	Main elements of story	Emplotment	Significance
The miners' collective struggle (cont.)	• the strikes of 1921 and 1926 • A. J. Cook led the British miners • Cook's passionate speeches, calling for 'justice' • Cook died and the miners were defeated, though not beaten.		voice is clearly 'of' the people, and his speech is accompanied by applause and shouts from the gathered crowd.
The depression 'The coal boom was over as the navies of the world switched to oil and foreign coalfields expanded. The great strike seemed in vain, nothing we did could stop the pits closing.'	• pits closed • mass and prolonged unemployment • exodus from the Valleys • by 1945 under half the miners in south Wales than twenty years earlier.	Bryn Rees narrates (voice-over with stills), in the past tense.	The Depression is seen as the result of global forces (the switch to oil). There is very little detail, however, on this period.

APPENDICES

Lexia	Main elements of story	Emplotment	Significance
The recovery 'Only the war effort made coal-miners wanted again, and in time, after the war, a Labour government did give us miners what we'd first asked for in 1912, that was nationalization. There was still 100,000 employed in the collieries of south Wales in 1958, so we haven't come to the end of the Black Gold story by any means.'	• the 'war effort' stimulated coal demand again • Labour government nationalized the mining industry • still 100,000 miners in south Wales in 1958.	As above. The final few minutes are interrupted by a cameo in which the figures of the manager and winder are lit up, discussing a problem with the winding engine. Bryn Rees then uses the present tense to give audiences instructions as to how to leave. The final cameo of the winder and manager shows that the problem has been resolved, and the cage can come up.	The renewed security of the industry in the 1950s is seen as due to nationalization and a Labour government. However, the spoken emphasis on '*seemed* more secure' suggests future problems. These are not referred to, however, and the story stops in 1958 on a note of optimism. Again this period is dealt with only cursorily.

TABLE A2: The fan-house show

Lexia	Main elements of story	Emplotment	Significance
Community without coal 'Anyone who's ever stood on a mountain top above the valley will have heard that sound: a distant, intriguing undercurrent of activity. The sound of people: busy, lively people. What one of Rhondda's writers called the hum of humanity. And somehow we've heard it most clearly when the wheels of industry were momentarily stopped and a community showed its best values of neighbourliness, resilience, the will to survive, together. Coal made the Rhondda but the Rhondda means much more than coal.'	• Rhondda people are active and lively • this community life is shown most clearly when the mines shut down • after the 1984–5 strike, they were defiant • this was the same in 1926 • the 1926 shutdown allowed beauty and calm to return to the hills • yet the human response was 'amazing and deafening' • the carnival spirit was usually reserved for the annual holidays • Rhondda joined the whole of the Valleys for the annual trip to Barry Island	Neil Kinnock narrates (voice-over with stills). He introduces Gwyn Thomas, whose (acted) voice takes over to read from the novel. Neil Kinnock resumes.	Here, the trope of community is activated through the device of the 'view from the hills'. Community is seen in terms of the qualities of energy, mutual aid, resilience and collectivity, and is presented as a property of people. It is seen as an entity that passes through time, whether or not the mines are there, and thereby outlasting all superficial change.

Lexia	Main elements of story	Emplotment	Significance
The 'women of the coal valleys' 'That day away from drudgery was sweetest and briefest, for the women of the coal valleys. In good times and bad, their toil was unremitting. From Monday wash-day to Saturday shopping, women followed a work routine as strictly patterned as any collier's.'	• the routines of women's work were 'strictly patterned' • women were 'essential parts of the workforce' • many died young of exhaustion • they put their husbands' and children's needs before their own. • miners worked for seven hours, but women for seventeen • miners coming off shift caused endless rounds of cleaning and preparation. • men were unaware of women's labour • men were vain about their clothes • women obtained satisfaction from doing the job well • women often judged other women in terms of household standards • women managed and controlled family life	Kinnock describes, in the past tense, the routines of the women's household work. Different voices of women are then heard one after the other, describing the hard conditions. Stills accompany.	Women's work is seen purely in terms of domestic labour, thus distancing the account from recent decades. The major characteristics emphasized are women's self-discipline, self-sacrifice and the constancy of their labour. Women are defined purely in terms of their household role. The trope of working-class matriarch/martyr is activated, though it is an 'inside account' concentrating on the hardship of the role. Gender difference is emphasized: men are seen as unaware and belonging to a different world.

Lexia	Main elements of story	Emplotment	Significance
Local institutions 'The chapels and churches, large enough in size, number and variety to accommodate every religious affiliation and any splinter thereof ... Education, in spite of the rigidity of schooling, was highly valued, both as a way out of the pit into security and respectability, and for many for the joy and illumination it could bring. The workmen's institutes with their splendid libraries were the seminaries of the coalfield and windows to a wider world.'	• chapels and churches reflected large number of affiliations • they were democratic places of oratory and political machinations • schools were strict and most left early for work • education was a way out of the pit, however, and a source of 'joy' • the workers' libraries offered wider views	Kinnock narrates (voice-over and stills), in the past tense	These passages cultivate further two major aspects of community: self-reliance (the Rhondda made its own institutions) and vibrancy (they were full of life and popular participation).
Social conditions 'The Rhondda was no backwater. For at least two generations it was one of the most vibrant places on earth ... There was, of course, dreadful overcrowding, with colliers often coming home to sleep	• newcomers were quickly crammed into the Valleys • building was 'frenzied' to keep pace • housing was inadequate • there was a middle class, too	As above	Here, there is a deliberate distancing from any notion of the 'underclass'. Instead, respectability, social order and the middle class are emphasized.

Lexia	Main elements of story	Emplotment	Significance
Social conditions (cont.) in beds still warm from a previous occupant ... In a community with strong social cohesion and family relationships, respectability and social order were cherished as valuable conditions of life. This was a tidy place.'	• social tension was rare, since the community was cohesive • 'respectability and social order' were collective values • the people made their own community • the community changed in character over the years, and grew up		The community is seen as 'natural': a product of the people's own needs. This is an organic view of community.
Popular culture 'The culture of the Rhondda was as deep as it was popular ... Sporting heroes brought pride in local identity and universal acclamation ... The mixture was rich and heady: from music hall and oratoria in the 1890s to rock and roll in the 1950s, and a thousand varieties since. The images were endless.'	• popular debate in pubs • champion boxers, rugby and soccer players • popular music • Italian coffee shops • picnics on the mountains • plays	As above	The self-provisioning of the Rhondda is emphasized, through the variety and energy of the cultural traditions. However, the section also helps establish the Rhondda's worldliness and participation in wider leisure networks.

Lexia	Main elements of story	Emplotment	Significance
Popular culture (cont.)			It thereby integrates community through delineating its internal cohesion, as well as differentiating community from others, by placing it within wider territorial formations.
The past in the present 'Maybe, inevitably, Rhondda, at work, at home and at play, will come to seem and look more like places *not* touched by its charged history between these enfolding hills. But if we have eyes to see and can still listen to the buzz of its history, the drama of the Rhondda will still inspire and still proclaim the vision of its human world.'	• Rhondda 'made its mark' • the age of *Black Gold* 'recedes' • 'scars' disappear • but memory survives • history will always be there	As above	History is seen as a resource that can be drawn on for enlightenment and inspiration in the present. This section emphasizes the essential continuity of history, set against the superficial changes of the physical landscape.

TABLE A3: The Trefor show

Lexia	Main elements of story	Emplotment	Significance
The path to the pit 'All of us boys in the village went down the pits. Couldn't wait really … well, it was like you'd become a man, see, and off you went, with your tommy box and jack of water, with the men to the pit. Couldn't wait, could we? Soon learned better, mind you.'	• I was born locally • I was the same as all the other boys in going down the pit • our mothers didn't like it • we wanted to dress as men • we couldn't wait to start work • but we 'soon learned better'	Bryn narrates. He addresses the audience in the present tense, as if he is directly present. He then switches to the past tense to recount his life story.	This story establishes the local hegemony of mining as an occupation. It positions mining as a marker of adult masculinity. A tragic structure of feeling is introduced through the contrast between boyish enthusiasm and the wisdom of experience.
Mining as a 'big concern' 'You'd be surprised how many different grades there are: colliers, of course, on the coal face but hauliers, engine men, pipe fitters … It's a big concern. Over 1,600 working here at one time.'	• there are many different grades • jobs both underground and on the surface • even surface jobs can cause lung disease • there were officials, clerks and managers too	Bryn asks the audience to 'imagine now that this is 1958'. The narration now oscillates between the present and the past tense: compare 'I've just become a safety officer' and 'then there were the officials'.	This story establishes the comprehensiveness and scale of colliery activity. The variety and specificity of skills are emphasized. The focus on the variety of skilled trades connected with mining endows it with status and an industrial pedigree.

Lexia	Main elements of story	Emplotment	Significance
The comradeship of danger 'All dependent on each other for safety. That's a big consideration underground. I think that's what gave mining such a sense of comradeship … Safety improved a lot after they nationalized the mines in 1947. But you can never make a pit fully safe, ever.'	• impossible to find 'better butties' • chatting before going underground helped to take your mind off the danger • all colliers share the strange experience of riding in the cage • the darkness • underground was unique • someone is always getting injured	Again, the narration oscillates between the past and the present tense.	This section establishes a relation between danger and comradeship, thus foregrounding the intensity and necessity of the bonds. This helps to construct a particular masculine version of friendship – based on mutual survival rather than sentiment alone.
High standards of discipline and maintenance 'This engine was put 'ere in the Trefor Winding House in 1890. Powerful thing it is …; Our lives were dependent on its maintenance … No matter what the mess of coal dust, oil and grease and muck elsewhere on the surface, this place was kept as spick and span as the engine itself.'	• the winding engine had to be powerful and reliable • it was winding continually • the ropes and brakes were rigorously maintained • the winding engine man had a very responsible job • the winders were very proud of the engine house • they kept it very clean and tidy	This section is narrated entirely in the past tense. Then, the lights dim and spotlights pick out two figures in a cameo: the winder and the cleaner. In the present tense, they joke about the speed at which the cage was dropped the day before, and the winder asks for another oiling of the rods.	Here, further elements of the industrial pedigree of mining are established: the high standards of cleanliness and rigorous maintenance suggest discipline and efficiency, a deep respect for machinery and the operation of a workplace hierarchy. The effect is

Lexia	Main elements of story	Emplotment	Significance
High standards of discipline and maintenance (cont.)	• yet the winder was just an ordinary man, liking a joke at the men's expense.		to produce an image of a tightly controlled and ordered workforce, where there is a symbiosis between men and machinery, and yet still a camaraderie and sense of humour among the workers.
The intensity and scale of mining in the Rhondda 'Collieries are peculiar animals . . . It's difficult to explain but, see, in the Rhondda the pits just dominated our lives . . . Rhondda was world famous, mun. And a magnet for people . . . I suppose, through it all, we survived because, in a way, the getting of coal had made us a community.	• there used to be 60 collieries working in the two valleys • there were 250,000 miners in south Wales • Rhondda coal was exported all over the world • coal was essential to the world economy • Rhondda suddenly became a 'magnet for people' • in the 1920s 168,000 people were 'crammed tight' in the Rhondda	Again there is a mix of past and present tense. The standpoint of the present is returned to: 'Looking back, it's funny how quick it's all changed.' Then the past tense resumes.	This long section turns its gaze outside Lewis Merthyr and elaborates on the penetration of the mining industry throughout the Valleys. The narrative echoes the other two *Black Gold* texts by underlining the intensity, scale and global importance of the Rhondda mining industry. The ebbs and flows of industrial expansion are seen as a result of fluctuating

Lexia	Main elements of story	Emplotment	Significance
The intensity and scale of mining in the Rhondda (cont.)	• half a century of growth, and then the sudden slump • there was no demand for coal • thousands were unemployed and left the Valleys • the war was our salvation • it was ordinary people who enabled us to survive		'demand'. Against the background of dramatic change, the continuity and survival of community is brought out, understood in terms of an ongoing vernacular identity ('ordinary people').
The danger and hardship of mining 'In the winter these were men who left for work in the dark and came back home in the dark ... Men worked in water for hours on end ... Their wives and mothers would know every day that there was a chance someone would only come back on a stretcher.'	• men only saw daylight once a week in the winter • the management demanded subservience • men who refused were sacked • men had to walk long distances to reach the coal face	Bryn Rees begins this section. Then the voices of men underground are heard, discussing the dismissal of a fellow miner for refusing deference to the manager. A jokey atmosphere is established, contrasting with the narration. Bryn Rees then resumes for a minute, before	This section further underlines and details the hardships and dangers of mining. The narrative juxtaposes the harshness of the conditions with the determined humour of the miners, thus emphasizing their

Lexia	Main elements of story	Emplotment	Significance
	• pay did not start until work began • men worked in terrible conditions • accidents happened all the time • men would walk to the streets to give news of an accident	one of the voices is heard again, talking about another recent accident.	resilience. Conflict with the management is configured in terms of interpersonal boss–worker relations. The routine nature and frequency of accidents are emphasized.
The reality of mining 'I'll tell you straight, I've never heard men singing when they come up the shaft, like they do in those 'ollywood films . . . But just to be back above ground was enough to make you want to sing. In your heart.'	• this engine has been here for 70 years • the rope drops down at an incredible rate • the engine used to be steam-driven but now runs on compressed air • men are too tired to sing after a shift • but the relief of coming to the surface was huge	Here, the time suddenly stabilizes in the present tense, located in the 1950s: 'a couple of years ago in the mid 1950s'. Bryn addresses the audience and instructs them to follow their guide.	The contrast with Hollywood sentimentality claims a down-to-earth ordinariness and realism for Bryn's own account. The narrative thus seeks to secure its authenticity by deliberately distancing itself from, and yet at the same time reminding the audience of, the familiar images of *How Green was My Valley*.

Appendix 2

The Rhondda Heritage Park case study: empirical research base

The research undertaken by the author at the RHP comprised four interlinked studies described below:

1. The decoding study

Interviews with 20 groups of visitors to the RHP took place in August 1995, over a period of three days (two weekdays and a Sunday). Interviewees were recruited whilst they were waiting for the half-hourly guided tour to start, in their own naturally occurring groups. A brief pre-visit interview sought to discover what preconceived ideas they already held (if any) about the Rhondda and its history, and semi-structured, in-depth post-visit interviews were conducted just before visitors left to go home. The objectives of the post-visit interviews were:

1. To discover what visitors remembered from the tour just undertaken.
2. To find out what ideas visitors now held about the Rhondda and its people.
3. To discover from what ideological angle, if any, visitors interpreted the historic events recounted.
4. To identify the range of interpretations that constitute heritage decoding, and to relate these back to encoding.

Interviews were then transcribed and analysed using a broad model of discourse analysis drawing on the principles of inter-textuality (Fairclough 1992).[1]

2. Trehafod Study

A small-scale and essentially exploratory qualitative study of local residents' attitudes to the Rhondda Heritage Park was carried out in the adjoining village, Trehafod. The rationale for this was twofold. Firstly, since this was a heritage centre which aimed to tell the story of *local* people, there was a question mark over what its subjects, local residents themselves, felt about 'their' history being turned into heritage. Secondly, I was aware that the RHP had encountered a significant amount of hostility from local residents during its development years, and I wanted to explore this further.

This study was necessarily limited in scope and did not aspire to provide a full account of the range of local opinion. Five focus groups were conducted with a selection of ex-mining households – residents who lived with the physical presence of the RHP on a daily basis, and who were ostensibly members of the RHP's imagined community: its history was their history.[2] Three groups comprised older residents (one mixed, one all-male and one all-female), and two smaller groups were made up of younger members (all female). The objective was to explore groups' responses to the RHP and their feelings about the local community and its history. Discourse analysis of the transcripts sought to identify how local voices made sense of the transformation of the Lewis Merthyr colliery into the Rhondda Heritage Park.

List of Focus Groups

Focus Group 1: Mixed gender group, 5 members, ex-miners and members of the Friends of the Rhondda Heritage Park, ages 45–75;
Focus Group 2: All male group, 4 members, ex-miners; aged 55–80;
Focus Group 3: All-female group, 10 members, wives of ex-miners, aged 50–75;
Focus Group 4: All-female group, 3 members, daughters/wives of ex-miners, aged 30–50;
Focus group 5: All-female group, 3 members, daughters of ex-miners, aged 25–35.

3. The encoding study

This study examined documents and interview data from a range of key informants who were central to the establishment and development of the Rhondda Heritage Park throughout the 1980s and the early 1990s. Three major groups of individuals were key to understanding how the museum came into being:

(a) Officers and councillors

The management and direction of the RHP's development was controlled by a coalition of co-opted local government officers, in the form of the Officers' Directing Group (ODG), and elected local councillors who sat on the Steering Group (SG). The Minutes of meetings of both these bodies were scrutinized at length, and I also had access to correspondence and other documentation archived at the Countryside and Tourism section of Mid Glamorgan County Council Planning Department, Cardiff, and at the Planning Department of Rhondda Borough Council (both now defunct).

These written empirical materials were supplemented by data collected by semi-structured interviews of key informants – officers and councillors who had been in office at the start and/or during the development of the RHP, and who were thus in a position to recount what they saw as the process of its development. Key informants were selected from each sponsoring agency/council, along with two of the directors of the Rhondda Heritage Park and key figures from the museums field in Wales.

(b) Consultants

A key research objective was to trace the process by which the heritage 'texts' were shaped, struggled over and defined during the course of the RHP's decade of development. The creative encoding of the displays and audio-visual shows had been entrusted to professional consultants from the heritage interpretation industry. Interviews were conducted with all the major consultancy firms involved in encoding, with the aim of identifying the frameworks of knowledge that consultants brought to their designs and the processes involved in implementing them. In addition, consultants' reports, which contained their proposals for development and design were scrutinized. These reports had been successively honed into a shape acceptable to all parties during a process of negotiation and rebriefing. To trace the outcome of this 'chain of encoding' meant analysing the reports alongside the minutes, interview material and documents of the public planning and sponsorship bodies.[3]

(c) Local informants

Certain local residents were key to the process of constructing the RHP historiography. These included founding members of the Friends of the Rhondda Heritage Park and guides that had worked at the Park both in the past and at the time of writing. In order to chart the complex interaction of officials, consultants and local informants, I carried out initial interviews with a small number of individuals who had been connected with the Park from the outset. These were later supplemented with interviews with the guides currently working at the Park.

Notes

1. Tourism and heritage in the Valleys: the local context

[1] Eventually, opposition (organized under the Heads of the Valleys Standing Conference) was sufficiently effective to instigate a public inquiry, which found against the initiative and resulted in the Welsh Office withdrawing its application (see Clavel, 1983: 100–4). This campaign built on the momentum established through the community-based activities of Tŷ Toronto, a voluntary group with church links set up to administer disaster funds at Aberfan.

[2] This hegemony had already been challenged, however, in Rhondda West in 1967, which saw Plaid Cymru managing to cut the Labour Party's majority from 17,000 to 2,306 (K. O. Morgan, 1995). At the time greeted as heralding a renewal and expansion of nationalist feeling in key new areas of Wales, such events came to seem a distant memory during the next three decades.

[3] Although it is true that local policy responses to restructuring have always had to be made in the context of the wider regional policies of the British governments, which have been dominated by the Conservative Party for much of the post-war era. The wider UK context has changed in various ways since the establishment of the Welsh Office in 1966, which has pursued different policy agendas at different periods (cf. K. O. Morgan, 1995; Rees, 1997). Local labourist political culture has had to adapt to these new climates in a pragmatic manner, particularly during the expansion of Welsh Office economic and political activity during the 1980s.

[4] Leisure and Tourism Unit, 1983: foreword by Wales Tourist Board, no page nos.

[5] The Richard Llewellyn novel and the Hollywood film *How Green was My Valley* furnish a handy *bête-noire* for anyone wanting to establish their credentials in identifying the 'true' identity of the Rhondda. All suspect and crass images of the area are safely contained within this single representation. Its frequent invocation suggests that there is an unease around Rhondda and Valleys place-myths and a concern about romanticization which are bound up with issues of historical

authenticity, reality, symbolic ownership and the question of who and what has the authority to represent the locality.

2. New vernacular heritage: wider cultural and economic contexts

[1] See *http://www.nmm.ac.uk/Index.htm*

3. Heritage debates

[1] This is the case even if we are talking about a long-established museum. Restructuring can result in concrete interventions, such as new heritage projects and developments, as well as a more diffuse transformation of the local sphere (economically, socially, culturally) which can profoundly affect the museum's need to justify its role in the locality by one means or another. It is important to remember that these transformations are not merely relevant to buildings, financial planning, administration, and so on, but are also constitutive of the realm of production itself, within which exhibitions and displays are put together. In this sense, we need to take seriously the notion of 'museums without walls' (Hetherington, 1996).

4. Wales in a glass case

[1] Whilst the rural/industrial split is a powerful 'internal' divide *within* Wales as imagined community, it needs to be remembered that this will not necessarily be visible from the 'outside'. For the non-Welsh gaze, 'Wales' may be the land of song and chapels, or the land of slag-heaps and unemployment (cf. Humphreys, 1995). Nevertheless, the internal purchase of the different versions of Wales does work to undermine/ promote different heritage identities in the minds of different social and cultural groups. Certainly, the level of cultural acceptance of the coal-mining heritage version was a major factor in destabilizing the Rhondda Heritage Park, as we shall see in chapter 6.

[2] The Folk Museum was committed to preserving the rural, not the urban, traditions of Wales, and thus for a long time ignored the industrial Valleys. However, Gruffudd (1999) argues that, in fact, Peate wanted to distance it from the mystical and romantic idealization of Welsh countryside that Plaid Cymru had often rather too readily embraced (he left the party early in his career). Instead, Peate's vision was of an active, productive Welsh countryside dominated by agriculture and (small-scale) industry, including the co-operative wool and wood-working industries. The essential point, however, is that the coalmining Valleys do not figure in this 'techno-arcadian' imagination.

3 In the nineteenth century, the *gwerin* were not imagined, however, as a purely rural ideal which excluded the mining communities of the south. Instead, as Morgan (1986) shows, the word was used as a romantic umbrella term to unite all the 'ordinary' people of Wales around a Nonconformist, classless, chapel-going, radical, Welsh-language ideal. Those who were specifically not included in the *gwerin* were the aristocrats, the landlords and the Anglican clerics. It was also, however, an image that was manifestly at odds with the ideal of a Welsh proletariat.

4 As both Boylan (1990) and Walsh (1992) point out, this term has been the source of some confusion in the UK, particularly since the publication of the collection *The New Museology* (Vergo, 1989), which used the term rather differently to describe the new modes of interpretation and display which came to the fore in the 1980s (see chapter 2). In Europe, on the other hand, new museology refers to the principles enshrined in the community or eco-museum movement.

5 There were, ironically, plans to effect such a transition at another ex-colliery site in the Rhondda (where the colliery buildings were already cleared) a few years ago, by erecting a Wild West theme park. Predictably, there was local (and national) outrage, and the scheme folded ignominiously.

5. The Black Gold community

1 This third discourse of community is a social-welfare usage, which classifies communities into those which are healthy and vibrant, and those which are dead-end, no-hope, sink-estate places. It raises the spectre of an 'underclass' community, a community of deprivation with a culture of poverty (see the discussion in Brook and Finn, 1978). This third usage is not displayed in vernacular heritage, but images of the political 'good community' and the anthropological 'community of the vanishing other' are locked in a kind of imaginary dialogue with it. Vernacular heritage museums rescue working-class communities from the 'condescension of history' (to borrow E. P. Thompson's phrase), and in so doing they banish images of urban dereliction and decay. However, by constructing a unitary identity for community, they help to invigorate a way of thinking about local culture which can potentially be filled by both positive and negative images. By drawing a boundary around social space, they increase the currency of notions of its 'otherness' and special nature. In this way, images of the good community can easily slide, within other institutional discourses and policy regimes, into images of the underclass and a self-perpetuating culture of poverty. For more discussion, see Dicks (1997b, 1999).

[2] It should be emphasized that this typology does not constitute a description of actual or previously existing mining communities. Bulmer intended the model as an ideal-type, and it is used in the present discussion in order to illustrate the discursive features of the mining-community imaginary. Some of the features are contradicted by reality: south Wales mining communities, for example, are not the geographically distinct settlements that are found in Scotland or south Yorkshire. These variations, however, do not challenge the mythology as a whole.

[3] From the Trefor audio-visual, narrated by Bryn Rees.

[4] It would be wrong to conflate the very different traditions of the socialist version and the communitarian version of the good community (the class-based anti-capitalist and emancipatory appeal of humanist socialism contrasts with the classless, conservative, moralist base of the communitarian tradition). However, they share a common discursive framework, in that their respective utopian visions rest upon the potential of locally placed individuals to join together in action geared towards the welfare and self-sufficiency of the collective.

[5] In the 1970s, for example, writers from the Birmingham Centre for Contemporary Cultural Studies (Taylor et al., 1976) deplored what they saw as a sociological tendency to fetishize community and thus fragment class analysis into the idiosyncrasies of place.

[6] From the Bertie Winding House audio-visual: W. T. Lewis was the owner of a string of collieries in the Rhondda, including the Lewis Merthyr colliery.

6. From mine to museum: the evolution of heritage in the Rhondda

[1] The account of the development of the Rhondda Heritage Park presented in this book, including the analysis of encoding (chapter 8), is based on empirical data collected by the author over a three-year period (please see Appendix 2).

[2] Personal interview with Rhondda Borough Council member, and with senior planning officer, Mid Glamorgan County Council.

[3] Indeed, Hetty was the name of W. T. Lewis's daughter, whilst Trefor and Bertie were his sons.

[4] Personal interviews with officials from the Welsh Development Agency and the Wales Tourist Board.

[5] This is the same John Brown who would the following year submit a notorious report to the Commons Select Committee on Welsh Affairs, which recommended letting the Valleys' population slowly die off (see chapter 1). His involvement in the Rhondda project made it even more controversial.

[6] Personal interview with senior planning officer, Mid Glamorgan County Council.

[7] Personal interview with councillor and planning officer from Rhondda Borough Council.

[8] Personal interview with planning officer, Taff Ely Borough Council.

[9] This package recommended a clichéd, any-time, nostalgic vision. 'The most important new feature would be the emphasis on people and activities rather than buildings and objects; for example, there might be a recreated cinema, actually showing period films, complete with organist; ice cream and fish and chips (wrapped in a reproduction period newspaper) might be sold from a period tricycle and shop respectively; perhaps visitors might even be given period money to use, at period prices, their "allowance" being equivalent to a miner's pay packet' (Welsh Development Agency, 1984: 28–30).

[10] The Officers Directing Group (ODG) was made up of planning and technical officers from Rhondda Borough Council and, before their withdrawal, from Taff Ely Borough Council; planning, tourism and financial officers from the then Mid Glamorgan County Council; planners from the Welsh Development Agency and from the Wales Tourist Board. Meetings would take place fortnightly, and would usually last a whole afternoon. From time to time, other organizations had representatives sitting in – such as planners and architects from the architectural firm Wyn Thomas and from William Gillespie & Partners (two of the consultancy firms), and from the Forestry Commission. Initially, members of the Friends of the Rhondda Heritage Park, the association set up by local people to support the museum plans, were invited to attend the meetings, but this participation was subsequently terminated, much to the annoyance of the Friends.

[11] Personal interview with planning officer and councillor, Rhondda Borough Council.

[12] Gillespie's (William Gillespie & Partners) are a high-profile UK firm of landscape architects who have specialized in large-scale tourism-orientated urban redevelopment projects. These have included the Liverpool Garden Festival, Birmingham Railway Museum, Castle Hill at Dudley.

[13] Personal interview with official from Welsh Development Agency.

[14] Personal interview with planning officer, Rhondda Borough Council.

[15] Cllr Clayton Jones was an elected member for Plaid Cymru in Taff Ely Borough Council, and was the RHP's most vociferous opponent.

[16] Letter to Officers Directing Group from County Planning Officer, 30 Oct. 1987, filed in minutes of the ODG meetings, Rhondda Heritage Park.

[17] Peter Walker, quoted in extracts from the Welsh Office Valleys Programme documents, 14 June 1988; my italics. These extracts are filed in the minutes of the ODG, 20 June 1988, Rhondda Heritage Park.

[18] Letter from Nicholas Bennett MP to Chair of Steering Group, 19 March 1991, filed in Rhondda Heritage Park Steering Group minutes, in Mid Glamorgan County Council Archives and at the Rhondda Heritage Park.

7. Heritage and local memory

[1] Interview with member of the Friends association.

[2] Letter from J. Cornwell to Rhondda Borough Secretary, dated 14 October 1983, filed in the Minutes of the Officers' Directing Group, at the Rhondda Heritage Park.

[3] From personal interview with Ivor.

[4] These included memories of the tin baths, the trips to Barry Island, the women judging each other's housekeeping, the Bracchi cafés and the shops, the self-education at the miners' institutes, the washing of pavements, etc. – all of which are to be found within the texts of *Black Gold*, see chapter 5.

8. The technologies of heritage encoding

[1] Management of the Rhondda project, in the form of the Officers' Directing Group (see chapter 6), comprised paid officers employed by the project's sponsors – the three local councils and the two public agencies – who were planning and tourism officers, engineers, architects and accountants. At the head of the group was the development officer, who had overall responsibility for managing the setting up of the project.

[2] Personal interview with researcher for *Black Gold*.

[3] In this regard, Bauman has argued that interpretation plays an increasingly important role in the 'postmodern habitat'. Whereas intellectuals used to *legislate* over questions of aesthetic taste, now their role has been reduced to that of *interpretation*: merely evaluating the system of knowledge from within its own terms, rather than pronouncing upon it in accordance with a prescribed hierarchy of value to which their audience can be expected to subscribe (Bauman, 1987). Urry points out that this interpretative voice can also be discerned in the less didactic tone of contemporary travel guides compared with their older equivalents, whereby 'visitors are encouraged to look with interest on an enormous diversity of artefacts, cultures and systems of meaning [of which] none are presumed to be superior, and the main role of the "expert" is to interpret them for the visitor' (1995: 146).

[4] Personal interview with Planning Officer, Mid Glamorgan County Council.

[5] Silverstone (1989) suggests considering three aspects of heritage textuality: its thematics (the choice of subject matter), poetics (narrative forms) and rhetoric (modes of addressing the visitor).

[6] See, for example, *Rhondda Leader* (1 Aug. 1991) and *South Wales Echo* (2 Oct. 1991).

[7] *Brief for the Visitor Design*, Rhondda Heritage Park Officers' Directing Group, Aug. 1988: 5.

[8] Most of this taped oral-history material has never really been put to use in the Park's displays; much of it was never transcribed, and presumably still exists to this day in the archives.

[9] Interview with researcher for *Black Gold*.

[10] Bryn Rees was an elderly ex-miner, a former Lewis Merthyr safety officer, living at the time in Trehafod. Sadly, he died soon after he was interviewed, before the full opening of *Black Gold*.

[11] The former UK Labour Party leader, who was born and bred in the south Wales Valleys and who, at the time of the encoding of *Black Gold*, was deemed likely to become the next British prime minister. Enlisting Neil Kinnock's participation in the RHP as narrator of the fan-house show was considered quite a coup at the time by the project's management.

[12] This was a method of calculating miners' wages, which tied their level to the price of sale-coal and was increasingly a focus of criticism by miners' representatives (see Francis and Smith, 1980).

9. The rhetoric of heritage: placing the visitor

[1] Children joined in the interviews but were not included in the analysis.

[2] The relatively high proportion of E-grade visitors (16 per cent) can be accounted for almost entirely by retired people. If these people are classified according to their last occupation, however, only two of the seven would move out of the manual grades (C2DE). This would make little difference to the overall profile.

[3] If we reclassify my interviewees on the basis of the occupation of head of household, the number of households whose members were interviewed, and which included a male adult head of household, is twenty. However, on this basis the social grade profile conforms even less closely to Prentice et al.'s findings. Of these twenty households represented, the male occupation falls within social grades ABC1 in only eight cases (40 per cent) while it is classified as C2DE in the remaining twelve (60 per cent). Again, only 15 per cent of the households have the male occupation in the AB categories, compared to Prentice et al.'s 63 per cent.

[4] It should be remembered, though, that these links do not imply in-depth knowledge of the Rhondda or its history – the next chapter will

discuss the range of different knowledge that the vistors brought to the vistor experience.

10. Visiting the Rhondda

1 All interviews were tape-recorded and transcribed, and analysed using a model of discourse analysis that identifies the cultural distinctions underpinning visitors' accounts (see Fairclough, 1992; Alasuutari, 1995).

2 These should not be thought of as categories of *visitor*; they are rather orientations visible in visitors' interview discourse. Many accounts seem to be oriented one way during one part of the interview, and another way at a different point.

3 Of the eight groups who did not make this assertion, seven offered no knowledge of the Rhondda, other than that 'coalmining comes to mind'. These seven groups are interesting, in that they are ostensibly the most akin to the 'black slate' visitor-type, upon which heritage texts can most readily 'write' their version of history.

4 There is space here to cite just one extract from the interview material, selected as exemplary of each positioning. All names have been changed.

5 There is no evidence in the complete interview sample of a straightforward class effect, nor of gender. In the first 'alien' framing, three groups belonged to social class C1, and the other six groups were C2, D and E. In the second, one group was A, one C1, and the other four were C2, D and E. The ambivalent framings were also mixed: with two from social class B, two C1s and an E. Although, as stated, there is some indication that male working-class occupation might be a factor, we need to be very careful here, since other working-class males produced the first reading (one of which, as a chimney sweep, had been closely connected to the coal industry for decades). The other potentially significant factor is local residence: having local links might plausibly result in less of a tendency to position local people/local past as an 'other'. However, there is no evidence of a local/non-local effect. Half (three of the six) 'alien' framing groups lived locally (that is, in Mid Glamorgan), while only one of the 'parallel' framing groups did.

6 Indeed, in two of the six 'parallel' readings (Mr R1 and Mr and Mrs W4), we find no instances of it. In three other cases (Mr A, Mr and Mrs M and Mr and Mrs J), we only find version 2, which imagines the people fighting back. In the final instance of the 'parallel' framing (Mr and Mrs H), it is the camaraderie of the workplace rather than of 'the community' which is pointed to.

7 In Hall's (1980) paper on encoding/decoding, there is considerable emphasis on the ideological message encoded into texts (the text's 'preferred meaning'). Hall suggests that the text's message can be

identified by the critic, who can then compare this with the meanings decoded by readers in order to see how far they accept this message (Hall theorizes three potential reading positions in relation to the preferred meaning: the negotiated, the dominant and the oppositional). In the present visitor study, we can see that negotiated meanings are not aspects of decoding alone, however. Rather, there is a negotiation or prevarication in the texts which is established through their conditions of production (see chapters 5 and 8). *Black Gold* is structured by a labourist discourse that presents the miners' struggles as legitimate, but there is no single preferred meaning that reflects a hegemonic world-view and which is passed directly from text to reader. The 'struggle for justice' theme is read in quite different ways by visitors, depending on the self/other relations that underpin their engagement with the heritage representations. Thus, the 'preferring' that the text accomplishes is relatively open, 'subject to more active transformations' in the interface with the visitor (Hall, 1980: 134). The question then becomes one of how visitors negotiate with the negotiation. It would be misleading, in this sense, to label the three framings identified as dominant, oppositional or negotiated readings, as in Hall's paper (see Dicks, 2000).

Appendix 1: *Black Gold* audio-visual shows

[1] The terms utilized here are drawn from narrative theory in film studies. Following Barthes, I call the 'terrain of meaning' of each substory its '*lexia*' (Barthes, 1977). Each substory consists of a series of events and descriptions that follow each other in a particular narrative order: this is called the story. The employment, on the other hand, refers to the ways in which the story is actually told, that is, as divided among narrators and scenes. Whereas the story is the logical and chronological order of events – in this case the vicissitudes of a century of Rhondda's mining industry and its fortunes – the plot is the artistic reordering of these events into an aesthetically pleasing form, using where appropriate the devices of flashbacks and flash-forwards, *in media res* constructions, and so on (Bordwell, 1985; Stam et al., 1992). The plot disrupts the predictable linearity and cause-and-effect sequencing of the story in order to hold the attention of the viewer more effectively.

Appendix 2: Rhondda Heritage Park case study

[1] Fairclough (1992) specifies two terms, *intertextuality* and *interdiscursivity*, which underpin critical discourse analysis These refer, respectively, to the presence of other texts within texts, and the configuration of discourse conventions that constitute a text. He uses this distinction in

the analysis of newspaper articles, which both implicitly refer to other
texts (public reports, etc.) – a practice he terms 'intertextuality' – and
also reproduce wider traces of ideologies and discourses circulating in
public culture, which he terms 'interdiscursivity'. I remain with the
generic term, intertextuality, to refer to the presence within texts both of
other constituted texts, and of wider ideological discourses not appearing therein as formal texts.

2 I do not want to suggest that non-mining families and ex-mining families
can be sharply distinguished; on the contrary, it is clear that many
current residents will have had mining connections that have long ago
been forgotten, or will have moved in from other mining areas. Those
who have moved in from non-mining areas, or whose families have had
no connection with mining, are equally interesting in terms of how they
make sense of community and respond to the RHP. However, such
questions are left to future projects to explore.

3 It is, in fact, somewhat artificial to separate out levels a) (officers and
councillors) and b) (consultants). It is clear that the 'heritage industry'
does not exist as an autonomous entity, but in a complex relationship
between commercial design companies and public funding bodies. It was
therefore essential to note the frequent cross-overs and inter-linkages
between and within officers', consultants' and councillors' accounts,
as all three groups together formed the field of negotiations and contrac-
tual relations within which the exhibits, narratives and designs were
drawn up

References

Abercrombie, N., Hill, S. and Turner, B. (1980). *The Dominant Ideology Thesis*, London, Allen & Unwin.

Adam, B. (1990). *Time and Social Theory*, Cambridge, Polity Press.

Adamson, D. L. (1991). *Class, Ideology and the Nation: A Theory of Welsh Nationalism*, Cardiff, University of Wales Press.

—— (1996). *Living on the Edge: Poverty and Deprivation in Wales*, Llandysul, Gomer.

—— (1999). 'Poverty and social exclusion in Wales today', in D. Dunkerley and A. Thompson (ed.), *Wales Today*, Cardiff, University of Wales Press.

Adorno, T. and Horkheimer, T. (1979 [1944]). *Dialectic of Enlightenment*, London and New York, Verso.

Agnew, J. (1989). 'The devaluation of place in social science', in J. Agnew and J. Duncan (eds.), *The Power of Place*, Boston, MA, Unwin Hyman, 9–29.

Alasuutari, P. (1995). *Researching Culture*, London, Sage.

Aldridge, D. (1989). 'How the ship of interpretation was blown off course in the tempest: some philosophical thoughts', in D. Uzzell (ed.), *Heritage Interpretation*, London and New York, Belhaven Press, 64–87.

Alonso, A. M. (1988). 'The effects of truth: re-presentations of the past and the imagining of community', *Journal of Historical Sociology*, 1(1), 33–57.

Anderson, B. (1991). *Imagined Communities*, 2nd edn, London and New York, Verso.

Appadurai, A. (1990). 'Disjuncture and difference in the global cultural economy', *Theory, Culture and Society*, 7, 295–310.

Ascherson, N. (1987). '"Heritage" as vulgar nationalism', *Observer*, (29 Nov.), 9.

—— (1997). 'Why "heritage" is right-wing', *Observer*, (8 Nov.), 9.

Bagguley, P., Mark-Lawson, J., Shapiro, D., Urry, J., Walby, S. and Warde, A. (1990). *Restructuring: Place, Class and Gender*, London, Sage.

Bal, M. (1996). 'The discourse of the museum', in R. Greenberg, B. W. Ferguson and S. Nairne (eds.), *Thinking about Exhibitions*, London and New York, Routledge.

Ballard, P. H. and Jones, E. (eds.), (1975). *The Valleys Call*, Ferndale, Ron Jones Publications.

Balsom, D. (1985). 'The three Wales model', in J. Osmond (ed.), *The National Question Again? Welsh Political Identity in the 1980s*, Llandysul, Gomer.

Barke, M. and Harrop, K. (1994). 'Selling the industrial town: identity, image and illusion', in J. R. Gold and S. V. Ward (eds.), *Place Promotion: The Use of Publicity and Marketing to Sell Towns and Regions*, Chichester, John Wiley & Sons, 93–114.

Barnie, J. (1985). 'Living by tourism?' Interview with Prys Edwards, chairman of the Wales Tourist Board', *Planet*, 52 (Aug./Sept.).

Barry, A. (1998). 'On interactivity: consumers, citizens and culture', in S. Macdonald (ed.), *The Politics of Display: Museums, Science, Culture*, London and New York, Routledge.

Barthes, R. (1973 [1957]). 'Myth today', in *Mythologies*, London, Paladin.

—— (1977). *Image-Music-Text*, essays selected and tr. by Stephen Heath, New York, Hill & Wang.

Bauman, Z. (1987). *Legislators and Interpreters*, Cambridge, Polity Press.

—— (1991). *Modernity and Ambivalence*, Oxford, Polity.

—— (1992). *Intimations of Postmodernity*, London and New York, Routledge.

Beatty, C., Fothergill, S., Gore, A. and Hereington, A. (1997). *The Real Level of Unemployment*, Sheffield, Centre for Regional and Economic Research, Sheffield Hallam University.

Benjamin, W. (1973). 'The work of art in the age of mechanical production', in *Illuminations*, London, Fontana.

Bennett, T. (1995). *The Birth of the Museum*, London, Routledge.

Benson, K. (1995). 'Community connections', *Forum*, 38(1), 9–13.

Berman, M. (1983). *All that is Solid Melts into Air: The Experience of Modernity*, London, Verso.

Betts, C. (1993). *The Political Conundrum: Wales and its Politics in the Century's Last Decade*, Llandysul, Gomer.

Bhabha, H. (1990). 'DissemiNation: time, narrative and the margins of the modern nation', in H. Bhabha (ed.), *Nation and Narration*, London and New York, Routledge, 291–322.

Bianchini, F. (1993). 'Remaking European cities: the role of cultural policies', in F. Bianchini and M. Parkinson (eds.), *Cultural Policy and Urban Regeneration: The West European Experience*, Manchester and New York, Manchester University Press.

—— and Schwengel, H. (1991). 'Re-imagining the city', in J. Corner and S. Harvey (eds.), *Enterprise and Heritage: Crosscurrents of National Culture*, London and New York, Routledge, 45–75.

Bicknell, S. and Farmelo, G. (eds.) (1994). *Museum Visitor Studies in the 1990s*, London, Science Museum.

Billig, M. (1995). *Banal Nationalism*, London, Sage.

Binks, G. (1989). 'Interpreters in the community: a discussion paper', in D. Uzzell (ed.), *Heritage Interpretation, 2: The Visitor Experience*, London and New York, Belhaven Press, 190–200.

Bommes, M. and Wright, P. (1982), 'Charms of residence: the public and the past', in R. Johnson, G. McLenon, W. Schwartz and D. Sutton (eds.), *Making Histories*, London, Hutchinson, 253–302.

Bordwell, D. (1985). *Narration in the Fiction Film*, Madison, WI, University of Wisconsin Press.

Bott, E. (1957). *Family and Social Network*, London, Tavistock.

Bourdieu, P. (1984). *Distinction: A Social Critique of the Judgement of Taste*, London, Routledge & Kegan Paul.

—— and Darbel, A. (1991 [1969]). *The Love of Art: European Art Museums and their Public*, Cambridge, Polity.

Boylan, P. (1990). 'Museums and cultural identity', *Museums Journal* (Oct.), 29–33.

Boyne, G. A., Griffiths, P., Lawton, A. and Law, J. (1991). *Local Government in Wales*, York, Joseph Rowntree Foundation.

Brewer, T. (1999). 'Heritage tourism: a mirror for Wales?', in D. Dunkerley and A. Thompson (eds.), *Wales Today*, Cardiff, University of Wales Press.

Brook, E. and Finn, D. (1978). 'Working class images of society and community studies', in Centre for Contemporary Cultural Studies (eds.), *On Ideology*, London, Hutchinson.

Browne, S. (1994). 'Heritage in Ireland's tourism recovery', in J. M. Fladmark (ed.), *Cultural Tourism*, London, Donhead, 13–25.

Bulmer, M. (1975). 'Sociological models of the mining community', *Sociological Review*, 23, 61–93.

Calhoun, C. (1983). 'The radicalism of tradition: community strength or venerable disguise and borrowed language?', *American Journal of Sociology*, 88(5), 886–915.

Casey, B. (1995). 'Museum and galleries', *Cultural Trends*, 25, London, Policy Studies Institute, 20–45.

Castells, M. (1989). *The Informational City*, Oxford, Basil Blackwell.

Chaney, D. (1993). *Fictions of Collective Life: Public Drama in Late Modern Culture*, London, Routledge.

Clavel, P. (1983). *Opposition Planning in Wales and Appalachia*, Philadelphia, Temple University Press.

Clifford, J. (1997). *Routes: Travel and Translation in the Late Twentieth Century*, Cambridge, MA, and London, Harvard University Press.

Cole, D. (1995). *Rhondda Tourism: A Strategic Overview: Report prepared for the Wales Tourist Board* (Cardiff, Wales Tourist Board).

Committee on Welsh Affairs (1986–7). *First Report, Tourism in Wales, 2*, London, Her Majesty's Stationery Office.

Cooke, P. (ed.) (1989). *Localities*, London, Unwin Hyman.

Cooke, P. (1982). 'Class relations and uneven development in Wales', in G. Day (ed.), *Diversity and Decomposition in the Labour Market*, Aldershot, Hants, Gower.

Coombes, A. E. (1992). 'Inventing the "postcolonial": hybridity and constituency in contemporary curating', *New Formations*, 18 (Winter), 39–52.

Corner, J. and Harvey, S. (1991). 'Mediating tradition and modernity', in J. Corner and S. Harvey (eds.), *Enterprise and Heritage: Crosscurrents of National Culture*, London and New York, Routledge, 45–75.

Craik, J. (1997). 'The culture of tourism', in C. Rojek and J. Urry (eds.), *Touring Cultures: Transformations in Leisure and Theory*, London and New York, Routledge.

Crang, M. (1994). 'On the heritage trail: maps of and journeys to Olde England', *Environment and Planning D: Society and Space*, 12, 341–55.

Critcher, C. (1979). 'Sociology, cultural studies and the post-war working class', in J. Clarke, C. Critcher and R. Johnson (eds.), *Working Class Culture: Studies in History and Theory*, London, Hutchinson, 13–40.

Crow, G. and Allan, G. (1994). *Community Life*, London, Harvester Wheatsheaf.

Curtis, T. (ed.) (1986). *Wales: The Imagined Nation*, Bridgend, Poetry Wales Press.

Davies, G. (1988). 'The end of the pier show?', *New Formations*, 5, 933–40.

Davis, F. (1979). *Yearning for Yesterday*, New York, The Free Press.

Day, G. (1989). 'Whatever happened to the sociology of Wales?', *Planet*, 77 (Oct./Nov.), 69–77.

—— (1998). 'A community of communities? Similarly and difference in Welsh rural community studies', *The Economic and Social Review*, 29, 3, 233–57.

Delaney, J. (1992). 'Ritual space in the Canadian Museum of Civilisation', in R. Shields (ed.), *Lifestyle Shopping: The Subject of Consumption*, London and New York, Routledge, 136–48.

Dennis, N., Henriques, F. and Slaughter, C. (1969). *Coal is our Life: An Analysis of a Yorkshire Mining Community*, London, Tavistock.

Dicks, B. (1996). 'Regeneration versus representation in the Rhondda: the story of the Rhondda Heritage Park', *Contemporary Wales*, 9, 56–73.

—— (1997a). 'The life and times of community: spectacles of collective identity at the Rhondda Heritage Park', *Time and Society*, 6(2/3), 195–212.

—— (1997b). 'The view of our town from the hill: an enquiry into the representation of community at the Rhondda Heritage Park', Ph.D. thesis, University of Wales.

—— (1999). 'The view of our town from the hill: communities on display as local heritage', *International Journal of Cultural Studies*, 2(3), 349–68.

—— (2000). 'Encoding and decoding the people: circuits of communication at a local heritage museum', *European Journal of Communication*, 15 (1), 61–78.

—— and Van Loon, J. (1999). 'Territoriality and heritage in south Wales: space, time and imagined communities', in R. Fevre and A. Thompson (eds.), *Nation, Identity and Social Theory*, Cardiff, University of Wales Press.

Divall, C. (1998). 'Transports of delight? Making and consuming histories at the National Railway Museum', in J. Arnold, K. Davies and S. Ditchfield (eds.), *History and Heritage: Consuming the Past in Contemporary Culture*, Shaftesbury, Donhead.

Dunkerley, D. (1999). 'Social Wales', in D. Dunkerley and A. Thompson, *Wales Today*, Cardiff, University of Wales Press.

East Midlands Museums Service (1996). *Knowing our Visitors: Market Survey 94/95* Nottingham: East Midlands Museums Service.

Eckstein, J. and Feist, A. (eds.) (1991). *Cultural Trends*, 12, London, Policy Studies Institute.

Eco, U. (1986). *Travels in Hyper Reality*, San Diego, Harcourt Brace & Co.

Ecotec Research and Consulting Ltd. (1993). *An Economic Development Strategy for Industrial South Wales*, Final report to the Standing Conference on Regional Policy in South Wales.

Edwards, J. A. and Llurdes i Coit, J. C. (1996). 'Mines and quarries: industrial heritage tourism', *Annals of Tourism Research*, 23(2), 341–63.

Ellis, J. (1982). *Visible Fictions*, London, Routledge.

Evans, J. (1994). *How Real is my Valley?* Pontypridd, Underground Press.

European Commission (1994–6). *Industrial South Wales: Single Programming Document (Objective 1)*, Brussels, European Commission.

Fabian, J. (1983). *Time and the Other: How Anthropology Makes its Object*, New York, Columbia University Press.

Fairclough, N. (1992). *Discourse and Social Change*, Cambridge, Polity.

Featherstone, M. (1991). *Consumer Culture and Postmodernism*, London, Sage.

—— (1993). 'Global and local cultures', in J. Bird, B. Curtis, T. Putnam, G. Robertson and L. Tickner (eds.), *Mapping the Futures: Local Cultures, Global Change*, London and New York, Routledge.

Foucault, M. (1977). *Discipline and Punish*, Harmondsworth, Penguin.

—— (1981). *The History of Sexuality*, Harmondsworth, Penguin.

Francis, H. (1981). 'A nation of museum attendants', *Arcade*, 16 Jan., 8–9.

—— (1990). 'The Valleys', in R. Jenkins and A. Edwards (eds.), *One Step Forward: Scotland and Wales towards the Year 2000*, Llandysul, Gomer.

—— and Smith, F. (1980). *The Fed: A History of the South Wales Miners in the Twentieth Century*, London, Lawrence & Wishart.

Fretter, A. D. (1993). 'Place marketing: a local authority perspective', in G. Kearns and C. Philo (eds.), *Selling Places*, Oxford, Pergamon Press, 175–92.

Fyfe, G. and Ross, M. (1996). 'Decoding the visitor's gaze: rethinking museum visiting', in S. Macdonald and G. Fyfe (eds.), *Theorising Museums*, Oxford, Blackwell, 127–52.

Gaffney, A. (1998). 'Monuments and memory: the Great War', in J. Arnold, K. Davies and S. Ditchfield (eds.), *History and Heritage: Consuming the Past in Contemporary Culture*, Shaftesbury, Donhead.

Giggs, J. and Pattie, C. (1992). 'Wales as a plural society', *Contemporary Wales*, 5, 25–63.

Gilbert, D. (1992). *Class, Community and Collective Action: Social Change in Two British Coalfields, 1850–1926*, Oxford, Clarendon Press.

Goodwin, M. (1993). 'The city as commodity: the contested spaces of urban development', in G. Kearns and C. Philo (eds.), *Selling Places: The City as Cultural Capital: Past and Present*, Oxford, Pergamon Press, 145–62.

Graf, B. (1994). 'Visitor studies in Germany: methods and examples', in R. Miles and L. Zavala (eds.), *Towards the Museum of the Future: New European Perspectives*, London and New York, Routledge, 75–80.

Griffiths, P. (1987). 'Mid Glamorgan County Council', in H. Elcock and G. Jordan (eds.), *Learning from Local Authority Budgeting*, Aldershot, Avebury.

Gruffudd, P. (1995). 'Heritage as national identity: histories and prospects of the national pasts', in D. T. Herbert (ed.), *Heritage, Tourism and Society*, London, Pinter.

—— (1999). 'Prospects of Wales: contested geographical imaginations', in R. Fevre and A. Thompson (eds.), *Nation, Identity and Social Theory*, Cardiff, University of Wales Press.

Hall, S. (1980). 'Encoding/decoding', in S. Hall, D. Hobson, A. Lowe and P. Willis (eds.), *Culture, Media, Language*, London, Hutchinson, 128–38.

Hall, T. (1997). '(Re)placing the city: cultural relocation and the city as centre', in S. Westwood and J. Williams (eds.), *Imagining Cities: Scripts, Signs, Memory*, London and New York, Routledge.

Hannan, P. (1999). *The Welsh Illusion*, Bridgend, Poetry Wales Press.

Harrison, R. (ed.) (1978). *Independent Collier: The Coal Miner as Archetypal Proletarian Reconsidered*, Hassocks, Harvester Press.

Harvey, D. (1989a). *The Condition of Postmodernity: An Enquiry into the Origins of Cultural Change*, Oxford, Basil Blackwell.

—— (1989b). 'From managerialism to entrepreneurialism: the transformation in urban governance in late capitalism', *Geografiska Annaler*, 71(1), 3–17.

Heady, P. (1984). *Visiting Museums: A Report of a Survey of Visitors to the Victoria and Albert, Science and Railway Museums for the Office of Arts and Libraries*, London, Office of Population and Census Surveys.

Hetherington, K. (1996). 'The Utopics of social ordering – Stonehenge as a museum without walls', in S. Macdonald and G. Fyfe (eds.), *Theorising Museums*, Oxford, Blackwell/*Sociological Review*, 153–76.

Hewison, R. (1987). *The Heritage Industry: Britain in a Climate of Decline*, London, Methuen.

—— (1989). 'Heritage: an interpretation', in D. Uzzell (ed.), *Heritage Interpretation*, 1: *The Natural and Built Environment*, London and New York, Belhaven Press.

Hobsbawm, E. and Ranger, T. (eds.) (1983). *The Invention of Tradition*, Oxford, Blackwell.

Holcomb, B. (1993). 'Revisioning place: de- and re-constructing the image of the industrial city', in G. Kearns and C. Philo (eds.), *Selling Places*, Oxford, Pergamon Press, 175–92.

Hooper-Greenhill, E. (1992). *Museums and the Shaping of Knowledge*, London and New York, Routledge.

—— (1994). *Museums and their Visitors*, London and New York, Routledge.

—— (1995). 'Audiences – a curatorial dilemma', in S. Pearce (ed.), *Art in Museums*, London, Athlone Press, 143–63.

Horne, D. (1984). *The Great Museum: The Re-presentation of History*, London, Pluto Press.

Hoyau, P. (1988). 'Heritage and the "conserver society": the French case', in R. Lumley (ed.), *The Museum Time-Machine*, London, Routledge, 27–35.

Humphreys, R. (1995). 'Images of Wales', in T. Herbert and G. E. Jones (eds.), *Post-War Wales*, Cardiff, University of Wales Press.

Huyssen, A. (1995). *Twilight Memories: Marking Time in a Culture of Amnesia*, London and New York, Routledge.

Jackson, B. (1968). *Working Class Community*, London, Penguin.

Jacobs, J. (1994). 'Negotiating the heart: heritage, development and identity in postimperial London', *Environment and Planning D: Society and Space*, 12, 751–72.

Jameson, F. (1984). 'Postmodernism, or the cultural logic of late capitalism', *New Left Review*, 146, 53–92.

—— (1991). *Postmodernism: Or, the Cultural Logic of Late Capitalism*, London and New York, Verso.

Jenkins, J. G. (1985). 'Wales in a glass case?', *Radical Wales*, 6 (Spring), 8–9.

—— (1986/7). 'Interpreting the heritage of Wales', *Folk Life: A Journal of Ethnological Studies*, 25, 5–17.

—— (1989). 'The collection of material objects and their interpretation' in S. M. Pearce (ed.), *Museum Studies in Material Culture*, London and New York, Leicester University Press, 153–71.

Jenkinson, P. (1989). 'Material culture, people's history and populism: where do we go from here?', in S. M. Pearce (ed.), *Museum Studies in Material Culture*, Leicester, Leicester University Press, 139–52.

Jess, P. and Massey, D. (1995). 'The contestation of place', in D. Massey and P. Jess (eds.), *A Place in the World?*, Oxford, Oxford University Press, in association with The Open University, 133–74.

Johnson, P. and Thomas, B. (1992). *Tourism, Museums and the Local Economy: The Economic Impact of the North of England Open Air Museum at Beamish*, Aldershot, Edward Elgar.

Johnstone, C. (1998). 'Your Granny had one of those! How visitors use museum collections', in J. Arnold, K. Davies and S. Ditchfield (eds.), *History and Heritage: Consuming the Past in Contemporary Culture*, Shaftesbury, Donhead.

Jones, R. (1986). 'Out of the past: pictures in theory and history', in T. Curtis (ed.), *Wales, The Imagined Nation*, Bridgend, Poetry Wales Press.

Jordanova, L. (1989). 'Objects of knowledge: a historical perspective on museums', in P. Vergo (ed.), *The New Museology*, London, Reaktion Books, 22–40.

Kahn, K. (1984). 'Land, language and community: a symbolic analysis of Welsh nationalism', *Michigan Discussions in Anthropology*, 7, 11–32.

Kamenka, E. (1982). 'Community and the socialist ideal', in E. Kamenka (ed.), *Community as a Social Ideal*, London, Edward Arnold, 3–26.

Kerr, C. and Siegel, A. (1954). 'The inter-industry propensity to strike: an international comparison', in A. Kornhauser, R. Dubin and A. Ross (eds.), *Industrial Conflict*, New York, McGraw, 189–212.

Lash, S. (1990). *Sociology of Postmodernism*, London, Routledge.

—— and Urry, J. (1987). *The End of Organised Capitalism*, Cambridge, Polity.

—— and —— (1994). *Economies of Signs and Space*, London, Sage.

Lee, D. and Newby, H. (1983). *The Problem of Sociology*, London, Harper & Row.

Leisure and Tourism Unit, Centre for Urban and Regional Studies, University of Birmingham (1983). *Realising the Tourism Potential of the South Wales Valleys*, Cardiff, Wales Tourist Board.

Lewis, P. (1980). 'The museum as an educational facility', *Museums Journal*, 80, 151–5.

Light, D. (1991). 'Heritage places in Wales and their interpretation: a study in applied recreational geography', unpublished Ph.D. thesis, University of Wales.

—— (1995). 'Heritage as informal education', in D. Herbert (ed.), *Heritage, Tourism and Society*, London, Pinter.

—— and Prentice, R. (1994). 'Who consumes the heritage product?', in G. J. Ashworth and P. J. Larkham (eds.), *Building a New Heritage: Tourism, Culture and Identity in the New Europe*, London and New York, Routledge.

Lovering, J. (1998). 'The "new regionalism" in Wales', *Contemporary Wales*, 11, 12–60.

Lowenthal, D. (1985). *The Past is a Foreign Country*, Cambridge, Cambridge University Press.

—— (1998). *The Heritage Crusade and the Spoils of History*, Cambridge, Cambridge University Press.

Lumley, R. (1988). 'Introduction', in R. Lumley (ed.), *The Museum Time Machine: Putting Cultures on Display*, London and New York, Routledge, 1–24.

—— (1994). 'The debate on heritage reviewed', in R. Miles and L. Zavala (eds.), *Towards the Museum of the Future: New European Perspectives*, London and New York, Routledge, 57–69.

McCrone, D., Morris, A. and Liely, R. (1995). *Scotland – the Brand*, Edinburgh, Edinburgh University Press.

Macdonald, S. (1995). 'Consuming science: public knowledge and the dispersed politics of reception among museum visitors', *Media, Culture and Society*, 17, 13–29.

—— (1997), 'A people's story: heritage, identity and authenticity', in C. Rojek and J. Urry (eds.), *Touring Cultures*, London, Routledge.

—— (1998). 'Exhibitions of power and powers of exhibition: an introduction to the politics of display', in S. Macdonald (ed.), *The Politics of Display: Museums, Science, Culture*, London and New York, Routledge.

McGuigan, J. (1999). *Modernity and Postmodern Culture*, Buckingham and Philadelphia, Open University Press.

McLees, D. (1997). 'Of chapels and working men's halls', *Heritage in Wales*, 8 (Summer), 20–1.

McManus, P. (1989). 'What people say and how they think in a science museum', in D. Uzzell (ed.), *Heritage Interpretation, 2: The Visitor Experience*, London and New York, Belhaven Press.

Maffesoli, M. (1995). *The Time of the Tribes*, London, Sage.

Marcus, G. E. (1994). 'The modernist sensibility in recent ethnographic writing and the cinematic metaphor of montage', in L. Taylor (ed.), *Visualising Theory*, London and New York, Routledge.

Marcuse, H. (1968). *One Dimensional Man: The Ideology of Industrial Society*, London, Sphere Books.

Marwick, S. (1995). 'Learning from each other: museums and older members of the community – the people's story', in E. Hooper-Greenhill (ed.), *Museum, Media Message*, London and New York, Routledge.

Massey, D. (1984). *Spatial Divisions of Labour: Social Structures and the Geography of Production*, Basingstoke, Macmillan.

—— (1991). 'The political place of locality studies', *Environment and Planning A*, 23, 267–81.

—— (1993). 'Power geometry and a progressive sense of place', in J. Bird, B. Curtis, T. Putman, G. Robertson and L. Tickner (eds.), *Mapping the Futures: Local Cultures, Global Change*, London and New York, Routledge, 59–69.

—— (1994). 'Double articulation: a place in the world', in A. Bammer (ed.), *Displacements: Cultural Identities in Question*, Bloomington and Indianapolis, Indiana University Press.

—— (1995a). 'The conceptualisation of place', in D. Massey and P. Jess (eds.), *A Place in the World? Places, Cultures and Globalisation*, Oxford, Oxford University Press, 45–86.

—— (1995b). 'Places and their pasts', *History Workshop Journal*, 39, 183–92.

Mellor, A. (1991). 'Enterprise and heritage in the dock', in J. Corner and S. Harvey (eds.), *Enterprise and Heritage: Crosscurrents of National Culture*, London and New York, Routledge, 93–115.

Merriman, N. (1989). 'Museum visiting as a cultural phenomenon', in P. Vergo (ed.), *The New Museology*, London, Reaktion Books, 149–204.

—— (1991). *Beyond the Glass Case: The Past, the Heritage and the Public in Britain*, Leicester, Leicester University Press.

Miliband, R. (1960). 'The sickness of labourism', *New Left Review*, 1, 5–9.

Morgan, B. (1997). 'LG', *Agenda*, Cardiff, Institute of Welsh Affairs, June.

Morgan, K. O. (1995). 'Wales since 1945: political culture', in T. Herbert and G. Elwyn Jones (eds.), *Post-War Wales*, Cardiff, University of Wales Press.

Morgan, P. (1983). 'From a death to a view: the hunt for the Welsh past in the romantic period', in E. Hobsbawm and T. Ranger (eds.), *The Invention of Tradition*, Cambridge: Cambridge University Press, 43–100.

—— (1986). 'Keeping the legends alive', in T. Curtis (ed.), *Wales: The Imagined Nation*, Bridgend, Poetry Wales Press.

Morley, D. (1992). *Television, Audiences and Cultural Studies*, London and New York, Routledge.

Morris, J. and Wilkinson, B. (1993). 'Poverty and prosperity in Wales: an analysis of socio-economic divisions', HTV Current Affairs Department, 'Wales this Week', unpublished report.

—— and —— (1995). 'Poverty and prosperity in Wales: polarisation and Los Angelisation', *Contemporary Wales*, 8, 29–45.

Morris, P. (1996). 'Community beyond tradition', in P. Heelas, S. Lash and P. Morris (eds.), *Detraditionalisation: Critical Reflections on Authority and Identity*, Oxford, Blackwell, pp. 223–49.

Myerscough, J. (1988). *The Economic Importance of the Arts in Britain*, London, Policy Studies Institute.

Nairn, T. (1988). *The Enchanted Glass: Britain and its Monarchy*, London, Hutchinson Radius.

Owen, T. M. (1985). 'Community studies in Wales: an overview', *Ethnologia Europaea*, 15, 27–52.

Peate, I. (1948). *Folk Museums*, Cardiff, University of Wales Press.

Peirson Jones, J. (1995). 'Communicating and learning in Gallery 33: evidence from a visitor study', in E. Hooper-Greenhill (ed.), *Museum, Media Message*, London and New York, Routledge.

Pitchford, S. R. (1994). 'The tourist trap', *Planet*, 104 (April/May), 3–7.

Poulot, D. (1994). 'Identity as self-discovery: the eco-museum in France', in D. J. Sherman and I. Rogoff (eds.), *Museum Culture: Histories, Discourses, Spectacles*, London, Routledge, 66–84.

Prentice, R. (1993). *Change and Policy in Wales: Wales in the Era of Privatism*, Llandysul, Gomer Press.

——, Witt, S. and Hamer, C. (1993). 'The experience of industrial heritage: the case of black gold', *Built Environment*, 19(2), 137–46.

Price, A., Morgan, K. and Cooke, P. (1994). *The Welsh Renaissance: Inward Investment and Industrial Innovation*, Regional Industrial Research Report 14, Cardiff Centre for Advanced Studies, University of Wales.

Price, D. (1992). 'Gazing at the valleys: representation and the cultural construction of south Wales', Ph.D. thesis, University of Birmingham.

Rees, A. (1951). *Life in a Welsh Countryside: A Social Study of Llanfihangel yng Ngwynfa*, Cardiff, University of Wales Press.

—— and Davies, E. (eds.) (1960). *Welsh Rural Communities*, Cardiff, University of Wales Press.

Rees, G. (1985). 'Regional restructuring, class change, and political action: preliminary comments on the 1984–1985 miners' strike in south Wales', *Environment and Planning D: Society and Space*, 3, 389–406.

—— (1997). 'The politics of regional development strategy: the programme for the valleys', in R. Macdonald and H. Thomas (eds.), *Nationality and Planning in Scotland and Wales*, Cardiff, University of Wales Press, 98–110.

—— and Morgan, K. (1991). 'Industrial restructuring, innovation systems and the regional state: south Wales in the 1990s', in G. Day and G. Rees (eds.), *Regions, Nations and European Integration: Remaking the Celtic Periphery*, Cardiff, University of Wales Press.

—— and Rees, T. (eds.) (1980). *Poverty and Social Inequality in Wales*, London, Croom Helm.

Reid, I. (1989). *Social Class Differences in Britain*, London, Fontana.

Ricoeur, P. (1984). *Time and Narrative, Volume 1*, Chicago, Chicago University Press.

—— (1985). *Time and Narrative, Volume 2*, Chicago, Chicago University Press.

—— (1988). *Time and Narrative, Volume 3*, Chicago, Chicago University Press.

Ritzer, G. (1996). *The McDonaldisation of Society*, revised edn., Thousand Oaks, CA, Pine Forge Press.

—— and Liska, A. (1997). '"McDisneyisation" and "post-tourism": complementary perspectives on contemporary tourism', in C. Rojek and J. Urry (eds.), *Touring Cultures: Transformations of Travel and Theory*, London and New York, Routledge.

Roberts, B. (1999). 'Welsh identity in a former mining community', in R. Fevre and A. Thompson (eds.), *Nation, Identity and Social Theory*, Cardiff, University of Wales Press.

Robertson, R. (1990). 'After nostalgia? Wilful nostalgia and the phases of globalisation', in B. Turner (ed.), *Theories of Modernity and Post-modernity*, London, Sage.

Robins, K. (1991). 'Tradition and translation: national culture in its global context', in J. Corner and S. Harvey (eds.), *Enterprise and Heritage: Crosscurrents of National Culture*, London and New York, Routledge, 21–44.

Rojek, C. (1993). *Ways of Escape: Modern Transformations in Leisure and Travel*, London, Macmillan.

Sadler, D. (1993). 'Place-marketing, competitive places and the construction of hegemony', in G. Kearns and C. Philo (eds.), *Selling Places*, Oxford, Pergamon Press, 175–92.

Samuel, R. (1994). *Theatres of Memory*, London, Verso.

—— (1998). *Island Stories: Unravelling Britain*, London, Verso.

Sandberg, M. B. (1995). 'Effigy and narrative: looking into the nineteenth century folk museum', in L. Charney and V. R. Schwartz (eds.), *Cinema and the Invention of Modern Life*, Berkeley, CA, University of California Press, 320–61.

Saville, J. (1973). 'The ideology of labourism', in R. Benewick, R. N. Berki and B. Parekh (eds.), *Knowledge and Belief in Politics: The Problem of Ideology*, London, Allen & Unwin, 213–26.

Selwood, S., Muir, A. and Moody, D. (1995). 'Museums and galleries statistics: the Domus Database', *Cultural Trends*, 28, London, Policy Studies Institute.

Shields, R. (1991). *Places on the Margin: Alternative Geographies of Modernity*, London and New York, Routledge.

Silverstone, R. (1988). 'Museums and the media: a theoretical and methodological exploration', *International Journal of Museum Management and Curatorship*, 7, 231–41.

—— (1989). 'Heritage as media', in D. Uzzell (ed.), *Heritage Interpretation, 2: The Visitor Experience*, London and New York, Belhaven Press.

—— (1994). 'The medium is the museum: on objects and logics in times and spaces', in R. Miles and L. Zavala (eds.), *Towards the Museum of the Future: New European Perspectives*, London and New York, Routledge, 161–76.

Smith, D. (1984). *Wales! Wales?* London, Allen & Unwin.

—— (1990/1) 'Labour history and heritage', *Social History Curators Group Journal*, 18, 3–6.

—— (1999). *Wales: A Question for History*, Bridgend, Poetry Wales Press.

Stam, R., Burgoyne, R. and Flitterman-Lewis, S. (1992). *New Vocabularies in Film Semiotics*, London and New York, Routledge.

Stead, P. (1986). 'Wales in the movies', in T. Curtis (ed.), *Wales, the Imagined Nation*, Bridgend, Poetry Wales Press.

Strangleman, T., Hollywood, E., Beynon, H., Bennett, K. and Hudson, R. (1999). 'Heritage work: re-representing the work ethic in the coalfields', *Sociological Research Online*, 4(3).

Tannock, S. (1995). 'Nostalgia critique', *Cultural Studies*, 9, 453–64.

Taylor, P., Brokes, E., Finn, D., Tolson, A., Willis, P. and Powell, R. (1976). *A Critique of Community Studies and its Role in Social Thought*, Birmingham, Centre for Contemporary Cultural Studies.

Thomas, A. (1999). 'Politics in Wales: a new era?', in D. Dunkerley and A. Thompson (eds.), *Wales Today*, Cardiff, University of Wales Press.

Thompson, J. B. (1995). *The Media and Modernity: A Social Theory of the Media*, Cambridge, Polity Press.

Thompson, W. (1993). *The Long Death of British Labourism: Interpreting a Political Culture*, London, Pluto Press.

Tonnies, F. (1955 [1887]). *Community and Association*, London, Routledge & Kegan Paul.

Tunbridge, J. E. and Ashworth, G. J. (1996). *Dissonant Heritage: The Management of the Past as Resource in Conflict*, Chichester, John Wiley.

Tunstall, J. (1962). *The Fishermen: The Sociology of an Extreme Occupation*, London, MacGibbon and Kee.

Turner, B. S. (1987). 'A note on nostalgia', *Theory, Culture and Society*, 4, 147–56.

Urry, J. (1990). *The Tourist Gaze: Leisure and Travel in Contemporary Societies*, London, Sage.

—— (1992). 'The tourist gaze "revisited"', *American Behavioural Scientist*, 36(2), 172–86.

—— (1994). 'Time, leisure and social identity', *Time and Society*, 3(2), 131–49.

—— (1995). *Consuming Places*, London and New York, Routledge.

—— (1996). 'How societies remember the past', in S. Macdonald and G. Fyfe (eds.), *Theorising Museums*, Oxford, Blackwell, 45–68.

Uzzell, D. (ed.) (1989). *Heritage Interpretation, 2: The Visitor Experience*, London and New York, Belhaven Press.

Vergo, P. (ed.) (1989). *The New Museology*, London, Reaktion Books Ltd.

Walsh, K. (1992). *The Representation of the Past: Museums and Heritage in the Post-Modern World*, London and New York, Routledge.

Ward, S. V. (1994). 'Time and place: key themes in place promotion in the USA, Canada and Britain since 1870', in J. R. Gold and S. V. Ward (eds.), *Place Promotion: The Use of Publicity and Marketing to Sell Towns and Regions*, Chichester, John Wiley & Sons, 53–74.

Welsh Office (1967). *Wales: The Way Ahead*, White Paper, London, Welsh Office.

—— (1999). *The Valleys: New Opportunities, New Future*, Cardiff, Welsh Office.

West, B. (1988). 'The making of the English working past: a critical view of the Ironbridge Gorge Museum', in R. Lumley (ed.), *The Museum Time Machine*, London, Routledge, 36–62.

Williams, C. (1996). *Democratic Rhondda: Politics and Society 1885–1951*, Cardiff, University of Wales Press.

Williams, G. A. (1985). *When was Wales?* London, Penguin.

Williams, R. (1961). *The Long Revolution*, London, Penguin.

—— (1978). *The Volunteers*, London, Methuen.

Williamson, B. (1982). *Class, Culture and Community: A Biographical Study of Social Change in Mining*, London, Routledge & Kegan Paul.

Willmott, P. (1986). *Social Networks, Informal Care and Public Policy*, London, Routledge & Kegan Paul.

Wilson, E. (1997). 'Looking backward: nostalgia and the city', in S. Westwood and J. Williams (eds.), *Imagining Cities: Scripts, Signs, Memory*, London and New York, Routledge.

Wright, P. (1985). *On Living in an Old Country*, London, Verso.

—— (1992). *A Journey through Ruins*, London, Paladin.

Young, I. M. (1990). 'The ideal of community and the politics of difference', in L. Nicholson (ed.), *Feminism/Postmodernism*, London and New York, Routledge, 301–23.

Young, M. and Willmott, P. (1957). *Family and Kinship in East London*, London, Routledge & Kegan Paul.

Zukin, S. (1991). *Landscapes of Power: From Detroit to Disney World*, Berkeley and Los Angeles, University of California Press.

—— (1995). *The Cultures of Cities*, Oxford, Blackwell.

Consultant, local authority and government agency reports

Centre Screen Productions Ltd. (n.d.). *Rhondda Heritage Park: Proposals and Creative Treatment*.

Coopers & Lybrand Deloitte (1992). *Rhondda Heritage Park: Marketing and Strategic Business Plan* (Jan.).

John Brown & Co., Sally Wright Associates, Wyn Thomas & Partners, Heritage Projects Ltd. and Frank Atkinson OBE (1988). *Rhondda Heritage Park Lewis Merthyr Site: Design for the Visitor Experience, Interim Report*, presented to Rhondda Heritage Park (Nov.).

——, ——, ——, —— and —— (1989). *Rhondda Heritage Park Lewis Merthyr Site: Design for the Visitor Experience, Final Report*, presented to Rhondda Heritage Park (Feb.).

Mid Glamorgan County Council (1982). *Mid Glamorgan County Structure Plan: Approved Plan*, Cardiff, Mid Glamorgan County Council.

Rhondda Borough Council (1983). *Lewis Merthyr Colliery: Development of Heritage Museum*, Report prepared by Borough Planning Officer, Borough Technical Officer, Borough Treasurer and Borough Leisure Services Officer (Nov.).

Rhondda Heritage Park, Officers' Directing Group (1988). *Brief for the Visitor Design* (Aug.).

Sally Wright Associates (1990a). *Rhondda Heritage Park, Black Gold: Report of Research for the Above Ground Experience*, for Heritage Projects Ltd.

—— (1990b). *Rhondda Heritage Park, Black Gold: Report of Research for the Above Ground Experience, Supplementary Report on Women's History*, for Heritage Projects Ltd.

Welsh Development Agency (1984). *Tŷ Mawr/Lewis Merthyr Colliery Sites Feasibility Study*, Report prepared by the study team for the WDA.

William Gillespie & Partners, Ove Arup & Partners, PEIDA and I. E. Symonds & Partners (1986). *Rhondda Heritage Park Development Plan Report* prepared for MGCC, RBC, TEBC, WDA and WTB (Feb.).

Index